Max Harrison, who lives in London, has written
extensively on both jazz and classical music.
Among his major contributions to jazz criticism
are the principal article on jazz in *The New Grove
Dictionary of Music and Musicians* (revised and
enlarged as *The New Grove Gospel, Blues and
Jazz*) and the two-volume work *Essential Jazz
Records*, prepared under his editorship and
written with (for Volume One) Eric Thacker and
Charles Fox. Volume Two is currently in
preparation.

a
jazz
retrospect

MAX HARRISON

With a Foreword by R. D. Cook

 QUARTET BOOKS

Published in Great Britain by Quartet Books Limited 1991
A member of the Namara Group
27/29 Goodge Street
London W1P 1FD

British Library Cataloguing in Publication Data

Harrison, Max
A jazz retrospect. – 2nd ed.
I. Title
781.65

ISBN 0 7043 0144 X

Reproduced, printed and bound in Great Britain by
Cox & Wyman Ltd, Reading, Berkshire

FOREWORD

For the most part, jazz literature is made up of either well-meaning biographies or histories of one sort or another. Jazz scholarship, despite the vast number of words expended in that direction, has never proceeded very far beyond sentimental hagiography on one hand and cloudy, idiosyncratic overviews on the other. Caught between art music and popular tastes, jazz has seldom attracted the kind of study which classical music receives as a matter of course, yet it has also been denied the kind of socio-political analysis which writers on rock have annexed for their field.

Since the 1970s, jazz criticism, always a somewhat embattled field, has fallen, if anything, further into disrepute. In Britain, a revival of interest in jazz, centred on the activities of a small new wave of young musicians, helped to create a fresh audience for music which had been increasingly marginalized by the inexorable rise of rock. Yet for the most part this was not an opportunity for a new wave of criticism to emerge alongside. Although a number of writers did make a particular mark, most criticism was dismissed as mere élitism in the rush to proselytize on behalf of jazz as a whole: club disc-jockeys and other personalities had more impact on the developing taste of the new audience, and the fashionable marketing of jazz had a far greater role to play than any critic could conceive of having. Which may account for the uneasy impression that, as the music entered the nineties, its place in contemporary culture was becoming more ephemeral than ever.

This is one reason why the reappearance of Max Harrison's book is particularly valuable. This kind of jazz volume – a collection of essays which have previously appeared in jazz and other periodicals – is still embarked upon by the small number of writers who have made it their business to discuss the music on a full-time basis. There have been, for example, fine collections by the American writers Gary Giddins and Francis Davis. Yet Mr Harrison's book is a rather different matter. These are not character sketches, or anecdotal memoirs, but sequences of intense – some might say ruthless – musical analysis. The author is not interested in what Miles Davis might have said to John Coltrane, or what the extent of Charles Mingus's temper was, or how much Fats Waller was able to drink without keeling over. In the very first essay here, devoted to some of the key recordings by Charlie Parker, Mr Harrison insists on the need to 'accept the allegorical nature of the creative life'. His point is that a greater, finer understanding of Parker's tragic genius is to be had by studying 'the order and integrity of his work' rather than the sensational revelations of any biography.

Needless to say, one can quarrel with this point of view. But an air of creative debate is one which the author actively seeks: he characterizes the book as 'an act of provocation' himself, and that spirit of contentiousness is a hallmark of the writing here. No received wisdom is allowed to go unquestioned if an alternative glimmer of interpretation is also available. The essay on Fats Waller, for instance, is a striking example of the kind of revisionism which requires considerable courage to express. Waller's reputation – and it is a substantial and very popular one – is based almost entirely on his greatest hits, the novelty and Tin Pan Alley tunes which have remained in many memories for over fifty years. Mr Harrison not only consigns nearly all this material to the realms of the inconsequential, he sounds the disquieting note that Waller was almost ashamed of his skills, and that 'jazz had no better use for his talent than to waste it'. It is by now a commonplace that Waller's piano solos contain some of the best of his work, yet the wider implications of this piece – which was first published as long ago as 1965 – have never been addressed.

This is, in part, because the context for such discussion has been in steady decline for twenty years. The oldest pieces here date from 1956, the most recent from the early 1970s, and *Jazz Monthly*, where many of them originally appeared, has long since vanished. The opportunities for publishing jazz criticism have now dwindled to a point where it seems unlikely that any periodical would, over the course of a year, indulge the possibility of publishing essays on such now-obscure figures as Miff Mole, Serge Chaloff and Hal McKusick. While the processing of information on music goes on unabated, the considered retrospective, the 'interesting footnote', is rare. Even such major figures as Miles Davis and Ornette Coleman are today discussed in terms of their relevance to the tide of pop culture: Davis as a bandleader who epitomizes popular cool, who blends funk and rock episodes with what remains of his jazz persuasions, and Coleman as the enigmatic purveyor of what he terms 'harmolodics'. Their work purely as *musicians* is by now impossible to discern as an issue within the verbiage expended on their mystique. For that alone, the pieces on Ornette Coleman in this book continue to be of exceptional value, even though they were written more than twenty years ago.

Within these essays, Mr Harrison is both critical and complimentary of Coleman's work, and that rigorous balance is something else which is scarce among serious jazz writing. Since the music is, in financial terms, such an underprivileged area of the arts, it is all too tempting to overcompensate sate for the lack of attention which most jazz musicians receive and indulge in special pleading on their behalf. The author states that this book has nothing to prove, and if anything he is more severe in dealing with the musicians than he is generous in handing out praise. Where he seeks to redress a balance – as in the pieces on Martial Solal, David Mack, Miff Mole and Paul Whiteman – one might consider that he is deliberately seeking out the obscure to act against the numbing and simplifying tendencies of large-scale acclaim; or that there is a certain amount of intellectual one-upmanship involved. Mr Harrison is quick to spot a phoney opinion, and there are plenty of stinging asides against inferior or lazy judgements scattered through these pages. There may be an element of what Tom Wolfe called 'the normal chuckly human satisfaction' in this, and it sometimes results in an air of reproof which every reader, no matter how conscientiously he or she strives to empathize with it, will feel they are smarting from.

But so be it. It is time that such an unforgiving and unsentimental approach was coming from at least one direction in jazz criticism again. A great deal, of course, has happened since this collection was originally published in 1976. Musicians such as Martial Solal, Ornette Coleman and Lennie Niehaus have been active in the interim, and the constant buzz of jazz activity – although that is not necessarily the same thing as progress – has increased to a substantial roar, with more records (and it should be noted that the author's discussions are almost exclusively confined to jazz as it has been preserved by the gramophone) emanating from more territories than ever before. Yet the careful delineation of Mr Harrison's themes, the interlocking theses on extending language and improving form, remain as cogent as when they were first published. Since scarcely any attempts have been made at re-evaluating the work of men such as Bunk Johnson, Jimmy Lunceford or Lennie Niehaus in the meantime, the author's essays remain entirely pertinent. And in at least one direction, Mr Harrison's work has proved to be prophetic. His discussion of the links between jazz and other musics anticipated the growing cross-fertilization between jazz and areas of contemporary composition which are currently underway in the work of many artists.

The example of *A Jazz Retrospect* is one that demands

another start on the road towards a diligent, clear-headed and unsparing jazz criticism. As to why such an approach is important in the wider sense, one need look no further than the author's own introduction here. For a jazz audience which comes fresh to the music, faced with a plethora of records and a sheaf of inherited folklore, one of the most fruitful ways to proceed is with a guide that is ready to pose as many challenges and encouragements to further search as possible.

R.D. Cook
July 1991

Contents

Introduction

I

Attempts have been made to define music not only in aesthetic, but also in moral, metaphysical, and even in purely decorative terms. Yet none of these offers a full explanation of its undeniable power to enrich and transmute, to achieve not merely an attack on its recipients' subjective emotions, but to uncover hitherto unsuspected aspects both of the world and of our own being, to contribute to the development of a higher state of consciousness that will lead to the evolution of a new kind of man. A true response to music confirms both Nietzsche's view of the art's life-enhancing role and Rilke's tribute to its ability to transform "a waiting world, expectant, unfinished, before the creation of sound".

Presumably it is the very irrationality of music which allows it to penetrate more deeply than literature or even painting into the remotest strata of emotion, into the interior life of the most varied times and places. As Romain Rolland pointed out long ago, music is always the first to reflect "tendencies which are later translated into words and still later into facts". It is a means of reconciliation between the individual and the universal, and, as Rolland added, a great musician is an intermediary between "the experience of his period and the timeless current of human feelings".

Certainly the shape of a particular time, its final presence in historical awareness, is often determined by what initially are hermetic insights, specialised lines of endeavour, private acts of which the crowd long remains unconscious. It is the critic's responsibility to find out about these, to sort the few grains of wheat from among vast consignments of contemporary chaff, and, though his labour is always arduous and sometimes lonely, he is very fortunate. It is both a challenge and a refreshment to deal with the past, present and future of so valuable an activity as music. One can never hear enough, know enough, feel enough, think enough. But one can try. To have one's perceptions seized by music and made to throb with the communicated force of another man's experience, to become implicated in

7

the act of creation which is life itself, is one of the greatest delights of the task. The critic must always remember that it is his duty to lead others towards these same delights, although this will not often be easy and he should not become discouraged if at first he appears to be talking to himself about his discoveries.

Jazz, a music that would be worthless if it bore much relation to its popular image, provides a good illustration of the critic's difficulties in this regard. Most habitual jazz listeners are quite primitive in their responses, which are too rudimentary to bring them a satisfaction of equal intensity to that of auditors more consciously and acutely involved in musical experience and better informed. Their appetites are strong but undiscriminating except in a purely sectarian sense, and much affected by inessentials such as the personality or reputation of a performer. Often they lack the self-discipline to entertain any opinion except their own.

Yet the critic as much as the non-professional listener is an instrument upon which the music plays, and, however objective and intellectual his conscious attitude, his interpretation of what he hears will always be deeply coloured by his own temperament. No music is ever solely an intellectual experience for a listener who is himself musical, but the critic—who, ideally, should never be entirely satisfied with his own views or with those of anyone else—must beware not only the hazards of personal bias, but, especially, the snares laid by the small percentage of genuinely new music, which may demand a restructuring of attitudes, responses and information which have already been processed into a pattern. He must particularly guard against habits of taste which masquerade, sometimes with great plausibility, as aesthetic laws. As Ibsen warned, "to write is to judge oneself".

And to write about music is soon to learn, from one's readers' letters, of the multiplicity of trees that listeners are barking up when they hear music, for there are as many modes of listening as there are listeners, each sealed in a private compartment though all apparently hearing the same performance. Despite this, and although a work of art must be experienced directly, no amount of explanation radically changing that experience, criticism may help the listener towards a fuller understanding of what his experience is. It can never reach the ultimate source of the revelatory power referred to above, because it is in its mystery that the inexplicable force and authority of music lies. But criticism may show the direction in which the art has moved and may be moving now, and it can demonstrate how one phase of development

8

is related to another. Individual works may be placed in perspective both historically and with regard to their expressive content and technical organisation. The final conclusions must be those of the individual listener himself, of course, and for him, as for the critic, spontaneous enjoyment of a given work must come first, as this alone unlocks the gate through which detailed explanations may constructively enter. Then study, comparison and analysis can widen horizons and intensify responses.

II

One produces an enormous quantity of material in the course of twenty years' writing for several periodicals, and maybe the author himself is the last person who should decide what is to live on between hard covers and what is to die in the diminishing number of extant copies of all those ephemeral magazines. Some of my work has already reappeared in other peoples' books, an instance being the essay on the Modern Jazz Quartet which is part of the *Art of Jazz* anthology edited by Martin Williams, and so the present volume makes no attempt at a full coverage of the subject. Several major figures and many lesser ones go unmentioned, and some of the pieces here are inconclusive, be it of necessity (James P. Johnson, Paul Whiteman) or of choice (Bunk Johnson, Hal McKusick). No bid is made, either, for an exhaustive study of those who do get in, and more space is given, for example, to Ornette Coleman's violin than to his alto saxophone playing. This may seem perverse, yet there is method in what might appear to be this book's madness, for whereas Coleman's work on the latter instrument has been widely discussed, his treatment of the violin has almost been ignored. Similarly, the piece on Fats Waller deals not with the records that won him fortune and fame, but with some of those which did not. There is nothing outrageously modern here, and that is because it takes the critic a while to do his job. If we evaluate too soon, the tender shoots of some new mode of consciousness may be smothered under irrelevant preconceptions. Distance does not *lend* enchantment but may be depended upon, eventually, to show in what direction it lies. We must hope there are still many chapters to be added to the story of jazz, and there is no doubt that our understanding of it is in its early stages.

Unlike some retrospective selections that might be named, this one certainly was not prepared in a spirit of getting the museum into good order before closing-time.

Nor, though it tries to be helpful, does this volume have anything to prove. In its pages a few heads may roll, yet no particular axe is ground. Ideas are offered which are the result of much listening and thinking in the hope that they will stimulate not agreement but listening and thinking on the reader's part. Few things, in this sphere, are more pernicious than a book which seeks to impose a rigid pattern on the chosen material and hence upon its readers' future reactions to that material. If we are to get anything out of jazz beyond the second-hand responses of others we must each make our own way, and so this collection is intended as an act of provocation, conscientiously seeking to raise more questions than it answers.

III

When writing over a period of two decades for periodicals such as *Jazz Monthly* which have relatively small circulations and constant readerships, one can make assumptions of shared knowledge to which the author of a single volume is not entitled. Consequently, changes have been made in the following texts for the benefit of the wider and more diverse audience a book may reasonably be expected to reach. Again, it was necessary to eliminate, so far as possible, various repetitions which, though essential in essays originally published years apart, became redundant as soon as they were brought together in this collection. One respect in which the past still exerts an influence, however, is in the relative lengths of these pieces: despite revision, these still reflect the amount of space I was allotted at the time of first publication rather than, in some cases, my present estimate of the subjects' importance.

Any writer who makes changes in such circumstances is automatically accused of profiting unfairly from hindsight, of being wise too long after the event, and in some instances that charge may be justified here. But some judgements do frankly need revision. For example, when I originally wrote my essay on the great baritone saxophonist Serge Chaloff I could not quite bring myself, perhaps because of a misplaced sense of loyalty to Harry Carney, the Ellington Orchestra's exponent of this instrument with whose work I had been longer acquainted, to say that Chaloff's *Blue Serge* LP contained the finest baritone playing I had ever heard, although this clearly was the case. That infirmity has been corrected here. ('Loyalty', so long as it is confined to their own especial favourites, is highly valued by jazz fans, but has no meaning in a true critic's vocabulary.)

A quite different, yet equally valid, reason for making changes is the vastly increased amount of material that has become available on disc over the past few years. It would have been small service to the contemporary reader, for instance, to reprint my essay on Jimmy Lunceford just as it stood, pretending that the four-LP American and six-LP French reissues of his band's output simply did not exist.

IV

Finally, I must acknowledge the kindness of my friends Michael James, Derek Langridge, Alun Morgan and Victor Schonfield in lending me a considerable number of records. And I must also thank Malcolm Walker of *Discographical Forum* who supplied information about various LPs.

Max Harrison
London NW11
1975

Some Attitudes to Improvisation:
four viewpoints

Discussions of the sharply contrasting ways jazzmen go about improvising, and the differing attitudes to music which accompany these.

Charlie Parker's Savoy Recordings

People often worry about contradictions between the chaos and confusion of an artist's life and the order and integrity of his work. Yet it is more profitable to concentrate on the latter rather than, as the jazz community usually does, upon the former. It is better to accept the allegorical nature of the creative life which, reverberating with the distant echoes of personal myth, so overlays the quotidian facts as to make them, finally, irrelevant. That life is a mystery which can only be explored—though never 'solved'—by attention to the collected works. These are a thousand times more revealing, and more interesting, than the collected deeds and misdeeds assembled by some biographer. With Parker, especially, it is study of the music which can most nearly reconcile the man's bluster and his recordings' austerely disciplined style, his con man antics and the wholeness of the secret pattern which coils behind the notes, his loud-mouthed contempt for modern (white American) society and his yearning for its rewards, his reckless high living and his gradually intensifying despair.

Such dichotomies must have seemed far off in 1945. During that year Parker was on several recordings under Dizzy Gillespie's name that are now recognised as being among the classics of jazz, and in the November he led a session for the Savoy company at which the music was shaped entirely on his terms. The result was an elimination of various inconsistencies that hitherto had marked his work on disc, and the performances set down at this date and those which followed, both for Savoy and for the Dial concern, demonstrated, like earlier records by Louis Armstrong and later ones by Ornette Coleman, a renewal of the language of jazz, an illustration of the organic growth of this music as both an art and a craft. Yet the repertoire of these sessions underlines, despite all the nonsense written about a 'revolution' within jazz during the 1940s, the rather strictly traditional basis of the changes Parker made. Twenty-two themes were recorded for Savoy of which nine are twelve-bar blues, six are based on the simple thirty-two-bar chord sequence of *I got rhythm*, and the remaining seven use the almost equally uncomplex harmonic frameworks of *Indiana*, *Honeysuckle rose* and similar popular songs from the 1920s and '30s.

This reflects the general pattern of his work, and of the 257 titles listed in Tony Williams's complete discography (1) 44% are themes on standard chord sequences— 19.5% blues and 24.5% popular ballads; these consist of only twenty-one harmonic sources, the blues plus twenty popular songs among which *I got rhythm* once more greatly predominates. On the Dial label there are a number of performances of popular ballads as such, where, as in *How deep is the ocean?* or *Out of nowhere*, Parker improvises on the original melodies, not just on the chords. Other categories are the strange aharmonic canons like *Chasing the Bird*, and the fast improvisations, such as *Klaunstance*, which state no theme. These latter have a precedent in themeless performances such as Armstrong's *Muggles* (whose third chorus, incidentally, is a reworking of King Oliver's solo on *Jazzing babies blues*).

Similarly, though much has been made of Parker and other jazzmen of his generation giving their music, through an interplay of cross-beat accents, an 8/8 instead of a 4/4 pulse, this was not quite the departure most commentators assume. Indeed, Virgil Thomson has suggested that "if you listen carefully to American music as performed by American artists, a very large part of what has been composed in the last forty years assumes the existence, whether or not this is overtly present at all times in the sound, of a steady continuity of eighth-notes, on top of which other metrical patterns, regular and irregular, lead an independent life" (2). Henry Cowell projected this tendency at least another generation further back when he wrote that "[Charles] Ives is addicted to the general twentieth-century practice of using a constant unit (normally an eighth-note) to underlie all the different metres" (3).

Although the conservative basis of Parker's music is significant, his solos develop their ideas—in terms of harmonic inflection and rhythmic variation as much as melody—with a precision quite foreign either to popular songwriting or to the reshuffling of stock phrases which constitute most blues 'improvisations'. His solos hold our attention through their unexpectedness and outward diversity, and satisfy us because of their underlying unity, which operates by subtle correspondences between different parts of the improvisation.

Like other greater and lesser creators, in and out of jazz, Parker had a number of musical fingerprints, basic phrases, some original, some less so, which recur throughout his mature work. Their constant presence is less of a limiting factor than might be imagined and for two reasons, the first being, alas, that from his achievement of a fully representative style with the November 1945 Savoy date to his death in 1955 was only a matter of ten years. Secondly, these basic linear shapes, while characteristic, are so simple as to permit almost infinite variation. Thus each one could start on any of the twelve notes of the chromatic scale and could be played in any one of the twenty-four keys (though in fact Parker's choice of keys was as lamentably restricted as that of most other jazz musicians); they could begin on any beat of the bar, or be played upsidedown or backwards; and the scope for rhythmic variation was nearly limitless, particularly at slow tempos where, departing from the quavers and semiquavers which dominate his faster pieces, the line blossoms into demisemiquavers, sometimes grouped in quintuplets, sextolets, etc. (e.g. *Parker's mood*).

Good instances of how these basic patterns are deployed can be found in the alto saxophone solo on take 3 of *Thriving from a riff* from that first Savoy date. There are close linear resemblances between the fourth bar of the first, second and fourth eight-bar phrases of the initial chorus, that is bars four, twelve and twenty-eight; also between bars three and eleven. In his second chorus Parker goes further and there are similar correspondences linking bars two, ten and sixteen, three and nine, twenty-five and twenty-seven; bar thirty-one exactly echoes bar fifteen, but such literal repetitions are rare. Normally when basic shapes recur he shifts them not only in pitch but also in relation to the bar-lines: thus the figure which occupies beats 2, 3 and 4 of bar eighteen and 1 and 2 of nineteen in the first chorus is moved to beats 1, 2, 3 and 4 of nineteen and 1 of twenty in the second. Again, when he shifts the position of a figure within a phrase like this it will often be played over different harmony from the rhythm section, and in the example just mentioned the notes are heard against a mediant seventh in the first chorus and against a submediant seventh in the second. The extent to which he was prepared to alter notes to fit the new harmony in such cases varied considerably, and in this instance Parker leaves the F-sharp and E-flat unchanged, so they are heard as chromatic inflections; a lot, though by no means all, of the altered notes in his phrases arise thus. It may be added that the use of 'melodic silence', often an important element in his solos (e.g. take A of *Klact-oveeseds-tene* on Dial), operates in the same way: in the first chorus of *Thriving from a riff* bars eight, twenty-six and thirty-two are empty whereas in the second it is bars eight, seventeen and twenty-four.

All this represents an attempt, often successful, to subvert the obvious cyclical repeats implied in the underlying chord sequence by imposing a more subtle kind of order. Also, the above are merely a random selection of rather obvious points, for many further relationships could be pointed out in this one solo—a matter of only sixty-four bars, which Parker improvised with such apparently artless spontaneity (4).

Because such procedures are open to so wide a degree of small-scale variation it obviously is instructive to hear different versions of the same piece recorded on the same day. The Savoy company's issue, in the late 1950s, of every scrap of music they had by Parker, including many incomplete performances, though widely criticised at the time, was a considerable aid to our understanding not only of his improvisatory processes but also, because of his wide influence, those of many other jazz musicians (5). It should not be imagined, however, that, say, each of the five takes of *Billie's bounce*, again from the initial Savoy date, marks a point of regular progress ending with the near-perfect final version. That kind of steady improvement is found in, for example, Bud Powell's three performances of *Un poco loco*, but with Parker the matter is less simple, his improvisations being in effect variations on each other, their range of meaning hard to assess. One does not wish to indulge in laboured cultural equations, but some remarks by Picasso seem relevant here: "When you begin a picture you often make some pretty discoveries. You must guard against these. Destroy the thing, do it several times. In each destroying of a beautiful discovery the artist does not really suppress it, but rather transforms it, condenses it, makes it more substantial. What comes out in the end is the result of rejected discoveries" (6).

Of course, a few of these series of performances do simply grow better organised and more expressive from one attempt to another, and *Parker's mood* is the best instance. Take 1, though it contains a few good ideas, is little more than a preliminary sketch, but 2 is far more to the point, and the listener is disturbed by its breaking down soon after the piano solo. Even so, take 3 marks a real leap forward, showing Parker in one of his most inspired moments. The tragic sense of life, "that awareness of man as being always poised between birth and death" (7), is lacking in much American culture, yet the deeper reality is affirmed with considerable power in jazz like this. The final version of *Parker's mood* is, indeed, one of the greatest blues improvisations ever to be recorded, and it vibrates in the mind for long afterwards, like a cry echoing through the dark and endless forests of a dream (8).

A different path is followed by the six takes of *Marmaduke*. The first four seem casual and under-motivated, and at the end of 4 itself we hear Parker asking the recording engineer to play the performance back to him. Evidently he is dissatisfied, and though take 5 soon breaks down it strikes us with its greater urgency. 6 is completed and the alto saxophone solo, if not on a level with Parker's finest, is markedly superior to anything that has gone before. There are several series like this, the four takes of *Barbados* and the five of *Buzzy* among them, where a sudden rise in quality is effected at the end, and they contradict Ross Russell's statement (9) that he was usually at his best on a first take.

Perhaps the most interesting category, however, and the one closest to what Picasso had in mind, is typified by the five versions of *Billie's bounce*. Any two or more solos on the same theme may be expected to have certain resemblances, but the relationship is particularly close in cases like this. After take 1 the following attempts give rise to comparatively little further invention and instead the same ideas are expressed in different ways. In this Parker stood close to Jelly Roll Morton, of whom Roy Carew said, "a dozen ways of expressing a musical idea were always flashing through his mind" (10). Thus each of the *Billie's bounce* alto solos begins with a phrase that is demonstrably based on the same idea though each has a somewhat different configuration.

Series of gradual improvements, sudden final accesses of inspiration, sets of variations round unchanging ideas—these are the three patterns into which most of the groups of Savoy recordings fit. Naturally there are exceptions and an interesting one is provided by takes 3 and 4 of *Now's the time*, a blues with obvious roots in the Kansas City riff music of Parker's youth. Each of his solos contains strong ideas which are most expressively played, yet it seems to the present writer that these are organised just a little more cogently in the later version. This is a subjective judgement, of course, and personal taste has led others to prefer take 3, but it is to be expected that sometimes Parker would improvise solos of virtually equal merit. It would be hard to choose between takes 1 and 3 of *Bluebird* or 1 and 4 of *Constellation* (11).

Ideally, the emotional drive behind the playing and the intellectual ordering of the musical material attain a simultaneous climax, as clearly happened with the second take of *Koko* or the third version of *Another hair-do*. Sometimes it took longer, half a dozen attempts being necessary to produce a satisfactory version of *Perhaps*, but inevitably there are relative failures, cases when it did not happen. Of the four *Donna Lee* takes the last is certainly the most finished and concise, yet the third, while rough and in some ways hesitant, communicates more forcefully: here the emotive peak was reached before the musical invention had been completely mastered. Just occasionally Parker forms an immediately satisfactory presentation of his ideas, as on the first attempt at *Bird gets the worm*, and is unable to recapture it in subsequent takes.

Such difficulties are unsurprising because while originality of style is fairly common in jazz, originality of content, genuine newness in what is expressed, is not, and it was the latter which kept Parker's music in ferment, discrediting Robert Reisner's preposterous assertion that "his style seems to have been fixed from the beginning" (9). True, it is hard to imagine the 1945 *Koko*, with its beautiful reconciliation of virtuosity and economy, being surpassed, yet if we attend carefully to the 1947 broadcast version or the 1948 performance recorded at the Royal Roost we find these show real advances, not least in that Parker seems even more unhurried, has still more time to pause, if he wishes, no matter how furious the tempo. Similarly, the alto solo on the 1949 Roost account of *Cheryl* is more closely argued than the Savoy version of two years before.

Progress can, of course, be observed among the Savoy titles themselves. For instance take 2 of the 1948 *Ah-leu-cha* exemplifies his skill in building solos out of a great variety of types of phrase. Long, short, smooth, angular, legato, staccato—all are thrown together in a seemingly arbitrary way. Yet Parker reconciles their differences of character and emphasis so completely that an improvisation of exceptional lucidity results, and one that is considerably more than the sum of its parts. This degree of spontaneous mastery would have been beyond him, say, three years before, although this type of solo was something of a speciality with the most gifted members of his generation, another superb example, also from 1948, being take 2 of Fats Navarro's *Symphonette*.

Ah-leu-cha, incidentally, is another piece with a contrapuntal theme statement, like *Chasing the Bird*, and the care that obviously went into these shows that the usual view of Parker as a pure improvisor unconcerned with such matters, which is suggested by themeless performances such as *Merry-go-round*, is, like so many ideas about him, too simple. What did remain constant, of course, was the power of invention. In some ways this is best experienced first in what may be called its primal form, on recordings of Parker in casual circumstances, like the three pieces on the Dial label called *Home cooking* (which employ different chord sequences although they share a title), or in Savoy rehearsal takes such as the 1945 *Warming up a riff*, a trial-run for *Koko*. This latter captures a degree of spontaneity rare in recordings of jazz or any music, and the phrases are like gold coins proudly flung down on a tabletop. Equally remarkable is the ineptly-titled *Meandering*, an improvisation on the chords of *Embraceable you* from the same date, which anticipates the extraordinary vein of fantasy displayed in the ballad performances recorded for Dial two years later. On pieces such as *Don't blame me* or *My old flame* even Parker's theme statements, full of feathery, form-making feints, are more imaginative than the actual improvisations of most jazz musicians.

By now there were few players, anyway, who could hope to match him—the trumpeter Fats Navarro, with whom he never made studio recordings, the drummer Max Roach, who is on nearly all his Savoy and Dial sessions, and the pianist Bud Powell, heard, in brilliant form, on the *Cheryl/Buzzy* date, almost complete the list. And certainly there was nobody from whom he could learn, if, except in the earliest stages, there ever had been. As Schoenberg says, "a talent learns from others, a genius from himself" (12). The vivid projection of Parker's unique abilities and position on the Savoy and Dial titles seems enough to justify the long-accepted view of them as being his greatest performances (and many of the relevant titles have not even been mentioned here).

Yet he was bound to continue refining his earlier achievements, and, though it seems like an act of perversity, he gave the most creative of all his recorded improvisations to the Clef label, who treated him with so much less understanding than Dial or Savoy. During his few remaining years, indeed, Parker had many albatrosses hung round his neck— light string orchestras, rhumba band rhythm sections, choirs, and the results were usually almost worthless. But scattered unobtrusively among all this evidence of bizarre incomprehension are a few small combo sessions, often with Roach behind the drums, sometimes with Al Haig at the piano, and these produced the most precious, and almost the least regarded, part of his legacy.

As noted, takes 3 and 4 of the 1945 *Now's the time* are very beautiful, yet the version recorded for Clef eight years later is more concentrated, more eventful. This is nothing to do with the 1953 performance's faster tempo but with the fact that more happens inside a given number of bars. It is the same in *Swedish schnapps* or *Back home blues*. The most urgent of the Dial and especially the Savoy improvisations remind us of the grimacing clay figurines the Aztecs used to bury with their dead: a great deal of anguish is expressed in a small space. But on his Clef *Confirmation* or *She rote* the overall design is more rigorous than in almost any of the recordings from the 1940s, the music lucid, almost serene. Despite the irrevocable chaos into which his personal life had now sunk, Parker was calmly certain of the exact expressive weight of each note, of every inflection, even when he repeatedly made changes, as between takes 1, 3 and 6 of *Chi chi*. Here he is shown to be one of those rare beings who can have it both ways, for he distills the complexity of his earlier music, retaining its old virtues and adding new ones (13).

Jazz Monthly, January 1959

Some Early Fats Waller Piano Solos

The several hundred recordings Waller made in the 1930s appear overwhelmingly to support the notion that jazz can only be an inconsequential music. A few grains of gold, such as his memorable anti-love song *Your feets' too big*, can be dredged from those vast mud deposits, but coherent purpose normally seems conspicuous by its absence. In fact, the matter is less simple, more depressing. Iain Lang, who often met the pianist on his visits to Britain, gives the jazz listener's viewpoint: "Waller, on the stage and in the recording studio, played brilliantly, yet never too brilliantly. . . . He accepted that there was no paying audience for the best he had to give." But in private, "time stood still while the music rolled on, audacity piled on audacity . . . newly-minted melodies toyed with and prodigally thrown away" (1).

If his recorded output is taken as a whole, though, it shows that Waller really was not able to solve his problems by clever departmentalisation, could not keep superficialities for the public while fully developing his gifts in private. Eugene Sedric, the tenor saxophonist who played with him in the 1930s, gives the jazz musician's viewpoint:

"He wanted to do great things on the organ and piano, which he could do. There were many times when . . . he felt like himself and wanted to play great. But, when he played as musically as he could, many people in the audience would think he was laying down and they'd yell 'Come on, Fats!' He'd take a swig of gin or something and say resignedly 'Aw right, here it is'. Fats really was a great artist. . . .

He could play all styles from modern on down. What is generally called the Waller style is more or less the style he became known by commercially. . . . He had a thorough knowledge of the classics and had a large library of classical music. He especially loved Bach" (2).

Recordings by 'Fats Waller and his Rhythm', a veritable ossuary of 1930s pop, were made to a formula that became rigid once it proved commercially successful. It was not simply that the standardisation thus entailed was inimical to the growth of his abilities, but, far worse, that the formula encouraged inherent weaknesses. We should be mistaken, however, in putting all the blame on business pressures because no matter how strong his fitful discontent, the formula was as congenial to Waller as it was commercially advantageous. This contradiction symbolises his whole position, for he possessed great gifts but not the temperament to go with them. His powers were manifest in a rare pianistic skill, fluent invention of musical ideas, a real feeling for structure. Yet Ed Kirkeby (3), his manager, spoke of his impatience with serious study, and from the countless anecdotes of his fecklessness one might deduce an absolute refusal to stand against the Gadarene momentum of events.

It fits this paradox that Waller's vital weakness lay in one of the most obvious aspects of his talent—a facility in manipulating standard musical materials. This assumed control whenever the pianist's little band tackled a melody from Tin Pan Alley: the glittering effects came easily and the crowd was pleased, so why should he engage in the intellectually and emotionally demanding task of bringing his gifts to their true fruition? Had he done so, he might well have created music comparable to that of his teacher, James P. Johnson, of Earl Hines, Art Tatum or Bud Powell, the masters of piano jazz. Even the *London suite*, whose six movements Waller recorded in 1939, sound like a next-to-last attempt, neither consistent nor well directed, to increase his range of expression. Yet by then it was too late, as it so often is in jazz, and if certain of his piano solos remain the least unsatisfying work he did, it is because in them the struggle between expressiveness and mere facility is still alive.

Even at his earliest sessions, however, the pianist revealed a tendency to repeat melodies rather than improvise on them, and the 1929 solos include several disappointments. *Baby, oh where can you be?* and *Turn on the heat* are nondescript tunes that are varied only in obvious ways, and it may be questioned whether he was even trying to create jazz here. *Love me or leave me* is better. Its first chorus is rather static, presenting the melody in pairs of chords that do not swing much, but this emphasises Waller's second-chorus feat of putting the tune into the bass yet swinging considerably. The last chorus again states the melody, with greater rhythmic emphasis, and if the final eight bars offer another real linear variation this still means there are only sixteen measures of proper improvisation out of one hundred and twenty.

Waller's own *Sweet Savannah Sue* is in popular ballad style, rather like Johnson's material in this genre, and, again, the sixteen-bar tune is not much departed from, simply being presented in differing keyboard layouts. However, the third chorus abruptly introduces new material that never reappears, this being a case of the principle of contrast, which elsewhere served Waller excellently, being applied in an irrational manner. There is something annoying, also, about the perfunctory way the introduction returns to serve as coda. *I've got a feeling I'm falling* has a four-bar introduction, sixteen-bar verse, three thirty-two-bar choruses and a four-bar coda—the same pattern as *Love me or leave me*. Here the introduction and coda are good, and different: one leads well into the delicately stated verse, the other arises naturally out of the final chorus's rhythmic attack. Once more, Waller does not leave the melody far behind; his second chorus includes a sixteen-bar high treble variation, but even this retains firm contact.

The practice of holding to the original melody almost throughout a performance was common to the whole New York 'stride' school of which Waller, through his link with Johnson, was a member, so it could be said he was conforming with tradition rather than lacking enterprise. But his treatments of popular material are strikingly inferior to Johnson's in terms of pianistic invention, as may be heard by comparing the above recordings with the older man's piano rolls of, say, *Vamping Liza Jane* or *Gypsy blues*. This process of using a melody—rather than its chords—as the scaffolding of an improvisation reached its height with Tatum, who acknowledged Waller's influence. Tatum 'analysed' the tune into basic motives which often were modified on recurrence, usually reharmonised and with counter-melodies added, the whole carried through over various sophistications of 'stride' bass patterns.

Blues playing was a problematical undertaking for Waller, and the pianist Dick Wellstood called his efforts "showbiz blues" (4) as they tended towards pensiveness rather than strong declaration. The sarcastically-titled *Numb fumbling* may be his best recording in this vein. It has six choruses and the structural idea is an alternation of solid rhythmic emphasis and fast-moving lyrical melodies, choruses three and five being the rhythmic ones. *Numb fumbling* gets its forward momentum from the parallel increase in complexity of both the melodic and rhythmic sections and so, for example, the continuous six-bar phrase in the fourth chorus is capped by almost eight bars of non-stop semiquavers in the sixth. There are clichés, such as the two-measure phrase that closes each chorus, yet the basic idea works, the choruses logically cohere, and this is easily the best piece discussed so far.

My feelings are hurt is another twelve-bar—one could hardly call it a blues. The main feature of the theme chorus is its opening, sinuous four-bar phrase, but Waller is unable to follow this adequately. Once again, there is much heavy rhythmic emphasis and for relief he uses high trills over a quasi-boogie bass in the second chorus (as in the second chorus of *Numb fumbling*) and double-time in the last. But these elements are handled arbitrarily and do not produce the rather satisfying formal shape of *Numb fumbling*.

The unification of a series of choruses is a problem for all jazz musicians but especially for solo pianists, being a tightrope between continuity and diversity of musical thought. Most of the 'stride' school had compositional abilities and this naturally comes out in their solutions to the difficulty. Johnson wrote pieces like *Carolina shout*, and even recordings such as his *Bleeding hearted blues* have a formal, worked-out air. However, it was in his answer to the problem of unification that Waller showed a skill that has been little remarked.

Basically, he used the principle of contrast in an unusually comprehensive way. This is dangerous to continuity, yet he employed the concept on a number of levels, occasionally interrelating them so well that part of the continuity actually derives from the consistency with which the principle of contrast operates. It is impossible to guess the proportions of spontaneity and preparation in the solos discussed below, but each is probably a crystallisation of a number of improvisations along similar lines.

Going about is a good elementary instance of Waller's methods. There are nine sixteen-bar choruses framed by an introduction and coda of eight bars each. The theme is a two-bar figure that is extended sequentially to fill sixteen bars, and the second chorus merely repeats this. In the next sequence, however, Waller does not produce new material so much as a variation based on the chords alone. The next chorus, while

25

adhering to the chords, is a deliberate variation on the theme. From then on, *Going about* consists of an alternation of what we may call thematic and harmonic variations. The weak point is the fifth chorus, in which he restates the theme literally in place of the variation on the chords which his formal scheme would lead us to expect. But there are several good things. For example, the seventh and ninth choruses—both harmonic variations—are linked by an emphasis on the high treble of which Waller was so fond. And in between comes a thematic variation to give us a final reminder of the opening material. Altogether he makes up for his lapse in the fifth chorus by handling the latter half of this solo well, even the coda flowing out of the final chorus to marked effect.

Better still is *Valentine stomp*. Outwardly a fast display vehicle, this is organised with subtlety. It consists of an introduction, two 'thematic' choruses, two interludes each followed by four choruses, and a coda; the choruses are of sixteen bars, the introduction, interludes and coda of four. The thematic motive is little more than a decorative turn which is spun out by sequence to cover the opening chorus, and a slight variant is provided by the second sixteen bars. Waller effectively contrasts the grouping of his two sets of four choruses: the first is 2+2, the second 1+2+1. After the first interlude come two choruses devoted to predominantly rhythmic ideas in full chords, followed by two presenting a more distant variation on the theme. The same type of contrast is used after the second interlude, but here two choruses of thematic variation are divided by two more of heavy rhythmic figures. Besides alternating variation on the thematic motive with passages of rhythmic emphasis, Waller also carefully manages contrasts of register: choruses one and two feature the high treble, after the first interlude we have two in the middle register followed by another two high, and after the second interlude two choruses set in the middle of the keyboard are flanked by two in the treble.

It need hardly be said that this somewhat numerical accounting can give little idea of the music's spontaneity and cohesion, its extroversion and carefully-judged formal relationships. But only a clarification of the ground-plans is intended here, as an aid to proper listening.

If this is difficult with *Valentine stomp*, it is almost impossible, without musical examples or at least a diagram, for the last item to be discussed. In *Smashing thirds* not only is there a more involved set of relationships, but the picture is complicated by Waller becoming uncertain over chorus structure. This is another fast stomp, the introduction and coda to which are unusually free and varied. All but one of the nine choruses are sixteen bars along. The theme is another two-bar figure sequentially filling eight bars which are then repeated. The second chorus gives the same material in a higher register. It is in the third chorus, while breaking away from the theme, that Waller apparently becomes confused: he abandons the 8+8 pattern of the preceding choruses and this sequence is instead 4+4+8. The fourth chorus is of twelve bars only (4+8). Chorus five is an 8+8 sixteen, but this is followed by a four-bar interlude. Finally come four more sixteen-bar choruses and a coda.

The irregular choruses are unusually related. Thus, the first four bars of chorus three are identical with the interlude following chorus five; the first four bars of chorus four repeat the second four bars of chorus three; the final eight bars of both these choruses are closely affined, being improvisations on the theme itself. Choruses three and four may be summarised as thematic improvisation mixed with four-bar sequences of unrelated material.

Again Waller has paired his choruses, and these two are well set off by choruses one and two, which were given over to simple thematic repetition. The weak point of *Smashing thirds*, as of *Going about*, is the fifth chorus, again devoted to an unnecessary restatement of the theme. But Waller makes up for it here, too, with another remarkable set of four choruses. First, choruses one, two and five are composed of harmonically identical halves; so, also, are choruses six and nine, but the halves of the intervening seven and eight are not identical. Thus we have the 1+2+1 pattern in the latter part of the solo contrasting with the earlier 2+2–just as in choruses three to ten of *Valentine stomp*. And, like *Smashing thirds*, both *Going about* and *Valentine stomp* began, remember, with pairs of choruses of thematic repetition: for all his concern with variety, Waller is not inconsistent.

Next, choruses six and eight are improvisations on the theme which, though related, are cleverly differentiated by being based on pairs of identical and non-identical halves respectively. They are divided by the new version of the theme given in chorus seven, which is an effective preparation for the return of the theme itself in chorus nine. Thus choruses six to nine again present a kind of alternation that was one of Waller's basic methods: improvisation on theme/thematic variant/improvisation on theme/theme proper. And he still has some good ideas left for the coda. Incidentally, of all the music discussed here, none shows James P. Johnson's stylistic influence so distinctly as the final eight bars of chorus four.

These solos, then, together with a few more Waller managed to set down in 1934, '37 and '41, are vastly superior to the records that won him fame and fortune. The latter show Tin Pan Alley ditties paralysing creativity whereas the minimal thematic content of his jazz pieces made him work harder to impart shape and depth to his music. In so doing he began to explore something of his real capabilities, and the best moments hint, no matter how incompletely, at what he might have achieved. Yet even they illustrate what exasperating stuff jazz can be, with its mixture of subtlety and carelessness, of cliché and inspiration. On even his finest records certain of Waller's procedures are really commonplace, and his musical language never approaches the masterful consistency of that of Hines or Powell. As Dick Wellstood wrote, "It's so hard to tell what Fats could do because he was always trying to entertain, and so made his playing entertaining at the damndest times. . . . The trouble with a lot of the guys of that age is that they really in a sense are ashamed of jazz" (4). Perhaps they cannot altogether be blamed. Attentative listeners gain the impression that Waller almost was ashamed of the skill and imagination which he sometimes could not help showing. But it is discouraging to have to accept that jazz had no better use for his talent than to waste it (5).

Jazz Monthly, December 1965

Thelonious Monk

If his singular originality was enough to ensure a hostile reception, it still is ironic that for many years comment on Monk centred around his supposed incompetence as a pianist. On his best days his public performances demonstrated, with a clarity which no recording ever could approach, that this musician was, in his highly individual command of the instrument and absolute control of his especial musical resources, as remarkable a virtuoso as, say, Earl Hines. The two transcendent techniques were, obviously, quite different, and in Hines's case the dazzling texture of his music, although shaped by an eminently characteristic melodic and rhythmic invention, was firmly rooted in the scale, arpeggio and chordal formations that have always provided the basis of tonal keyboard music.

In sharp contrast, Monk's pianism, strictly in accord with other aspects of his work, if it did not lead us to go quite so far as André Brassaï, who wrote "awkwardness means greatness and lack of skill means talent and these things are signs of genuine creativity" (1), still had little connection with established conventions, and was of a purer, more directly musical order. His strength lay not in complex executive feats but in a deployment, at once sensitive and vividly incisive, of some of the basic elements of jazz: time, metre, accent, space. This is why, with minor exceptions like the Dutchman Stido Astrom, his influence was not on other pianists but on players of other instruments: the lessons he offered were purely musical, not arising of necessity out of the keyboard.

Certain of Monk's recorded solos, or sections of them, consist of rhythmic variations on the thematic line with shifting metres and evolving patterns of accentual displacement. When he first appeared, in the 1940s, such a method seemed dangerously radical in comparison with the then usual system of basing improvised lines solely on the chordal harmonisation of the theme, not on the theme itself. That was because people who listened to Monk had never heard Jelly Roll Morton, and people who knew of Morton's use of motivic development wished to hear nothing of Monk. To both, of course, thematic variation was an essential process.

Much was made of Monk's harmonic innovations, and his pungent, hard-biting sonorities were the aspect of his language which aroused nearly as much adverse criticism as his playing. Yet this shows how right Stanley Dance, a tireless advocate of progress in jazz, always a friend of the latest development, was to complain of the jazz audience's frequent "inability to appreciate the joy of the musician in expression through harmonies rich and strange", of listeners' "narrowed sensibility which does not permit them to perceive, through its subtlety and complexity, the inner integrity of much of the later jazz" (2). Certainly in Monk's harmony, and perhaps more immediately than in his exceptionally subtle rhythm, we apprehend a needle-sharp intelligence which rigorously avoids the commonplace.

Yet however striking this music may be on rhythmic and harmonic planes, it is always informed and directed by the requirements of melody. If the melodic construction is often severe in its economy this is because Monk knew precisely what he wanted to say and how to say it, because he had full command both of his ideas and their means of communication. Thus is explained much of the immense temperamental drive and magnetic cogency of his finest work—again, not fully conveyed on any recording. In his most representative moments all effort was devoted to the true expressive aim, none wasted on mere decoration. Such control is an authentic sign of mastery, but naturally Monk could not bring it off every time; indeed, he was in the same situation as a sculptor for whom one false stroke could ruin the whole statue.

In fact it is misleading to discuss the separate aspects of Monk's work too much in isolation. All elements of rhythm, melody and harmony interact so closely that it is unrealistic to consider one without the others. Monk did not offer an assemblage of easily identifiable trade marks in the manner of a popular soloist: his improvisations are new wholes, not just accumulations of pleasing objects. He was, in short, a composer, not simply because he wrote many 'tunes', or even themes, but because the compositional mode of thinking is evident in everything he did. One instance is his accompanying of other improvisers, for, instead of providing the normal type of chordal support, he often set modified fragments of the theme beside—not behind—the soloist's line in such a way as to give extended performances a closer-knit feeling of thematic reference. A different illustration is his treatment of popular songs like *Smoke gets in your eyes*, where he abstracts and rearranges the components to a quite drastic extent.

Just as Monk's pianism was unusually direct in its musicality, so his recordings, for all their self-consistent idiosyncrasies, have a curious air of objectivity. Even when the choruses follow the conventional AABA pattern of four eight-bar phrases, they are in the tradition of 'compositions for band', like Morton's *Cannonball blues* or Bix Beiderbecke's *Humpty Dumpty*, rather than jazz versions of mere songs. As such, pieces like *Epistrophy* or *Criss cross* are altogether foreign to the world of popular music in a way that, for example, even masterpieces of transmutation such as Coleman Hawkins's *Talk of the town* or Charlie Parker's *Embraceable you* can never quite be. And, with a few exceptions like the train piece *Little rootie-tootie*, his works never attempt to establish a particular atmosphere, as does *Mood indigo* by Duke Ellington, or to suggest a specific place, like Tadd Dameron's *Fontainebleau*.

They are, rather, investigations of perfectly specific musical ideas, such as the minor seconds idea of *Mysterioso* or the diminished fifth ideas of *Skippy*, which arise out of his unusually acute awareness of the expressive weight of a given melodic interval or rhythmic or harmonic pattern (3). If, however, there remains, even in the most violent passages, a kind of detachment, a feeling of objective exploration, it should not be imagined that all Monk offers is a series of abstractions. It is his achievement that in following such a path he created jazz which balances the rival claims of surprise and inevitability. Such music, to quote Brassai again, is "a rebellion against the misdeeds of a mechanised civilisation" (1), but also shows the artist, at an extreme pitch of technical and psychic tension, coming to terms with violence and disorder in the self and in the public world; indeed, that presumably is what its reconciliation of opposites is really about.

Monk's best jazz has, then, a more substantial intellectual content than most, and, while it would be naïve to imagine that lessens its power to move us, this world is not the easiest to enter. The private, self-contained nature of his music, its strange, mineral toughness, make it hard to grasp, and help explain the disproportionate popularity of a relatively untypical piece like *Round about midnight*. It may also account for undue emphasis on the humour in his work. A sharp wit, as ever manifesting itself in directly musical terms, is clear in such things as his caricature of *Tea for two*, with sophisticated bitonal harmony countered with deliberately stiff rhythms. But whenever we saw Monk at the piano he presented that admirable and, in the jazz world, rare spectacle of a serious artist wholly possessed by the urgency of the matter in hand, the creation of music. Humour was evident in his eccentric platform demeanour—away from the instrument—which, however offhand, clearly aimed if not to amuse then at least to disconcert. This may be regarded as a characteristically oblique comment on the social isolationism and outright rejection of the audience practised by other musicians of his generation, such as Charlie Parker. With typical parochialism, the jazz community believed the boppers' attitude to be unique, and uniquely reprehensible, while, as Monk's very dryness implies, it was a mild gesture compared, say, with the cubist painters' hermeticisation of content several decades earlier in protest against a commercialised academic tradition.

It is a deceptive simplification to say that we get the art we need and deserve, yet it may be that Monk was a little like the court jesters of old, who clothed their home-truths in just sufficient foolery. Whenever we saw him, the stiff-limbed, ungainly movements and bland smile appeared to be those of a buffoon, yet the harsh rhythms and acidulated dissonance of the music he played us said something altogether different (4).

Jazz Journal, June 1961

Lionel Hampton's RCA Recordings

The first recordings under Hampton's name were made in February 1937, while he was playing for Benny Goodman. From then until April 1941, by which time he had left Goodman and formed his own large band, he led a series of small combo recordings for the RCA company (1). There were twenty-three sessions from which nearly a hundred titles have been issued, and it is characteristic of Hampton's entire career that in quality they range from classic performances on a level with the finest jazz of their time to ones that show all too clearly what another vibraharpist, Teddy Charles, meant by "the heavy-footed jungle of swing" (2).

Usually the procedure was to make up his units largely from the personnels of established big ensembles, and it might have been assumed that men accustomed to working together would produce well-integrated performances, even on unfamiliar material. In fact, the best music came from groups of players not regularly associated with each other, although Hampton's choices were quite erratic. For example, though he occasionally invited fine trumpeters like Cootie Williams or Henry Allen to record with him, a place was repeatedly found for an abysmal vulgarian such as Ziggy Elman. These decisions would obviously be affected by the availability of musicians, but it is not surprising that the series is as inconsistent in style as it is uneven in quality.

His first date, using players exclusively from the Goodman band, was not a success, and *Jiving the vibes* is a fair sample. Based on a slight yet typical Hampton riff, this is an average snippet of mid-1930s swing, the best passage being the opening, which has the leader soloing over the saxophone section—a texture he used a number of times and obviously liked. Two months later he employed a more enterprising personnel taken from both Goodman and Duke Ellington ensembles, and it is apparent how much of their seemingly powerful identities the Ellingtonians lose when parted from his composing and orchestration. Lawrence Brown (trombone) is quite good on *Stompology*, but his *Buzzing around with the bee* solo is frankly nondescript. Cootie Williams is less at sea, though it is a pity that his solo on the latter piece was interrupted by a pointless spoken comment. Jess Stacy makes interjections of a different kind during the horn solos, and one is reminded of how personal a tone he always seemed able to draw from the piano.

Occasionally Hampton tried instrumentations which, regarding the conventions of the period, were a little unusual. One such used Buster Bailey and Johnny Hodges as front line, recalling the Apex Club sessions of almost a decade earlier by Jimmy Noone and Joe Poston. On *I know that you know* clarinet and alto saxophone achieve a perfectly equal-voiced contrapuntal texture: no composer's art could much improve on this. The horns then solo and the remainder of the piece is given over to a drumming exhibition by Hampton. At these dates, besides playing the vibraharp, he sang and resorted to drums and piano, though nothing of value emerged from his work—or rather assaults—on the latter instruments and *I know that you know* is an unfortunate example of how he might reduce to musical stupidity a performance that had begun on a level of most sensitive expression. However, it would be mistaken to assume that Hampton was only capable of the sort of drumming heard, say, on *Jiving with Jack the bellboy*, for with Goodman he often drummed far more musically, as the Trio's *I must have that man*, or *Smokehouse rhythm* with the full band show. His work on the blues singer Ida Cox's 1939 sessions, also, is a model of restraint and insight that would surprise those who have only heard him with his large band, when he usually sounds like the necessary man for a brutal and unsavoury occasion.

Several of the vibraharp solos do give an idea, though, of Hampton's real strengths and weaknesses as an improvisor, and his most obvious skill is an extreme facility, a seemingly unhesitating invention—and an apparent inability to sustain a line of musical argument for more than about sixteen bars. Much of his 'invention' proves to be a memorised stock of riff-type motives from which he compiles solos, although these figures are genuinely personal, and their influence on Goodman recordings such as *Shivers* is clear. Yet with most improvisors of stature remembered material is fused with properly fresh invention and the new ideas give further meaning to the old, partly through setting them in a novel context. What is discouraging about Hampton is that he is so ready to fall back on a juxtaposition of ready-made patterns without much effort at connecting them in a musically significant way.

Stompology and *Rhythm, rhythm* illustrate this. On the former he follows Cootie Williams's trumpet solo with a good, rather unexpected idea, developing it quite well for sixteen bars; then he breaks off, throwing in an entirely unrelated motive, and in the final eight measures he falls back on a riff from the piece's opening chorus. In *Rhythm, rhythm* his first thirty-two bars are excellent, particularly the latter sixteen, but the second chorus is far less convincing; its line has no follow-through beyond that supplied, from outside as it were, by the beat, and it is patched together of purposeless runs and bits and pieces from the previous chorus.

To mean anything substantial emotionally, music needs to possess its own kind of logic and unity, and Hampton's frequent stopping short of total involvement and refusal to bring the full weight of his talent to bear on the development of completed musical structures rob his up-tempo solos on so many of these records of much of their possible meaning. His chief reputation is as a hard and insistent swinger, but this public image is partial, even unjust, and ignores the deeper potential of his gifts. That first chorus on *Rhythm, rhythm* hints at the true state of affairs: he plays therein good, rather delicate, ideas which are robbed of their full effect by the rhythm section's pushing too hard. The fact is that although Hampton is especially associated with riff pieces and fast tempos they rarely bring out the best in him—rather as Art Tatum's trio recordings display only the most superficial aspect of his ability. With Hampton, unless he is in exceptional company, creative performance usually begins when the tempos are down and the pressure off. His refined linear sense is well exemplified by the Goodman Sextet's *Stardust* and by his own *I surrender, dear*, which he shows in a new light by revising the melody's phrasing and shifting its accents.

Yet how typical of Hampton's extreme variability that *Drum stomp* and *Piano stomp* should also have come from the session which produced the latter piece! Both are almost everything that the enemies of jazz imagine it always to be, and a heavy, thudding beat is used as the basis of the most pointless sort of virtuoso display. With rare exceptions like *Denison swing,* Hampton normally approaches the piano as a vibraharp, using his two forefingers like mallets, a self-defeating method that takes little account of the instrument's real nature, and, aside from a few cases such as his much later *Walking at the Trocadero*, one that has produced no worthwhile results (3).

1938 began with another date employing Hodges and Williams in which the latter's trumpet playing is the most notable feature. On *Ring dem bells* his entry is perfectly timed and the crescendo on his opening sustained note faultlessly graduated; how strangely this intense utterance contrasts with the inconsequential scat singing by Hampton which precedes it! Both here and in *You're my ideal* Edgar Sampson plays strikingly good baritone saxophone which, as his reputation scarcely survived the 1930s, would surprise many listeners, particularly on *Ring dem bells* where he has time to make a rounded statement. His tone and flexibility compare favourably with Jack Washington's playing in, say, Count Basie's *Somebody stole my gal*, and, were his ideas more original, could almost stand beside Harry Carney's work on the Ellington *New black and tan fantasy*.

The session of July 1938 was one of the two most nearly perfect of this entire series. Benny Carter's *I'm in the mood for swing* and *Shoe shiner's drag* (alias *London blues*) composed by Jelly Roll Morton are classics ranking with the best recorded jazz of their decade. Carter scored all four items, and in reality the date was more his than Hampton's, providing a fine illustration of some of his gifts. He is one of the most complete examples of musical talent known to jazz, though, as one might expect in view of the limitations imposed on this music, circumstances never allowed his full potential to be realised. He is a convincing multi-instrumentalist, above all a great alto saxophonist, and one of the few creative jazz arrangers. The beauty of Carter's alto solos is in no way lessened by their slight air of detachment; the tone has an almost luminous quality and the phrases seem sculpted out of the air, having a curiously three-dimensional effect. Very rare is the formal balance of these improvisations, and in his reconciliation of spontaneity with structural balance Carter may be compared with Fats Navarro. He contributes a magnificent solo to *I'm in the mood for swing*, yet it is chiefly through his arranging that he dominates the session, his influence being evident in many details on all four tracks, not least in the uncommonly well rehearsed ensemble choruses.

These show Carter's ability to bring off an unusual combination of punch and refinement, and each piece has an integrated wholeness and seeming inevitability to its development. The participants respond with admirably concise and pointed solos: note the sure calculation with which Harry James places the climax of his twelve bars on *Shoe shiner's drag*. This item in particular is a model of how to fit several quite varied solos into a confined space without any impression of overcrowding, and in this respect stands with Earl Hines's *Yellow fire*, almost with Ellington's *Jack the bear*. As in his recordings with Goodman, Hampton reacts to positive leadership and a clearly defined ensemble style with a much fuller exercise of his powers, and on

Muskrat ramble he plays what is probably the best solo he had recorded up to that time.

The group sound is dominated by the four saxophones, but Carter makes telling ensemble use of the vibraharp, especially in the opening sequences of *Shoe shiner's drag*, and the latter half of Hampton's *Mood for swing* solo unfolds in dialogue with the horns. The exchange between vibraharp and ensemble in *Muskrat ramble*, however, is rather obvious, and this, along with the triteness of Billy Kyle's piano solo, robs it of the classic wholeness of the other two pieces. There is further meaningful interplay between Hampton and the rest of the ensemble on the fourth item, *Anytime at all*, but this is a typical pop song of the time and very inferior in musical substance to its companions. Hearing it one realises that the other three performances derive at least some of their force from being based on intrinsically good themes.

Little space is usually given to the bandsmen on Hampton's piano features so *Rockhill special* is unusual in containing good music along with the keyboard antics. Goodman's band (with Hampton) was apparently in Chicago at the time of this date and opportune use was made of players from Hines's group. This was probably the sole occasion that employing several men from a permanent ensemble did pay dividends in terms of superior integration. Indeed, from this viewpoint the titles almost rank with those from the Carter session and, again, the hand of an outstanding arranger, Hines's Budd Johnson, is felt in the rounded completeness of each performance. Alvin Burroughs's splendid drumming provides exceptional lift, and its effect is felt in the surprisingly powerful ensemble playing. The tenor saxophone solo on *Rockhill special* is from Bob Crowder, one of several excellent but forgotten tenors of that decade.

Like *Muskrat ramble* or *Shoe shiner's drag*, *High society* was an odd choice for Hampton to record at his next date, the first of 1939. The reed section is again remarkable, but the leader can make little of this piece's traditional clarinet solo, though it is amusing to hear it on the vibraharp. There is a suggestion of real mastery in the shaping of Chew Berry's short tenor saxophone solo, and this musician's work, like Crowder's on *Rockhill special*, suggests that the neat division of 1930s tenor playing into the Coleman Hawkins and Lester Young schools is a considerable oversimplification. As performances with Cab Calloway such as *Lonesome nights* and *Ghost of a chance* show, Berry, in particular, was a major figure on the instrument, although there has been much inconsistency in the assessment of his work (4). Its tone, grainy and unusually hard for the period, represents an independent concept of saxophone timbre, and the structure of his solos, with their careful ordering of short phrases, shows real imagination. He was on his most persuasive form at Hampton's next session, monopolising the listener's attention not only during his *Sweethearts on parade* solo and behind the leader's singing, but also throughout what was clearly intended to be the vibraharp solo. Hampton begins decisively enough, yet is soon compelled to fall back into second place, and the result is an intriguing duet improvisation.

Something rather similar happens on *Shuffling at the Hollywood*, and at first sight it is surprising that these musicians should have been so adept at what amounts to a form of collective improvisation, for such playing was rare in the 1930s. However, Bailey and Hodges on the first chorus of *I know that you know*, Hawkins and Buck Washington in the last chorus of the former's *I ain't got nobody*, and Hampton and Goodman throughout the latter's *AC-DC current* are further examples, and, as the counterpoint of collective improvising is one of the most singular jazz achievements, it is perhaps latent in each phase of this music's development, surfacing whenever conditions allow. The sort of collaboration heard on *Shuffling at the Hollywood* or *AC-DC current* may represent one of the unfulfilled potentialities of 1930s swing.

In September 1939 Hampton assembled the most impressive personnel with which he ever recorded: Dizzy Gillespie, Benny Carter, Coleman Hawkins, Chew Berry, Ben Webster, Clyde Hart, Charlie Christian, Milt Hinton and Cozy Cole. While fully comparable with the session of July 1938, the results are less consistent despite some of the music reaching a still higher level. Carter's hand is again evident in the ensembles' potency, yet, almost inevitably, it is Hawkins who predominates. His exploitation of the rhapsodic vein of tenor saxophone playing was then at a peak and *One sweet letter* includes one of the supreme recorded examples of the genre from this period. Even so, his supremacy is less complete than might be supposed, and the leader especially is on his mettle in this company, perhaps too much so, for while on *One sweet letter* he reaches the standard he attained in *Muskrat ramble*, on the faster *Hot mallets* there is more than a hint of prefabrication to his solo. *When lights are low*, however, maintains so high a level in ensembles and improvising as to stand with *Shoe shiner's drag* and *I'm in the mood for swing*. Hampton's vocal alone robs *One sweet letter* of like status.

The highest pitch of interaction between individual players and the ensemble of which they are part is necessarily rare, especially in ad hoc groups; it should always be prized, yet its attainment ought never to be regarded as the sole criterion of quality. In their extreme unevenness Hampton's RCA sessions are typical of jazz as a whole, and it is important to recognise that the playing of Hawkins, Carter, the whole September 1939 rhythm team, and, on several titles, of the leader himself, embodies a kind of perfection. The very completeness of that perfection, however, of itself implied that there soon would be changes in jazz. Henry Allen's contribution to an October 1939 session gives rise to similar thoughts, albeit for a different reason. *I'm on my way from you* is mainly of interest for his trumpet solo, which is striking in its use of controlled slurs allied to an unexpected placing of accents. This kind of rhythmic freedom looks forward to the innovations of the 1940s, just as Chew Berry's short, detached phrases at faster tempos anticipate the melodic fragmentation of bop. The more we listen to recordings of the swing period with a knowledge of postwar jazz the less tenable does the notion of a 1940s musical 'revolution' become. Certainly Hampton's RCA dates are no less characteristic of their period for embodying hints of the future.

Remaining highlights are few, but *I can't get started* and *Blue because of you* should be noted. The latter, from 1940, is probably Hampton's finest ballad solo of the series: in logically sustained invention it points towards such mature works in this genre as his 1953 *September in the rain* and *I only have eyes for you*. He is nearly as good on *I can't get started*, but the cloying saxes and Elman's sentimental passage in the first chorus lessen the effect.

Granting the inevitable variation of musical quality in all these recordings, and the fact that the outputs of many jazzmen are blighted harvests, there remain the implications, for Hampton, of their stylistic inconsistency. That during the same period men with such differing aims and methods as Teddy Wilson and Sidney Bechet made far more unified series of recordings with similarly inconstant personnels must lead to Hampton's musical capabilities as a leader being questioned. It may appear absurd to entertain such doubts of a man who fronted a large band for several decades, yet it is important to locate where his gifts achieve their best expression. Although the vibraharp is the identifying link between all his recordings, it is undeniable that, especially when working beside his peers, he never imposes his personality on a group as true leaders always do. On the contrary, Hampton might be characterised as a lazy giant who only exercises his powers to the full when leadership and, if possible, a well-conceived ensemble style and framework are provided by others. But when that happens he can stand with the finest musicians of his generation.

Jazz Monthly, March 1963

Group Relations:
five commentaries

Different approaches to the problems of collective creation that, within the Western tradition, are almost unique to jazz.

Teddy Charles

The growth of a taste for music has several almost disconcerting aspects. Providing we do not restrict ourselves to an unduly narrow range of experience, we often find on returning to a piece that we have not heard for a long period that our reaction to it has markedly changed. This does not refer merely to the truism that fine music takes a while to yield all its secrets, or even to the half-truth that yesterday's revolutionary is tomorrow's reactionary. The point is, rather, that as experience grows the way in which we apprehend music subtly alters, that as time passes our sensibility itself is modified by our continuing involvement with the art.

To return after many years to some of Charles's New Directions recordings of the early 1950s is to be reminded of this rather forcibly. They were never touched, luckily, by the erratic flame of popular success, but on first appearance many of these performances had an almost wilful air of eccentricity, their procedures seeming to bear little relation to what was then going forward in jazz. Yet none of them was a mere *farce d'atelier*, and certain items could later be recognised as among the earliest intimations of what was going to happen during the 1960s. An obvious example is the 1953 *Variations on a motive by Bud*, which does not have the sort of repeating chord sequence that formed the basis of nearly all jazz then, and which, in its structural aspect, glances forward to the music of Ornette Coleman and more particularly John Coltrane.

In those years Charles remarked (1) on the need he felt for a jazz performance to be as integrated as possible, chiefly through an interaction between composing and improvisation. His attitude is here similar to that of all real jazz composers from Jelly Roll Morton to George Russell, and it is unsurprising that he had decided views on the desirability of using pieces written specifically for jazz purposes rather than taking material from the world of popular entertainment. Remembering the many fine improvisations jazz musicians have based on the latter, however, it is not surprising that Charles has been inconsistent here, and has included items such as *Nature boy* and *When your lover has gone* on his LPs.

He was correct to emphasise the influence good themes should have on a man's improvising, but found that not a few performers offered resistance to the challenges inherent to the sort of music he wished to present. Others had the same trouble, of course, and of all the players who recorded with Thelonious Monk perhaps only Milt Jackson, Art Blakey, Lucky Thompson, Thad Jones and possibly Max Roach and Sonny Rollins can be said to have produced genuinely organic improvisations on his themes. Despite the predictable discouragements, Charles repeatedly composed and commissioned pieces which lead players to attempt new areas of extemporisation, to evolve not only a larger melodic vocabulary but freer harmonic relationships and more varied formal patterns. This recalls George Russell's endeavours, but whereas that unique innovator developed a central, strikingly original theory (2), Charles was an empiricist, trying first one approach then another.

In view of his association with Charles Mingus's Jazz Workshop, it was not surprising to find him, on *Wailing Dervish* and *Further out*, trying for contrapuntal textures not only in the pre-set theme statements but in the improvised choruses also. These attempts are not maintained throughout the performances as during Shorty Rogers's trumpet solos the leader sets down quiet supporting chords on his vibraharp. Yet when it is Charles's turn to solo Rogers plays sequences of phrases that are not just accompaniment but form an independent, though fully related, line. It is noteworthy in both these pieces, and in *Etudiez le cahier* from the same 1953 date, that this extempore interweaving is more convincing in its effect than the fully written-out counterpoint of, say, *Composition for four pieces* dating from the previous year.

Jazzmen at that time were extremely conservative in their adherence to the twelve-bar format of the blues and to the thirty-two-bar chorus of most popular songs—arranged in an AABA pattern of four eight-bar phrases. There were exceptions, like Duke Ellington's *Hip chick* (12+8+12) and John Lewis's *S'il vous plaît* (12+12+8+12), but Charles did well to try something more adventurous. *Variations on a motive by Bud*, for example, has a forty-eight-bar chorus in six eight-bar sections (ABCDED), and *Wailing Dervish* is an interesting embodiment of rondo format. Following an eight-bar introduction, the thematic material is of sixty-four bars length—ABACADA—and each segment is again of eight bars except D, which is sixteen. However, the improvised choruses are of only fifty-six bars and it would seem that the D section is therein halved. Although these ventures found an echo in a few pieces such as Duane Tatro's *Dollar day* (12+12+12+4+12) and Pepper Adams's *Adams in the Apple* (12+8+12+8+8), it cannot be said that this aspect of Charles's ideas ever met with much response, and this is unfortunate.

A broader kind of formal working is demonstrated on several tracks of the *Tentet* and *Word from Bird* LPs. The eponymous piece from the latter, with its constantly shifting balance between soloists and ensemble, the transitions from one chorus to another, the ways in which passage from one chorus to another is disguised, is especially typical of Charles's initiatives at their most immediately fruitful. Even better here is the skilful manner in which the soloists are, as it were, absorbed into the ensemble, the way, as the performance unfolds, that the character of the group is increasingly asserted and the improvisors made part of a larger unity.

Yet it may be that Charles's harmonic sense is his strongest single quality. Sometimes, as in *Edging out*, he is content to make conventional use of a chord sequence which repeats, basically unchanged, throughout the performance. But the altered harmonies of *Nature boy* and *Night in Tunisia* (which has altered rhythms, too), the dense chromaticism of *Green blues* or the modal ideas of *Etudiez le cahier* show him at his best. In *Further out* Charles said he used "non-triadic harmonies to see what kind of blowing [improvising] would come out of using just a simple bass line". This has polytonal elements—in the accompaniment to Rogers's first solo, for example—and perhaps to counterbalance the unusual chordal framework, the theme is an orthodox thirty-two-bar AABA.

Variations on a motive by Bud was particularly adventurous for its time as, instead of the usual recurring harmonic sequence, it employs a left-hand device of Bud Powell's which results in a constant, though irregular, fluctuation between the tonalities of F and G-flat. Eliptical yet expressively resonant, Charles's two solo choruses at the vibraharp most intelligently exploit the ambiguities which thus arise. Elsewhere, as on *Night in Tunisia*, he displays remarkable virtuosity, but his finest recorded improvisations are probably in *Green blues*, *The quiet time* and *When your lover has gone*. Other excellent solos came from the guitarist Jimmy Raney, who has an attractive melodic sense the obliqueness of which is enhanced by his curiously muffled tone; to *Night in Tunisia* and *Nature boy*, especially, he contributes pieces of closely-argued linear invention which fully justify the leader's altered harmonisations.

Though less overtly exploratory than the New Directions series, a number of the pieces Charles recorded with larger ensembles still offer considerable satisfactions. These include the tense yet furiously mobile lines of Russell's *Lydian M-1*, the well calculated ensemble dissonance of Charles's own *Emperor*, Gil Evans's beautiful recomposition of *You go to my head*, and Mal Waldron's *Vibrations*. Besides fine solos from Gigi Gryce (alto saxophone) and Raney, this last has two themes, one agitated and rhythmic, the other smoothly romantic, that are combined at the close with a skill reminiscent of Ellington's *Hot and bothered*.

From such varied endeavour it obviously must be hard to decide Charles's exact position. Perhaps at times more interested in experiments with the musical language of jazz than in communication, he was, as already noted, essentially an empiricist who anticipated various procedures which came to have central significance in later jazz. But that should be enough to challenge stereotyped ways of thinking about this music. Each new major figure is praised and condemned as 'revolutionary' and his work taken to mark a completely fresh departure. Yet the music of lesser men often shows that even the most arresting of 'new' ideas have been in the air for years beforehand. Even the most iconoclastic apparent trail-blazer may reflect a general situation—albeit in an intensified way—more than he institutes radical changes. The pioneer explorer and the builder of a new city are rarely the same man.

Jazz Monthly, November 1962

Bunk Johnson

Concern with New Orleans jazz, of all varieties, has declined since the high fanaticism of the 1940s and that is not surprising, as fanaticism is hard to keep up. Yet, remembering the fever-pitch of interest during that intolerant decade, it is surprising that we have so little exact knowledge of what happened to jazz, at various times, in New Orleans. Among the chief relevant happenings of the 1940s were William Russell's recording sessions for his American Music label, which brought us performances that were in several respects new and puzzling. And it is typical of our ignorance that while there is general agreement, among European listeners (1), on the fine quality of this music, we remain uncertain of its historical significance. What stage, or stages, of jazz development does the work of Bunk Johnson, of Wooden Joe Nicholas, of George Lewis and of the others represent?

When their discs first appeared they were assessed by standards derived from recordings made in the 1920s by King Oliver, Jelly Roll Morton and Louis Armstrong that were almost universally thought to exemplify 'classic New Orleans jazz'. The long-term effect of the American Musics, plus associated material on the Delta, Climax and other labels, was, finally, to show how untenable that over-simplified notion was. In the end, such performances "changed the way we listened to jazz" (2), but at first they were judged and inevitably found wanting because the criteria used were irrelevant. Following this, it was decided that this must be the music of the inferior players left behind when the money and real opportunities went North. Yet it cannot be shown that all good musicians left the South—the recordings made in New Orleans by Sam Morgan's band are enough to prove otherwise—or that they necessarily followed Oliver, Morton & Co. into the Chicago recording studios. Bunk Johnson, to take an obvious instance, was professionally active throughout the period during which the 'classics' of New Orleans jazz were set down, but, due to extensive touring and other reasons, never then recorded.

A more sophisticated line was that American Music and similar catalogues represented a stage of jazz earlier than that of the long-familiar and widely distributed recordings of the 1920s. As such they were dismissed because of the music's supposedly obvious crudity. Much self-interest was involved here. A number of writers had established their reputations establishing the 'classic New Orleans' status of the Morton, Oliver and Armstrong recordings, and to have re-examined the whole question of what really happened to New Orleans jazz, both at home and away, clearly would have been too much trouble. Easier to dismiss the new records out of hand and hope that everybody would forget them (3).

Naturally, some people did not. They praised this unfamiliar jazz as 'urban folk music', yet this was no more perceptive. If a music is functional and strictly related to its immediate use it is truly folk music, but it was never explained how, or why, this particular variety of 'urban folk music' had been preserved unaltered over several decades in a constantly changing society. The theory is, anyway, exploded by the ages of most of the musicians who made these recordings. Some, like Alcide Pavageau and Wooden Joe Nicholas, are of Oliver's and Morton's generation, while others, such as Kid Rena and Shots

Madison, are of Armstrong's. These men were working musicians, not antiquaries. Why should they, just for recording purposes, revert to the jazz of some unspecified generation earlier than their own?

Bruce King once suggested that the discs "represent a slightly corrupted version of New Orleans jazz as it was played after the migration of Ory, Oliver and Louis to the West and North" (4). How long after? It is hard to believe that at the time they left New Orleans jazz was at all close to what we hear on the American Music and similar recordings of the 1940s or else the discs they made in the North would show similar characteristics. True, the Oliver Creole Band of 1923 must have had to tighten-up its performances for recording purposes, and the textures might well have been more relaxed when they played in public. But the structure is quite different from anything on American Music. The lead is always firmly held by the two cornets, not passed around from one part to another with the remarkable fluency we find on Johnson's or Nicholas's records. Nor, recording limitations aside and despite Baby Dodds being the drummer both with Oliver and on the finest of Johnson's American Musics, is there any real evidence of the sometimes quite complex relation between horns and percussion heard on some of the discs made in the 1940s.

Is it reasonable to suggest that these changes must have come about gradually as the result of steady development rather than of King's "slight corruption"? Is it possible that the music we hear on American Music and similar labels was actually perfected in the late 1930s? After all, the titles Ory made in Los Angeles in 1922 show no sign of a development in that direction. Nor do recordings produced in New Orleans itself during the 1920s, such as the Oscar Celestins of 1925 (which use Shots Madison), the excellent Sam Morgans of 1927 (which include Jim Robinson), or the Jones-Collins Astoria Hot Eights of 1929. Perhaps one of our difficulties is that we have never completely got rid of the up-the-river-from-New Orleans interpretation of jazz history. Certainly jazz went to Chicago and passed through important changes there, but is there any reason to suppose it did not continue developing, along other lines, in New Orleans as we know it did in the Southwest (5)? Do the American Musics simply mark the stage reached by the mid-1940s, with subsequent records, such as the Icons by Punch Miller, Thomas Valentine and others, representing later changes?

This is an attractive idea yet still too simple, for different generations and therefore divergent, though closely-related, attitudes to jazz are represented on the same performances. Johnson's regular band is the best instance: he was born in 1879, Robinson, the trombonist, was born in '92 and was roughly of the Oliver-Morton age-group, Lewis, the clarinetist, was born in 1900 and was the same age as Armstrong. It will be useful to summarise so far as possible the three main approaches that can be detected on the American Music and similar recordings. Clearly we shall never know what Buddy Bolden (born *c* 1868) himself sounded like, but, to judge from Johnson's work, jazz was played by that generation with quite legitimate instrumental technique, without the smears and slurs from one note to another that were apparently introduced later. There was little swing in the post-Armstrong sense and melodies were subject to rather formal variations, perhaps influenced by piano ragtime and earlier dance musics. So far as we can tell from records made in the early and middle 1920s, jazz was, for Oliver's and Morton's generation, still a quite deliberate type of music-making. The discipline of Oliver's Creole Band could scarcely be more obvious, and the best of Morton's Red Hot Peppers present a composer's formalisation of this. Progress in the real sense is marked by the music's greater emotional impact, which derives from its absorption of the blues, and, probably, superior standards of performance.

Perhaps it was with this generation, however, that a split began to appear, the first sign of the myriad styles jazz was to develop later. Born in 1883, Wooden Joe Nicholas was of Oliver's age-group but on his 1945 American Music dates plays extremely varied music, quite unlike Oliver's, or Morton's. Of course, it does not follow that Nicholas would, or could, have performed in this manner, say, twenty years before, yet the differences between his trumpeting and Oliver's show that even within a single generation jazz could grow in quite divergent ways. With the next generation, that of Armstrong, the split became more obvious. Some of them, as we know, went North, and, in company with certain of their elders such as Morton and Oliver, made the recordings which until the arrival of the Deltas, Climaxes and American Musics were thought to be 'typical' New Orleans jazz but which can now be recognised as an independent and essentially post-New Orleans—indeed, Chicagoan—development.

Those who remained at home may slowly have grown towards the kind of jazz caught on American Music in the mid-1940s. This meant looser, more open ensemble textures, lighter rhythm, easier swing. Common to both branches of this generation, as Samuel Charters has pointed out (6), is their abandonment of elaborate, multi-strain rags for simpler material which facilitates a more continuous style of extempore playing. Those in the North, led by Armstrong, perfected solo improvisation and went on to popular ballads which led to the harmonic sophistication of swing and bop. The others appear to have developed a form of jazz whose chief means of expression were contrapuntal subtlety—on both melodic and rhythmic levels—and variety of ensemble texture.

We should also remember the personal tastes, and theories, of the men who supervised the recording sessions, a matter first raised by Jerome Shipman (7). Writing of George Lewis's 1943 Climaxes he said "[William] Russell picked the personnel (not to say the instrumentation), the repertoire and in New York even arranged the way the music was presented. In a way the Climax records are as much his as they are Lewis's, and if Lewis furnished the raw genius, Russell brought out what was in him". And there are definite instances of musicians and supervisors disagreeing. When Johnson recorded with members of the Lu Watters band he wanted to do current hits like *Mairzy doats* but ended with the more 'acceptable' *Careless love, Ory's Creole trombone*, etc. Later, when taping regular working New Orleans bands, recording supervisors replaced saxophones with clarinets, in accordance with long-untenable purist theories on jazz. Sometimes one feels that records such as the American Musics embody so many on-the-spot compromises—between different generations of musicians, between the players' abilities and experience and the supervisors' preconceptions and misconceptions that their historical significance must be slight. Is there much more to it than that?

Even if this were the answer it would not, of course, diminish the high quality of the jazz on American Music and Climax in particular. Indeed, that worth suggests that in these circumstances compromise may be no bad thing. Johnson's regular band, with Lewis and Robinson, was once famous for its internal dissensions, yet the leader was either one or two generations away from his various players and so differences were to be expected. It might be apt to polarise the disagreements by saying that they wanted to give rather complex ensemble treatments to simple material while he wished to play straightforward performances of fairly elaborate rags and similar pieces.

On the vexed question of supervision, whether it be considered enlightened guidance or puritanical interference, it is now impossible to find out how much control Johnson had over his recording sessions. According to Harold Drob (8), the 1947 Columbia dates, his last, were the only ones really to accord with Johnson's ideas. But the 1944 broadcast titles are so very similar that we can assume he had his own way there also. In his 1942 notes for the Jazz Information sides of that same year, Eugene Williams wrote "Bunk himself selected the tunes, directed the rehearsals and the recording session". Now although Johnson's reputation chiefly rests on his American Musics, it clearly is important that jazz recorded at sessions over which we can assume he had control is so strikingly different in repertoire and especially in organisation. Comparisons suggest that he must have had to alter his preferred way of playing quite considerably to create properly integrated music with Robinson and Lewis, and credit is due to him, particularly in view of his age, for being able to do so.

Although his own attitude is presumably represented by the fact that, according to Drob, he wanted, during the band's New York engagements, to replace Robinson with Sandy Williams, he played the rather involved ensemble style of the American Musics with real skill and imagination. Neither Lewis nor Robinson would have had the musicianship to adapt themselves so much. Continued listening to Johnson's records over several decades convinces one of two things. First that he was far from being a decrepit has-been who could only just manage to stutter out the notes—indeed, this is a view which survives little contact with his actual music. Second, that he knew all along what he wanted to do musically and what he was equipped for. It can easily be shown that, despite the decided contrary views of recording men, he held to these aims with remarkable consistency on the few sessions at which he had real freedom. None of this is to attack the American Music recordings, which include some very beautiful performances, but any view of Johnson based solely on this label is bound to be partial.

His first recordings, for Jazz Man and Jazz Information in 1942, are by no means of merely historical interest, and each of the two dates has its own particular characteristics and values. Common to both is the poor recording and balance, for they were made with limited equipment, especially the Jazz Mans. On the second, Jazz Information, session the beat is quite raggy, more driving than freely swinging. Because of this the parts occasionally sound cramped, almost stiff, yet this date produced generally better music. The two versions of *Sobbing blues*, for example, are of considerable interest. *No. 2*—which actually was recorded first—is the slower, and here the rhythm section is rather too heavy, but in both versions there is good counterpoint between trumpet and clarinet, and at the close Lewis plays the melody against a

hot 'second trumpet' part by the leader. This is a genuinely imaginative passage that is more effective at the faster tempo of *No. 1*.

On neither of these sessions did Lewis's playing show much of the
feeling for the blues which, with its searingly-accented flat thirds and
sevenths, so marked his American Music work. A partial exception,
though, is the Jazz Information *Franklin Street blues*, on which he takes
two choruses which are easily his most lucid playing up to that point.
To get an idea of his variability in those days, contrast this with his solo
on *Bluebells goodbye*, which is merely a confusedly decorated version of
the original melody.

More important, however, are the two general insights which
emerge about Johnson. The first is his apparently constant preoccupation with variety of ensemble texture. Immediately disposed of is the
widely-propagated notion that he dropped out of ensembles due to
exhaustion. On the Jazz Information *Weary blues*, recorded at the end
of a twelve-title session, he blows just as powerfully as in *Big Chief Battle-
axe* cut at the beginning. Further, the technical control of his playing
on the 1947 Columbias, made two years before his death, should be
obvious to anyone who takes the trouble to listen to the records. The
simple truth is that Johnson fell out of definite parts of some pieces to
produce striking effects of contrast, the Jazz Man *Panama* and Jazz
Information *Thriller rag* being clear instances. (A trouble on the latter
session, though, is that Johnson's silences expose the extraordinarily
square trombone playing of Albert Warner.)

This kind of shifting of interest led to the subtle passing of the lead
from one instrument to another that is so striking a feature of Johnson's
best American Music titles. He, Lewis and Robinson did not invent
this procedure, of course, for it is almost equally evident on, say,
Wooden Joe Nicholas's recordings, as already noted. It was, perhaps,
the result of a long tradition of collectively-improvised ensemble playing, was 'in the air' in New Orleans jazz during the 1940s, and came to
the surface no matter what compromises or other unfavourable conditions affected any particular date. Certainly it is noteworthy that
Johnson and his men, whatever their differences of outlook, began to
move towards this sort of complexity as soon as they started playing
together, and even on such tentative sessions as these. As indicated,
Johnson was aiming at something quite different all along, and,
although to a fastidious and honest temperament no conformity comes
easily, he seems to have got involved almost despite himself.

Luckily these tendencies within New Orleans jazz of that time sorted very well with his search for textural variety. For example, in *Down by the riverside*, one of the best of the Jazz Mans, Robinson, though badly off-mike, clearly takes the lead for two sixteen-bar periods with Lewis playing a subsidiary part. Nobody takes a solo; this is all ensemble; when Johnson falls out there is simply a change of overall sound. On *Storyville blues* he plays the usual kind of lead during the first two choruses but it is hard to say who is leading in the third. The trumpet is still there, yet, especially in the earlier bars, it plays subordinate figures, and the lead is, as it were, suspended between all three horns.

To generalise, Johnson's silence in the fourth chorus is prepared by his being progressively less assertive in the first three. More than any other title recorded that day, *Make me a pallet on the floor* looks forward to their later achievements together. The ensemble is in three real—that is, independent—parts almost throughout and it is especially regrettable here that the front-line could not be properly balanced so far as recording was concerned. Still, the texture is sufficiently open for almost everything to be heard. Again, there is a kind of 'suspended' lead in the earlier part of the second chorus, in the fourth, and to some degree elsewhere. On the second chorus of *Moose march* Lewis takes the lead, but at the opening and again at the close of this chorus Johnson plays subsidiary figures: he did not always simply drop out.

Most instructive of the trumpeter's concern, even at this early stage, with variety is to compare the Jazz Man and Jazz Information accounts of *Weary blues*. The Jazz Man is more relaxed, has a more genuine swing, yet is a far cruder performance. This is not simply because Johnson and the others had slightly less technical command than a few months later, but because on Jazz Information the trumpet lead is deliberately organised chorus by chorus. Johnson lessens the force of his attack in the fourth and seventh choruses, decreases further in the eighth, falls out of the fifth and ninth and plays with especial force, for contrast, in the sixth and tenth. Lewis, despite poor balance, gains greater prominence during the fourth, seventh and eighth choruses as well as the fifth and ninth. Yet while it would be only a slight exaggeration to say the clarinet moves progressively forward from the fourth to the ninth choruses, Johnson retains the lead throughout. In fact there is scarcely any lead-passing on the Jazz Information titles, presumably on account of the trombonist's weakness.

The consistency of Johnson's musical aims is less surprising than may appear at first sight. He has often been written about as if it were a miracle that he was able to play at all in the 1940s, as if he had been out of music for about twenty years. In fact he retired in 1932, was first contacted by jazz researchers in '38, and so was completely out of sight for only six years. Although the Jazz Information account of *Weary blues* is better done and more interesting than the Jazz Man of a few months before, no attentive listener could miss that he tried to follow the same basic concept of the piece on both occasions. This is even clearer with his two versions of *Balling the jack*. The earlier of these comes from his first, Jazz Man, session and the second from the San Francisco broadcast of two years later. While it is true the latter has solos from Wade Whaley on clarinet and from Floyd O'Brien's trombone, it is essentially a more completely realised performance of what Johnson had tried to do two years before. He had at his disposal, of course, musicians of greater technical accomplishment who, besides O'Brien and Whaley, included Red Callender and Lee Young. These are not the kind of players with whom Johnson is popularly associated, yet the records show that he was able to get along with them admirably.

Indeed, his adaptability was one of his most remarkable and least recognised qualities. He had one way of playing and organising a performance on 'his' sessions and another for Lewis, Robinson (and William Russell) on American Music. Nor is this all. In 1943, after the Jazz Man and Jazz Information dates and before the San Francisco session, he recorded eleven items with members of Lu Watters's Yerba Buena Band. Here his approach is different again. During the ensembles he firmly occupies the centre of the stage, playing the most skilfully-varied continuous leads, with no real gaps. Although the effect of his playing is heightened by the inept, entirely derivative work of the Yerba Buena yobs, Johnson, who must have felt like a panther yoked to a plough, was particularly fluent and imaginative on this session. His solo in *Careless love*, for example, is excellent by any relevant standards. It also is most instructive to compare *The girls go crazy about the way I walk* from this date with the following year's account of the tune for American Music (on which it is sensitively retitled *All the whores like the way I ride*). Probably neither version was ideal from Johnson's point of view, yet these are both masterly readings.

So far as critical attention is concerned, Johnson's unique session with Sidney Bechet is the most neglected part of his output. But here is shown yet another side of his musical personality, another way of playing. Bechet, of course, was one of the virtuosos who helped perfect solo improvisation, and so from an 'historical' or 'evolutionary' angle this date represents the meeting of two very different views of jazz. It is even more surprising that Johnson and Bechet produced such fine results together than it is that the trumpeter did so well with Lewis and Robinson. The biggest surprise, however, is that three of the four issued titles show such marked differences from the normal run of Bechet recordings and give every indication of being organised according to Johnson's ideas. This must be one of the very few sessions in which Bechet took part that he did not dominate completely.

Perhaps the most beautiful passage is the opening choruses of the slow *Days beyond recall*. These have a two-part interplay between trumpet and Bechet's clarinet, some of it in closely-argued counterpoint near—in quality, not style—to Armstrong and Johnny Dodds on the 1927 *Potato head blues*. The two-part texture continues during Bechet's solo with fill-ins from Sandy Williams's trombone, and then Bechet fills-in throughout Williams's solo, a quiet third part being added by Johnson. Some of the intensity of the final ensemble comes from the equality of the three voices, each most beautifully adjusted to the other two. The ensembles of *Milenburg joys* are a trifle more stereotyped, and almost the best passages are the trumpet, trombone and clarinet solos, each with counterpoint by the other two horns. Again, though, the crown of the performance is the closing equal-voiced ensemble, so much richer musically than the near-dixieland patterns of the final choruses of some of Bechet's other recordings. *Up in Sidney's flat* is dominated by Williams's eloquent trombone, but its 'solo' is always accompanied by the other horns. Johnson's playing is then set in a like context and he leads into another magnificent closing ensemble (9).

Jazz Monthly, March 1967

Hal McKusick

McKusick was never lucky with the LPs he had issued in this country. On records such as *Jazz at the Academy* or *East Coast Jazz* the tracks' shortness prevented any sustained development of ideas and all we hear are brief solos. Not that McKusick cannot improvise. He usually

is dismissed as being a disciple of Lee Konitz, though in fact his work on clarinet, bass clarinet and tenor saxophone, as well as alto saxophone, his main instrument, avoids that musician's sometimes rather pointless harmonic ingenuity and ranges from the clear-toned blues distillation heard in George Russell's *Night sound* to an acid gaiety on *Round Johnny rondo*.

He is, of course, an entirely minor figure, but one who understands his limitations and knows what to do about them. Only the masters of jazz can, through the sheer quality of their musical thought, hold our interest over long distances with solo improvisation alone, and McKusick needs to offer something more, his most satisfying discs being the most carefully planned. Indeed, he is perhaps best thought of as the finest kind of executant—one who provides opportunities for others more creative than himself. *Jazz Workshop* (1) and *Cross Section Saxes* (2) may have slipped through the coarse net of contemporary attention, a crude web that, for a while, holds many gaudier objects, yet this is because their message is not a simple one. McKusick aimed, firstly, at achieving as much outward diversity as possible—through groups of varied size and instrumentation, through employing writers with quite different approaches. Secondly, he wanted to produce what may be termed 'composer's jazz', but, as this art has few composers, the result was unavoidably a mixture of composers' and arrangers' music. Indeed, the main point about these records is that they usefully illustrate differences between composer and arranger, between artist and craftsman, between creating new ideas and reshuffling old.

The basis of the 1956 *Workshop* disc was a quartet McKusick led during the 1950s. Although it fulfilled a number of public engagements—of which *Jazz at the Academy* is a recorded instance—this was mainly a private rehearsal group that played for its own satisfaction and Al Cohn's *Ain't nothing but a memory now* is typical of what they did. This is a thirty-two-bar AABA that uses McKusick's alto saxophone and Barry Galbraith's guitar sometimes antiphonally, sometimes together in the rather fragmentary A section which contrasts quite effectively with the flowing four-bar phrases carried by the leader in B. On its return A is cut to six bars to accommodate a guitar break, and the thematic restatement at the end is also only six bars—a pleasing formal aberration.

Upon his well-integrated quartet McKusick built a quintet, an octet, a nonet and a dectet. Manny Albam's *Alto cumulus* and Johnny Mandel's *Tommyhawk* are played by an octet, and, despite the substitution of electric guitar for french horn, resemblances to Miles Davis's Capitol recordings, some of which are discussed on another page, are obvious. In this respect they should be heard in conjunction with Gerry Mulligan Tentet pieces such as *Ballad* and the rather earlier Shorty Rogers items with a comparable instrumentation, like *Sam and the lady*. On the 1958 *Cross Section Saxes* LP are several titles scored for a four-piece saxophone section (two altos, tenor and baritone) and rhythm which, though obviously making a very different sound, demonstrate the same craftsmanlike handling of established ideas. Of these McKusick wrote in the sleeve note, "the sax players were chosen for their ability to work as a section. We aimed for a feeling of unity, a togetherness that is best illustrated by the sax sections of the early Benny Goodman band, and the Count Basie crew which recorded *Jump the blues away*". Fortunately, however, the results speak of their own time, rather than for some kind of 'mainstream' revivalism.

Two of them are scored by Ernie Wilkins, a highly competent, totally uninspired craftsman if ever there was one, and he catches the subdued moodiness of Benny Golson's *Whisper not* quite well. But *Now's the time*, Charlie Parker's recordings of which are dealt with elsewhere in this book, here emerges as a curiosity, with the original 1945 alto solo arranged for the whole reed section. This practice, strange though it might be, is not uncommon, and among early examples may be cited Don Redman's 1928 score of *Milenburg joys* for McKinney's Cotton Pickers, which includes Leon Roppolo's clarinet solo from the 1923 New Orleans Rhythm Kings recording written out for the whole reed section. In the case of *Now's the time* the resulting blandness shows that despite the melodic, rhythmic and harmonic richness that make Parker's music an analyst's paradise, much of its expressive force derives from his acutely personal tone and inflection.

Disappointing in a rather different way are *La rue* and *The last day of fall*, arranged by George Handy. These are tepid indeed beside the agreeable density of musical incident packed into his scores for the underrated Boyd Raeburn band of the mid-1940s, particularly if one recalls such items as *Yerxa*, which featured McKusick (then a Raeburn bandsman) and made intelligent use of Ellingtonian procedures. *La rue*, like *Whisper not*, is redeemed by a Bill Evans piano solo which probes considerably deeper than the arrangement. But none of the writing discussed so far, though successful in achieving its modest aims, communicates any fresh experience, embodies any technical discoveries: it can offer nothing beyond entertainment. It is an indication of McKusick's ability that he sought more complex challenges, and, on his humbler level, the listener, too, as these discs become familiar, turns increasingly to those tracks whereon musical material is handled in a more uncompromising way.

Dividing an artist's output into the customary early, middle and late periods is usually a drastic simplification, yet, if not applied too rigidly, can help us to see the pattern of his development more clearly. And it works quite well in George Russell's case. His initial phase is represented by a few isolated pieces like *Cubana be/ bop* written for Dizzy Gillespie's band, and *Odjenar* and the first version of *Ezz-thetic* recorded by the youthful Lee Konitz and Miles Davis. These showed little sense of direction and were frankly exploratory. Hints of later maturity can be found in the highly eventful *Bird in Igor's yard* recorded by Buddy deFranco, however, and formulation, after several years' work, of the Lydian Concept of Tonal Organisation (3) led to the 'middle period' scores found on the two McKusick LPs discussed here, on Russell's own *Jazz Workshop* disc of 1956 (4), and elsewhere. The third phase came with his remarkable, though little-known, series of Sextet records, which showed a general loosening-up in his theories and their application. Theories are always suspect in the arts, and rightly so, but the *Workshop* and associated LPs show that what Russell offered was no mere theory, no private system of little use to others.

Simply, he examined the entire harmonic resources of Western music, saw and systematised an entirely fresh set of relationships that had always been present within the traditional framework and which, as it were, only awaited discovery. Far from being a constricting set of regulations, Russell's precepts made available resources whose full possibilities, in the composer John Benson Brooks's words, "may take as much as a century to work out" (5). And according to Art Farmer, trumpeter on many of these discs, the Lydian Concept "opens the doors to countless means of melodic expression. It also dispels many of the don'ts and can'ts that, to various degrees, have been imposed on the improvisor through the study of traditional harmony" (6). Of course, it is necessary to remember Schoenberg's words, "ideas can only be honoured by one who has some of his own" (7)—that is to say Russell offers no magic formula to transform mediocre soloists into good ones. But the gifted improvisor is not the only one to benefit. These investigations led Russell to produce music that has strong individuality yet which is very subtle, that teems with invention but is absolutely consistent stylistically. And in the sheer variety of his thematic materials he surpasses all jazz composers except Duke Ellington.

Many of the *Workshop* items, recorded under both Russell's and McKusick's names, demonstrate this variety, and two of them, *Night sound* and *Jack's blues*, however different, might both be called jazz nocturnes. The theme section of the latter, although having a definite pulse, conveys an impression of a mobile, undecided tempo, and evolves from a sinuous, blues-derived melody; *Night sound*, with its shifting tonal centres, has contrapuntal lines which are distinct yet constantly overlap. These are masterly scores, as intricate and nearly as functional as watches, with a quiet intensity that is peculiarly Russell's; no words could hope even to suggest the searching originality with which each instrumental part is organised, nor the constantly changing ensemble textures.

In contrast, *Miss Clara* has cranky, angular thematic lines, suggesting the lady may have something in common with Auden's Miss Edith Gee. The most striking passage is perhaps the unaccompanied contrapuntal opening between Farmer's trumpet and Jimmy Cleveland's trombone, though elsewhere the jerky linear movement is tellingly accentuated by thick scoring. In each of these pieces the composer's originality qualifies every detail, so that apparently nothing is determined by mere formula. It is no paradox that, at the same time, Russell seems here the most sophisticated of jazzmen, with a greater awareness of the outside musical world than others. The Stravinskian ostinatos of *Ye hypocrite, ye Beelzebub* are noticeable enough, and on pieces like *Fellow delegates* percussion is used with almost Bartokian sensitivity.

Again, when Russell has a soloist improvise in one key with an accompaniment in another (e.g. Farmer in A minor against a B-flat minor background on *Knights of the steamtable*), it recalls Bartók's device, in his String Quartets and elsewhere, of accompanying a melody only with notes that do not occur in the melody itself: in each case a tension between unlike and unlike is produced. The *Workshop* LPs' rigorous yet never academic application of Russell's ideas hints, also, at his awareness of Schoenbergian continuous variation technique (anticipated, in jazz, by Ellington's *Old King Dooji*, but never followed up), and his recurring aim of expressing several contrasted moods during one piece, as in *Jack's blues* or the alfresco *Ballad of Hix Blewitt*, similarly parallels that master's lifelong preoccupation with fusing several movements into one (e.g. String Quartet Op. 7, Piano

Concerto Op. 42).

Undoubtedly the best instances of this are *Lydian lullaby* and *The day John Brown was hanged*, both recorded by McKusick, the latter being the most substantial of Russell's 'middle period' works. Both are played by a quartet (with the composer as extra percussionist in the second piece), and both involve the transformation, as well as the contrast, of quite different shades of feeling. *Lullaby* opens with the kind of restlessness also found amid the agitated geometry of *Livingstone, I presume,* and resolves to an overtly romantic mood whose continuing uneasiness is conveyed by a mixture of tense and of rather languorous phrases. Gradually this assumes a more dancelike character, but the restlessness, which was never far away, cannot be held off, and returns.

In *The day John Brown was hanged* the same formal and emotional scheme is written larger and more elaborately. Again the opening presents agitated, highly rhythmic non-imitative counterpoint with strongly differentiated figures set beside each other and across the beat. This is suddenly broken off for the statement by Galbraith's guitar of *The battle hymn of the Republic* ("John Brown's body . . .") which, against eerily sustained notes of desolation sounded by McKusick's alto, seems bizarre, unreal. The intended effect is, in fact, rather like that of Schoenberg's quotation of *O du lieber Augustin* in his String Quartet Op. 10, for in each case the melody's diatonic squareness throws into relief the emotional and technical complexity of the surroundings. It should be compared with the references to boogie piano in the third of Michael Tippett's *Songs for Dov* and, more particularly, with Gunther Schuller's integration of the Bessie Smith *Nobody knows you when you're down and out* into his Kafka opera *The Visitation*, whose score, indeed, is flecked with echoes of jazz, for those with the ears to hear.

The second part of *The day John Brown was hanged* begins as a dance. This, also, is highly rhythmic, yet the texture is too discontinuous, the musical gesture too varied, for its attempted gaiety to be properly convincing, and it gradually transforms itself into an oddly disembodied, intensely sad blues. This moves to a shorter quotation from *The battle hymn* that leads into the opening restlessness which, again, has never been far distant.

Another blues is Russell's *Stratusphunk*, on the *Cross Section Saxes* LP, and this, although simpler than the middle section of *John Brown*, raises more acutely the question of how much musical sophistication the blues can absorb before its characteristic climate of feeling is dissipated. John Carisi's *Israel*, another modal piece, with grave Dorian lines, had earlier drawn attention to this point, and while obviously neither the blues, nor jazz itself, should stand still, Cecil Taylor performances such as *Luyah!*, a blues in the Aeolian mode, suggest that once the dissonance level reaches a certain point the blues disappears, as a feeling if not as a form. (The regressive formal and harmonic simplicity of successful latter-day blues like John Coltrane's *Mr Syms* is of obvious significance here.) Although *Stratusphunk* emerges as a bluer piece in later recordings by Russell's Sextet and by Gil Evans than in this McKusick performance, maybe the question did not much concern the composer, for it remains an excellent piece of writing which always retains its essential character.

Just as personal is Russell's treatment of that other jazz staple, the popular song, and from *You're my thrill* and *The end of a love affair* he distills intense rhythmic and contrapuntal activity. Although there can be little doubt that his own pieces carry more weight, these are fine examples of what he describes as a composer improvising on a melody. If both sound like uncommonly successful collective extemporisations by the whole ensemble it must be at least partly because here as elsewhere, he aroused the full sympathies of the performers, including McKusick, Farmer, Evans, Galbraith and several others. In this connection Russell once wrote "Everyone wants to preserve the intuitive nature of jazz, even the composer. He wants his written lines to sound as intuitive as possible, no matter how much organisation there is behind them. I think the point is that music should always sound intuitive, as though it is being improvised" (8).

Perhaps in our time more than any other, being intelligent is not simply a matter of being rational, but also means being subtle and flexible enough to accommodate the irrational. Russell, as if sending a rich report from an arid place, offers music whose rigorous, almost mathematical, method renders its highly emotional impact all the more disturbing. To put it the other way, in several of his pieces, like *The day John Brown was hanged*, the urgently convoluted *Witch hunt*, or the mysterious *Night sound*, he achieves an extraordinary reconciliation between the vividness of a dream and a submission to logical order (9).

Jazz Monthly, March 1965

Jimmy Lunceford

In their best moments, which, alas, were none too frequent in the recording studio, Lunceford's band offered a style so well integrated as almost to deflect speculation about its origin. Perhaps that is why prospective listeners to their music have received no guides beyond fatuous expressions of hero-worship that, in Hume's useful phrase, are "distorted by the frenzies of enthusiasm", but which a certain kind of jazz commentator imagines to express real insight.

True, the initial questions are not easy, although it can be taken that Lunceford himself was not responsible for his band's style. He was the front-man in dance halls and theatres, the orchestral disciplinarian at rehearsals, and, with Harold Oxley—the band's manager and, according to some (1), its owner—he was the businessman. The Lunceford style is assumed to have been created solely by Sy Oliver, the trumpeter and arranger, and he is supposed to have worked it out beforehand in Zack Whyte's band, perhaps under the influence of Gus Wilson's ambitious scores for Alphonso Trent, by whom he also had been employed. It is less simple than that.

Whyte's few records were not made when Oliver was with him and so prove nothing, while Edwin Wilcox, Lunceford's pianist, denies credit to Oliver (2). One or two early Wilcox arrangements, such as *Flaming reeds and screaming brass*, recorded before Oliver joined, certainly contain the mature style's embryo, and Oliver himself claimed that "the fellows were all creative in their playing, I just wrote it all down. I was the band's Boswell" (3). However, other influences were at work.

For one, the Casa Loma band cannot be easily dismissed. The widespread effect of this group in the early 1930s is remarked on another page, and the first Lunceford records to make an impression were *Jazznocracy* and *White heat* by Will Hudson, both exercises in the Casa Loma manner—as were Fletcher Henderson's *Tidal wave*, the Blue Rhythm Band's *Blue rhythm* and Benny Goodman's *Nitwit serenade*. Oliver's use of plunger-muted brass might seem to point to Duke Ellington as a further influence, and this appears confirmed by certain aspects of the 1930 *In dat mornin'* and *Sweet rhythm*, almost the earliest Lunceford recordings. But they were unable to make anything of *Rhapsody junior* or *Bird of paradise*, two Ellington items unrecorded by the composer, and Willie Smith's arrangement of *Mood indigo* is so jumpy as to seem a deliberate caricature of the original's hushed reverence.

Louis Armstrong must appear a less likely influence, yet, quite apart from the fact that *Rhythm is our business*, a piece credited to Lunceford himself, has a melody almost identical with Armstrong's *Ding dong daddy*, the trumpet-and-drums coda to *Running wild*, another Smith score, is modelled on Armstrong's *Shine*. Having virtuoso trumpeters on board, it was predictable the band should echo Armstrong's celebrated high-note endings, and this is occasionally done to excellent effect, as on *Lunceford special*. But whereas Armstrong's use of the upper register is never musically illogical, even in extreme cases such as his 1933 *High society*, the Lunceford band's often was. Paul Webster's playing in the final moments of *Harlem shout* is a debasement of Armstrong's practice while on *Belgium stomp* he is worse, and in *Rose room* Tommy Stevenson is worst of all.

The prevailing influences, then, were quite diverse, some being well used, others not, as we should expect with a still-immature ensemble. Oliver's *Stomp it off* is supposed to be the first typically Luncefordian record, yet, although the brass and reed sections interlock in ways that we recognise as characteristic, this piece retains a slightly cold, almost mechanical Casa Loma air. The earlier *Breakfast ball* likewise is too busy, and may be a score Oliver brought with him from Whyte, but his *Swinging uptown* and, though still earlier, *Chillun get up* (both versions) convey the exuberant warmth associated with this band in its maturity.

What these various items suggest is that Oliver found some elements of the Lunceford style already present when he arrived late in 1933 and brought others with him; his first personal contribution was to draw them all together, so intensifying their effect. The relationship between writer and performers was two-way, as it must be in jazz, but the fact Oliver was no mere Boswell is proved by two things. First, others found it hard to imitate his style, as Eddie Durham's *Harlem shout*, and, even more, his earlier *Oh boy* show. Second, Oliver himself had no difficulty in recreating it elsewhere, as in *Opus 1* or *Easy does it* for Tommy Dorsey—though it must be noted that he was never able significantly to develop it further (4). Supposed adepts at the Oliver style, like Billy Moore, his replacement when he quit Lunceford in 1939, made no impression elsewhere when they in turn left.

If the band is overpraised for its virtues it has also been unduly condemned for its weaknesses, although these exist side by side and both are inherent in what may be called Oliver's system of contrasts, which operates on both a large and small scale. The slightly sour muted trumpets sounding against Ted Buckner's creamy alto saxophone in *Ain't she sweet?*, the juxtaposition of Al Norris's guitar and the full, roaring ensemble on *Sweet Sue*, or a fierce, plunger-muted trumpet accompanied by soothing saxophones in *Love nest* show how this principle affected the scores' detail. At this level Oliver was extremely inventive, even if the result sometimes is fanciful rather than deeply imaginative. Aside from a ridiculous non-jazz piano interruption, the *Swanee river* score consists of an entire sequence of such contrasts, one arising out of another, while on *Pigeon walk*, written by Durham after he had got right inside Oliver's style, the shifts of emphasis are even sharper yet never lead to disunity nor detract from the music's impetus. The highest application of Oliver's concept, however, is found in his own *Organ grinder's swing*, one of the swing bands' few masterpieces. Almost every change of colour or texture is extreme yet seems inevitable; each detail is unexpected but absolutely right—the woodblocks behind the celeste, the dialogue between guitar and legatissimo saxes; there is not one extraneous note. With this recording, made in 1936, the Lunceford band set themselves a dauntingly high standard, and it is not surprising that, on disc at least, they rarely lived up to it.

As *Coquette* or *I'm in an awful mood* further illustrate, Oliver took four-, eight- and sixteen-bar segments by soloists and band, and set them in kaleidoscopically varied sequences. This mosaic technique could obviously be applied in many ways, and *Avalon*, another exercise by Durham in the Oliver manner, was an influential score several of whose procedures were borrowed by others; Oliver's own *Shake your head* had its effect, also, to judge from Edgar Sampson's *Facts and figures* recorded under a year later by Chick Webb and much less well played (5). In fact, Oliver's devices have become so much part of the common practice of arranging that it is now hard to grasp their originality unless an effort of historical imagination is made and they are heard in the context of their time; failure to do this has resulted in misunderstanding of the band's achievement.

For example, an American critic was under a serious misapprehension when he wrote that "with rare exceptions Lunceford was not interested in his soloists for the best that soloists can contribute, but only as pieces in a pattern of ensemble discipline and showmanship. Solos were effects to this band, effects among all the other effects it could achieve, and not the chief effects" (6). The jumbled bits and pieces which lead into Dan Grissom's frightful singing on *The best things in life are free* might seem to justify these comments all too well, yet sometimes the connections between one sequence and another are excellently made, as in *Yard dog mazurka*. The basically orchestral stance of Lunceford's music was established in the *Jazznocracy* days, and it scarcely makes sense to condemn orchestral music for emphasising the ensemble: Ellington's *Koko* does not make its impact through the soloists. *Hi spook*—by Gerald Wilson, not Oliver—deploys the ensemble's disciplined power in an almost classic demonstration of the swing bands' finest qualities, and is unthinkable except in orchestral terms. So, too, is Leon Carr's *'Frisco fog* or Oliver's own *For dancers only*, which builds tension remorselessly over several choruses without any extraneous gestures yet fully justifies Webster's high-note climax. *Annie Laurie*, also, is true orchestral jazz, and achieves a remarkable conversion of non-jazz material; surely the pavonine trumpet phrases get close to equalling that devastating performance at Jericho some years before the swing era.

Soloists in this band were numerous and well varied, and it cannot be said that Lunceford gave them insufficient freedom when they achieved such individual expression as Willie Smith's volatile alto saxophone improvisation on *Uptown blues*, or the solo by Snooky Young which follows and is probably the best constructed which that trumpeter ever recorded. Though *Lonesome road* is supposed to be a virtuoso ensemble display piece the main thread is carried by soloists almost throughout, as it is in *What's your story, morning glory?* Notice, also, the long series of solos fitted deftly into *Shake your head*, and the developed statements made by the tenor saxophonist Joe Thomas on *Baby, won't you please come home?* or *I'm in an awful mood*. And hear Willie Smith on *Flight of the jitterbug*.

Further, these soloists, like most ex-Ellingtonians, counted for little once they left the Oliver/Lunceford ambit. Each of the more prominent made a few good records on his own account, such as Thomas's *Harlem hop* and *Big foot*, or Trummy Young's *Behind the eight bar* and *Man I love*, while Smith played excellent solos on pieces like Charlie Barnet's *Lumby* and *Blue hound bus grays*. Yet even the most sympathetic listener could not pretend these were a major contribution to jazz such as they made while playing for Lunceford.

There is no denying the band's technical weaknesses, of course, particularly in the earlier years. There is bad voice-leading in all sections, most obviously in the saxophones, who also had their intonation problems, and internal balance within a section is sometimes poor. Yet rarely can things be had both ways. In 1957 Billy May meticulously reconstructed some Lunceford scores and re-recorded them with top Los Angeles sessionmen: the result was better intonation and finer section balance, yet the spirit of the music, its warmth and good humour, had departed (7). According to at least one eye-witness (8), the band played items like *For dancers only* for as long as half an hour, and, although this presumably involved considerable repetition, it suggests the crude transitions on some Lunceford records may be due not to poor writing but to Procrustean editing to fit three-minute 78 r.p.m. discs.

However, the arrangements themselves sometimes did not help, and whereas in *Yard dog mazurka* the guitar interlude most tellingly subdues the contrapuntal pile-up of riffs, providing a moment of calm amidst the storm, on the earlier *Sleepy time gal* the sudden piano interruption is devoid of musical sense. It was up to the bandsmen to make things flow, and in cases such as the latter they could not succeed. With increasing frequency, though, the ensemble playing was superb, with finely-shaded dynamics, well matched articulation and attack. Oliver's choice of tempos was occasionally surprising—as in the very fast *Lonesome road*—but nearly always effective. These various points are illustrated by *Organ grinder's swing, Hi spook* and a few others, yet wherever one looks in Lunceford's output one finds glaring contrasts of quality. For example, the backgrounds to solos by Thomas on *Ragging the scale* or to Buckner in *By the river of Saint Marie* are jerky and too prominent, but hear the saxophones propelling Trummy Young's trombone through *Lunceford special* and the splendid exchanges between trombones and growling trumpets behind Thomas on *Well alright then*.

Despite the band's skill, even virtuosity, there apparently was nobody with the musical equipment to correct the various faults; this sometimes happened with the swing bands and their descendants, and John Lewis spoke of a comparable situation with Dizzy Gillespie's ensemble in the late 1940s (9). Oliver's reputation as one of the great jazz arrangers might suggest otherwise, yet the weaknesses are a fact, and, of course, he was perfectly capable of writing dull scores, like *Four or five times*. On occasion the other arrangers were no better. Hear the saccharine opening to Bud Estes's *I'm alone with you*, or Wilcox's *While love lasts*, the ensemble writing of which could be that of any tenth-rate commercial band. One must also regret the illiterate trifling with great composers in Billy Moore's *Chopin Prelude No. 7* and Chappie Willett's *Beethoven Sonata Pathetique*.

It seems typical of jazz in general and Lunceford in particular that the enervated *I met her on the beach at Bali-Bali* was recorded the day after the classic *Organ grinder's swing*. Similarly, the blandness of *Me and the moon* or the dreadful singing on *Honest and truly* lead one to speculate as to Lunceford's, and Oliver's, true aims. In the course of a Leonard Feather blindfold test (10), during a negative reaction to Charlie Parker's beautiful *Relaxing with Lee*, Oliver said, "I think in the final analysis the music that lives is the music the greatest number of people buy". Maybe this is enough to explain why he never achieved any advance on what he did with Lunceford, but he has also been quoted (11) as saying his favourite among all his Lunceford scores was *By the river of Saint Marie*. This is one of the dullest pieces they ever recorded, some of the writing, as Bill Russo has said (12), being worse than that of a publisher's stock orchestration. The vocalist is Dan Grissom, and one is not surprised to learn that he was known as "Dan Gruesome" (11); in fact Oliver said "nobody in the group could really sing" (11), and on the Panglossian *Life is fine* the vocal exchanges between Trummy Young and the rest of the ensemble sound like a case of the bland leading the bland. Occasionally this was mitigated, as in *Ain't she sweet?*, where the vocal quartet's chanting is supported with terse brass interjections and an intimately murmuring guitar. Once in a while, as if in apology, the band strikes out with almost savage force after some wretched singing, as on *Down by the old mill stream*.

Perhaps all the sickly ballads are best explained as a disconcerting reverse image of the up-tempo stomps—except that the playing can sometimes be as bad. Hear Smith's clarinet, with scarcely a note in tune, on *Siesta at the fiesta*, the cocktail lounge piano of *Sophisticated lady*, or Young's vulgar entry on *Annie Laurie*, anticipating his crude and widely-praised work with Armstrong in the 1950s. But hear also Young's splendid playing on *Think of me, little daddy*, or Smith in *Lunceford special*, where, above his usual form, he can stand with Johnny Hodges, even with Benny Carter.

Those who saw the band (11) emphasise its showmanship, but that is of no significance to us now, being left only with the records. Lunceford was able to communicate with his dancing public and occasionally to do fine things musically—though rarely at the same time. Despite the exclusive and puritanical attitude adopted by ageing swing fans towards later jazz, the big bands of the 1930s were in effect touring entertainment troups who spent a lot of their time not playing jazz, a fact naturally reflected in their gramophone output. At public engagements they had to provide something for everyone, and although their jazz capability is their sole interest for us now it was a marginal concern to most of their audiences. The abysmal *Merry-go-round broke down* may be the point at which latter-day explorers of Lunceford's music come nearest to despair, yet it is no more than his equivalent to Claude Hopkins's *Trees*, to Gillespie's *You stole my wife, you horse-thief*, to Basie's *I'm drowning in your deep blue eyes*.

Though most of us have met the jazz dilettante who says "very interesting sociologically" when he feels there may be something in a piece of music but cannot think of much to say about it, one should not too insistently explore the social setting of stylistic change and of individual invention (or of the failure of these). It can so easily become a diversion from, and a diminishment of, a direct feeling for the absolute value of inspired discovery in art; sociologically-inclined analysis, if pursued too methodically, clouds aesthetic enlightenment, reducing it to a duller form of understanding and a covert revenge of the academic intellect upon the senses. The use of conventions of entertainment music to express something deeper is not peculiar to jazz, still less to the 1930s, but goes back at least to Elizabethan lutenists such as John Dowland. Communication in all those urban dance halls Lunceford played as he crossed and recrossed the United States during that decade (13) may have been aided by the music's folk roots not going at all deep: *Uptown blues* and *Barefoot blues* are distinguished orchestral pieces, but they are not particularly blue. Count Basie, when he broke out of Kansas City, offered a massive simplicity of ensemble which complemented Lunceford's relative complexity quite well. But he retained less and less contact with his music's origins, and ended up accompanying Tony Bennet, Frank Sinatra, and, final ignominy, recording Beatle songs and themes from James Bond films.

Lunceford's group was lucky not to survive that long. The 1942 *Strictly instrumental* was their last characteristic recording. The band struggled on, even past Lunceford's own death in 1947, but it had long since become irrelevant. Their appalling 1946 titles, such as *Cement mixer* or *Call the police*, marked a final closing of horizons.

Oliver's claim that "those arrangements, they were all just alike" (11) stands as his most incomprehensible remark. The Lunceford band and soloists, while highly inventive at their rare best, never significantly extended jazz as a musical language as Ellington's ensemble and, for a short while, the finest of Basie's players did. But their style, in its highest application, lies at the centre of the relatively brief swing band tradition. It achieved an integration that became impossible soon after: consider Woody Herman's eclecticism, Gillespie's failure to devise an orchestral equivalent to bop, Stan Kenton's pseudo-symphonic perversions, Basie's sell-out to mindless simplicity. *What's your story, morning glory?*, *Organ grinder's swing* and the few other Lunceford tracks of permanent worth may not be the most exciting swing band records, nor the most innovatory, yet they are among the most beautiful. Their warmth and essential simplicity speak, perhaps rather better than it deserves, of a time that has gone and will not return.

Jazz Monthly, March 1956

The *Music for Brass* LP

Jazz still awaits its satirist. Should he ever appear, he will make great play with the exaggerated claims advanced on its behalf. For example, the notion that this rather simple and conservative art is 'the music of the century' ought to generate as much amusement as the claims made regarding the 'fantastic' virtuosity of its average player. Jazz has indeed had more than its fair share of remarkable executants, but they by no means overshadow the skills of European concert artists, or of distinguished exponents of African and Far-Eastern musics. The apologists are on safer ground when speaking of the originality with which the instruments are handled, the new ways of playing that jazz musicians have discovered, though here also the achievement has been uneven. After several centuries' intensive exploitation of the piano and its forebears by a line of great masters there were few resources left even for Art Tatum to discover. Yet the saxophone is virtually a jazz invention for what little, and ineffectual, use straight composers have made of it. Probably it is on brass instruments, however, that jazz musicians' 'handling of sound' is heard at its most creative, especially in the plunger-muted techniques which characterise an important vein of Duke Ellington's music.

Yet it is interesting to see what happens when jazzmen go, as it were, in the opposite direction, virtually confining themselves to 'legitimate' procedures. That is one way the *Music for Brass* LP (1) can be heard, as a jazz exercise in the deployment of conventional devices of brass scoring which never obscures the quite different attitudes of the three musicians chiefly concerned.

As a virtuoso trombonist, J. J. Johnson obviously has an intimate knowledge of the ensemble's capabilities and yet, rather paradoxically, his writing is the most conservative here, as if he were too acutely aware of performers' difficulties. In contrast, while Jimmy Giuffre's piece is thoroughly effective, he drives his players harder because the character of a musical idea for him outweighs any idiosyncrasies of the instrument to which it is assigned. John Lewis reconciles these extremes, though, quite apart from their rather different harmonic vocabularies, each draws a distinct sound from the ensemble, which is made up of six trumpets, four french horns, three trombones, two baritone horns, tuba and percussion.

Although the musical language of these pieces may seem conservative for 1956, there is an important link with formal explorations then being conducted in supposedly more advanced sectors. Just as Charles Mingus, on records such as *Love chant* (1956), or, still earlier, Lennie Tristano, with *Digression* and *Intuition* (both 1949), broke away from the normal repeating twelve- and thirty-two-bar choruses of jazz, so Johnson, Lewis and Giuffre here undertake free composition, accepting the challenge of finding unity by other means. Each, of course, reacts in a different way.

Both the Lewis and Johnson pieces are in three movements, and both have Miles Davis and Johnson himself as improvising soloists. The latter's *Poem for brass* opens with an almost ponderous introduction which implies the first movement's theme. Alternating various brass textures with side drum then cymbal rolls, this is the first of a series of dialogues between wind and percussion heard from each composer. The rapid pace of the movement proper comes as a surprise, and dark mixtures of open and muted sound lead quickly to Davis's first contribution. He is heard on flugelhorn, and, in combination with the swift tempo, his melancholy creates an ambiguous feeling that is resolved by the extroversion of the composer's solo, which follows. Each improvises on the theme, thereby strengthening the movement's unity, and the ensemble is pointedly active behind them, not just accompanying but adding a further perspective to their discoveries. Indeed, while the main thread is undoubtedly held by the soloists, the writing is everywhere precise in its intention, a genuine, if oblique, extension of Johnson's remarkable trombone playing.

It is the more surprising, then, to find that his slow movement falls into two unrelated halves. First comes a section with beautiful parallel harmony on french horns and tuba, then a sharply contrasting ballad-like section with a trumpet solo by Joe Wilder: perhaps one should regard these as two linked interludes rather than a unified statement. The third movement reminds us, no doubt intentionally, of the first by opening with another dialogue between brass and cymbal. Soon, however, Johnson resorts to that familiar solution to the finale problem, a fugue. Its theme is first heard from the trumpets, but the tuba starts the fugue itself. Other instruments make their expected entries until five lines are on the go, making harmonic sense together and melodic sense individually. This is a respectable technical achievement, and George Russell has detected the influence of Hindemith (2). If the climax is convincing this is because it arises from an intensification of the musical argument, not a resorting to Kentonesque volume.

Lewis's *Three little feelings* has remained one of his best pieces. Its lines are sometimes eloquent yet have an irreducible simplicity which, like his finest piano solos, can make even the most disciplined virtuosity seem unduly rhetorical. The blues are evoked, particularly in the first movement, yet the mood is not one of protest but of intimate expression allied to sombre richness. This is, in fact, a romantic score, although one that uses terse thematic material adroitly. In the beginning three motives are announced, then piled on top of each other. Davis, on trumpet this time, improvises around one of them, a chromatic four-note figure. He sounds even more forsaken than in Johnson's *Poem*, but is, of course, responding to the more emotional nature of the musical material. It is noteworthy that his acutely subjective art can fit into so deliberately organised a setting, but perhaps that is a commentary on both desire for freedom and desire for discipline.

Davis has the central movement almost to himself and the music floats, seemingly weightless and outside time, as the trombones and baritone horns alternate two unrelated chords in a way reminiscent of *Neptune*, farthest-out of Holst's *Planets*. Across this the flugelhorn wanders, forlorn yet never losing direction. Though minor-keyed, the finale is more rugged, and its opening solo french horn call echoes that which begins the *Lento moderato* of Vaughan Williams's Pastoral Symphony. This call is often present in one form or another, and the movement is especially well tied together—so well, indeed, that

Johnson's forty-bar solo does not seem altogether relevant. But there is an excellent use of timpani. Lewis does not employ percussion, like Johnson, to get movements going, but sets it in structurally significant dialogues with the brass to build this movement's, and the work's, climax. Afterwards tension eases, and a recapitulation of the horn call, this time on all four instruments, makes an ending that is expected yet has the stamp of comprehended truth.

Pharaoh is the most tightly constructed of these works but the one whose unity is hardest to account for. Giuffre's structure is sectional and each part deals with different fragments of thematic substance. As these all derive from the same source, hearing it is something—though not too much—like viewing a statue from a series of different angles. Many interesting textures are heard on the way, such as the six-part writing for trumpets, and these arise from *Pharaoh's* unflagging counterpoint. This gives it a leaner sound than the other scores, partly explains its musical concentration, and justifies both its brevity and the absence of improvised solos.

Giuffre, then, emerges as the composer most independent of cherished jazz conventions, perhaps even the one best to profit from the pre-set limitations of this undertaking. *Pharaoh* points, also, towards more rarefied areas of American music and one is reminded of the long melodic lines with leaping sevenths and ninths, the pounding timpani and fierce dissonance of Carl Ruggles's *Sun treader*.

This record was a byproduct of the rather spasmodic activities of the Jazz and Classical Music Society founded in New York during 1955 by Lewis and Gunther Schuller—who conducts the above performances. It may be regarded as both a sophisticated comment on the big band tradition and as a demonstration of various compositional procedures whose jazz application ought to have been taken further.

Jazz Monthly, August 1966

INTERLUDE I

Continental jazz—notes on two anthologies

Considering that jazz, as an artistic phenomenon, was discovered by Europeans and that for many years all critical commentary originated here, it is surprising our pioneer American visitors and the local musicians who early learnt from them have received so little attention (1). Both a cause and a consequence of this neglect was that for several decades the pertinent recordings were unobtainable, but various anthologies now exist which prove how fruitful an area of study this is, from both musical and historical viewpoints.

Several tracks on *La Prèhistoire du Jazz en France* (2) do not seriously pretend to be jazz, yet it is futile to dismiss them for not sounding exactly like King Oliver, or because the participants had no contact with the vocal blues idiom. Writers on jazz often make that kind of mistake, and we should beware the facile perspectives of hindsight, be less concerned with ministering to our own present state of mind and try to enter into the imaginations, motives and experiences of these distant people.

Following on the wide distribution of commercialised ragtime, the rhythmic and tonal qualities of such performances helped establish a climate favourable to European recognition of jazz, and they illustrate the necessarily slow mastering of the appropriate executive techniques by local men. For instance, the melody of *Smiles*, recorded by Marcel's Jazz Band des Folies Bergère in 1919, is not much departed from, and, though its effect is varied by ragtime ostinatos from banjo and percussion, the spirit of older popular music remains strong.

A pioneer of comment on early jazz in Europe was Robert Goffin (3), who, in discussing the Southern Rag-a-Jazz Band's 1921 recordings, said "there is not yet any great individual improvisation, but rather a kind of ragged bouncing by all the musicians". This applies to several items on *La Préhistoire*, such as the Melody Six's *Georgia blues*, which confirms the inevitably uneven progress made by local players, being a much superior example of the approach found in Marcel's *Smiles* though recorded a year earlier. Again its melody—not a real blues—is rarely departed from in concerted passages, and there are no improvised solos; but there is a profusion of breaks full of ragtime syncopations, and further textural diversity is obtained by distributing the melodic phrases round the ensemble, with considerable rhythmic variation.

That ragtime concepts of rhythm still dominate the 1923 performances of Billy Arnold suggests the great impact they had on European besides American popular music, for ragtime had been introduced here almost a quarter of a century before, by Sousa's band, in Paris during 1900. Perhaps, indeed, it affected twentieth-century popular music even more fundamentally than jazz, at least in providing a considerable rhythmic shaking-up; later, the very pervasiveness of its influence, working through the music publishing and record industries, imposed a uniformity which contrasts unpleasantly with the myriad styles of popular music in the nineteenth century and earlier, and prefigures the rigid conformism of pop songs in our own time.

With Arnold—whose band's performances in Paris were cited by Darius Milhaud (4) as having introduced him to jazz—the melodies still are faithfully adhered to, and, as with the previous groups, the approach is orchestral, not soloistic. Yet the invention and deftness of these scores show a real advance: overlapping antiphonal phrases reach towards counterpoint, and after hearing *Carolina in the morning* (which opens by quoting *Morning* from Grieg's *Peer Gynt* music) few people would any longer agree that antiphonal duets between reed and brass sections were innovated a few years later by Fletcher Henderson. As treatments of popular material Arnold's compare favourably with almost anything then being written in America, and are superior to the 1924 Doc Cook recordings, although these latter obviously have a pedigree more acceptable to jazz orthodoxy. Arnold's scores are very demanding for their period, yet are executed with precision, with a kind of post-ragtime, pre-jazz momentum, and with a spirit which leaves one wanting to know more about these unidentified musicians.

Their approach is taken further in L'Orchestre du Moulin-Rouge's *Zululand*, a 1926 semi-jazz piece whose almost virtuosic ensemble writing must have been still harder to play but which is even better performed. Here the overlapping antiphony draws still nearer to counterpoint, and, no matter how different the style, we receive a hint of the complex arrangements that Sy Oliver would be producing for

Jimmy Lunceford's band a decade later. It is hard to imagine how this sort of orchestral, almost compositional, treatment could have been pushed further at that time, and the development of European jazz towards the orthodox solo improvising heard on Grégor's *Le rugissement du tigre (Tiger rag)* was probably inevitable, even if hints of other possibilities were given in England by Fred Elizalde and Reginald Forsythe. This level of achievement emphasises how deep were the roots put down by the pioneer groups.

Supposedly, the earliest pioneer bands were led by Louis Mitchell, who visited Europe several times and is represented with three 1922 performances by his Jazz Kings, the ensemble with which he won fortune and fame in Paris. They are distressingly poor in musical quality, and as inconsistent both in style and intent as work by several other widely praised American pioneers, such as Charlie Creath and Fate Marable, who recorded at home. *Turkish ideals*, in particular, is backward in comparison with, say, 1917 recordings by a quite marginal group like the 'Frisco Jazz Band. There scarcely is a hint of ragtime here, let alone jazz, and even a tinge of that quasi-oriental vein which persisted for so long in jazz (5) cannot identify this as anything other than pre-rag light music. Mitchell's *Sheik of Araby* shows little improvement, yet *Wabash blues* is so different as almost to sound like the work of another ensemble altogether. Here antiphony, first between trumpet and alto saxophone, then trumpet and trombone, overlaps to the point where it virtually becomes counterpoint, and there is an attempt at polyphony by the other melody instruments. This is more jazz-orientated than anything else in *Le Préhistoire* except Grégor's *Tiger rag*.

Twenty-first-century musicologists would draw wildly inaccurate conclusions on Louis Armstrong were their study confined to *Was it a dream?*, *Me and brother Bill* and *Takes two to tango*, so one cannot venture even a provisional opinion about Mitchell's contribution on the basis of three items selected by the chance survival of exceedingly rare 78 r.p.m. discs. But we must note the wide discrepancy between these records and Goffin's and other eye-witness accounts, and also that they do not even square with contemporary journalistic comment. Thus when Mitchell played at Ciro's in London during 1916-17 (admittedly with a different personnel from that used on the above records) one newspaper complained "Only the loud-lunged have a chance, for at one end of the room are many indefatigable black men who bang drums and cymbals, and even sound motor-horns". And Jean Cocteau wrote entertainingly (6) of how the Jazz Kings had "domesticated catastrophe". Yet not a single motor-horn blast splits one's ear during the numbingly sedate periods of *Turkish ideals,* or even in *Wabash blues.* Further, many comments were published on Mitchell as a "whirlwind ragtime drummer", "noise artist supreme" and the like, but his playing, which evidently dominated his bands during their public appearances, is scarcely apparent on these performances. Nor, according to the discographies (7), did he record any of the pieces, such as *Jada* or *Hindustan,* which Goffin heard him play in 1919, when Sidney Bechet was a member of the band.

The relationship is unclear between Mitchell's Jazz Kings and a group rejoicing under the name of Ciro's Club Coon Orchestra which recorded quite frequently in London during 1916-17, the period of one of Mitchell's visits here. The personnel given by Rust and others (7) is identical with that listed by Goffin for Mitchell's band of the time, except that Harry Pollard appears as drummer instead of Mitchell. Yet a contemporary poster (8) carries photographs of each member of the ensemble, including Mitchell, who is named as drummer, not Pollard; and the band is here called the Seven Spades, the title by which Mitchell's group was known on the Continent. He seems, in fact, to have had something of a career in Britain prior to his big Paris success, appearing at Glasgow, Belfast and Liverpool besides London. Nor was he alone. An ensemble called the Versatile Four was playing in London as early as 1910 and recorded such items as *Down home rag* in 1916. Earlier still, the Black Diamond Band recorded *Wild cherries rag* in 1912, Olly Oakley recorded *Hiawatha rag* as a banjo solo on an Edison cylinder in 1904, and Burt Earle's cylinder of *Hot foot Sue,* also a banjo piece, is dated 1899. This is a minute random sampling of pre-jazz syncopated music recorded here prior to Mitchell's appearances, but is enough to invalidate his claim—which he repeated in several interviews—to have been the first in bringing such music across the Atlantic. The same is obviously true of the Original Dixieland Jazz Band's stay in 1919, and, indeed, the notion of a definite 'first' here is meaningless because then as now jazz was subject to constant change and, on closer examination, supposed boundary lines shade off into a variety of transitional phenomena.

Of course, this is equally the case for developments elsewhere, and an album called *Czechoslovakian Jazz 1920-60* (9) shows that the gradual absorption of jazz techniques in another part of Europe followed a similar path, despite the cultural background being very different from that of France or Britain, let alone the U.S.A. As a two-LP set, this has room for enlightening subsidiary material of a sort not found on the single French *Préhistoire* disc, an example being the *Shimmy* from Ervin Schulhoff's 1919 *Partita* for piano. This is an early instance of the use of jazz—not ragtime—devices in straight composition, and anticipates what Hindemith soon did more pungently in his suite *1922*.

Schulhoff was among the most prolific in this line, writing incidental music in the jazz idiom for Molière's *Bourgeois Gentilhomme*, a Sonata for alto saxophone and piano, plus many other things. More aggressive is the *Charleston* from Bohuslav Martinů's 1927 ballet *Kuchyňská Revue*, a disquietingly brilliant caricature of Jelly Roll Morton from the man who in this score, in his *Trois Esquisses* (1927), Jazz Suite (1928) and Sextet (1929) made a more perceptive use of jazz devices in the contexts of European composition than almost anyone else. Perhaps only Milhaud's *La Création du Monde* can stand beside these works.

Kirkilis-shimmy is a 1923 piece by R. A. Dvorský, a pioneer Czech jazzman, recorded, unaccountably, in London by the Mayfair Dance Orchestra, the Gramophone Company's house band of 1914-25. The performance predictably lacks jazz feeling, but this was creditable writing for a Central European at that time, and the ambiguity between the tune's melancholy inflections and its jolly underlying rhythm is reminiscent of the New Orleans Rhythm Kings' *Farewell blues* of a year before. Of course, this early instance of Czech understanding ought not to surprise us for E. F. Burian's *Jazz* was published in Prague during 1928—four years ahead of Goffin's *Aux Frontières du Jazz*, which we in Western Europe tend to think of as the first significant book on the subject.

Generally these two LPs follow chronological order, yet it was perceptive to insert Jaroslav Ježek's 1936 *Rapsodie kroavého měsíce* at this point. This appears to seek the limits of stylistic incongruity, but is an instructive example of the sort of glaring mistakes that can be made by players skilled enough to imitate an idiom's gestures yet who do not really understand how it works. The oblique influences are early-1930s Ellington and the beautifully scored *Andante* of Gershwin's Piano Concerto (1926), and Ježek combines sensitivity to colour and texture with clumsiness of structure. As an instance of how uneven progress in such matters usually must be, however, *Rapsodie kroavého měsíce* should be compared with Jan Sima's *Feeling low* of the same year, which achieves stylistic consistency through having less ambitious aims. Indeed, it is interesting to observe, as with the French performances, how ensemble playing, arranging and even composing in the jazz idiom are mastered before genuinely individual solo improvisation appears.

Perhaps the stage before *Feeling low* is best represented by Sam Baskini's *Navigator*, recorded in Berlin during 1930 by mainly unidentified musicians though including Dvorský at the piano. This sounds like a jazz-influenced theatre band which boasts no soloist of distinction but whose section playing is disciplined and relaxed. The stage after *Feeling low* is marked by Karl Vlach's *Ráda zpívám hot* of 1939, where the ensemble playing is as good as that of any non-American large combo of the time. Later still, the 1945 *Alexander's ragtime band* of Ladislav Harbart, with its late-Lunceford overtones, achieves a standard that would only be surpassed by the top U.S. groups. Again, in Kamil Behounek's *Jubilejní dan*, also of 1945, while the ensemble shows Czech jazz moving away from swing, the solos, especially that by Vladimir Horčík at the piano, look backwards with some determination.

Similar in its way is *Improvisace*, which finds another pianist, Jan Verberger, as having mastered Earl Hines's procedures but with nothing of his own to add. Yet inconsistency remained the rule, and a perfect reverse image of the unidentified singer's incomprehension of *Beale Street blues* (recorded by Sima's group) is the glowing, authentically blues-inflected clarinet which redeems an anonymous band's *Strejček hlad*, cut the same year (1936). This is so good that one suspects the presence of an unknown migrant Negro player, but if a Czech was responsible it is satisfying to contrast this isolated voice with Vlach's 1959 *Na počátku bylo blues*, where the whole band clearly understands the idiom very well.

Remembering that during the late 1940s there was a New Orleans revivalist band in London of whose King Oliver plagiarisms it used to be said that one could tell whether they were performing the Okeh or Gennett version of certain items, it is to the Czechs' credit that, so far as this no doubt carefully selected anthology shows, they rarely lent too heavily on their models. For example, although *Feeling low* is Ellingtonian in mood it uses none of his specific devices, and while Karl Slavík's *Basin Street blues* is frankly derived from Armstrong's 1928 recording, it offers an intelligent variant, not a copy, with very skilled trumpeting from F. Diaz. True, the piano on Emil Ludvík's *Inspiration* sounds much like Teddy Wilson and is further evidence of Verberger's imitative skill, but V. Novák's clarinet playing is not in the least like Benny Goodman's, and one may disagree with this album's commendably thorough and detailed notes and assert that on Rytmus 42's *Topsy* the trumpet of Lumir Brož is not particularly close to Armstrong, nor Horčík's piano to Fats Waller.

In fact the nicely poised solos on Arnosta Kavky's *Man I love* of 1946 show that by this time the Czechs had thoroughly mastered the concept of solo improvisation in all its aspects and several styles, except that nobody apparently had anything very individual to say, and so the music, rather paradoxically, sounds independent yet impersonal. However, Vlach's *Caravan* (1948) demonstrates the progress being made on the orchestral front, and Alexej Fried's score—calmly ignoring Ellington's own treatment of this piece—develops the rather facilely exotic theme most intelligently; the latter half of Ludvík's *Sjezd swingařů* had shown what a lifting rhythmic pulse these musicians could generate by 1940, but *Caravan* is a splendid ensemble performance in all respects, with real power and collective drive, plus a communicative warmth that many groups would miss.

When they first attempted postwar styles the Czechs seemed, not surprisingly, to become more dependent on their models. Rytmus 48's *Night and day* proves that by 1948 Charlie Parker Quintet records had penetrated to Central Europe, and this is a worthy attempt at bop for that time and place. Four years later *Kriminologie* is in the mode of Parker's aharmonic canons such as *Ah-leu-cha*, and Karel Krautgartner shows himself to be a remarkable musician in European terms, possibly an equal of Arne Domnerus, the outstanding Swedish alto saxophonist of those years. It is true that the other participants in *Kriminologie* have little idea of the rhythmic basis of bop, yet as much could be said of many American players at that late date.

Krautgartner's 1957 *Foggy day* is chastening, also, if one recalls how spineless the British jazz scene was at that time, and both here and in Jaromir Hnilička's trumpeting on *Indiana club* by the Gustav Brom Orchestra, notice is given of the achievements that were to come in the 1960s (10). These two recordings, along with Vlach's *Na počátku bylo blues*, show the refinement and consolidation of what had gone before.

As in other European jazz of this 1920-60 period, there is still little here which is specifically new, beyond the personal inflections of some of the later solos. Of necessity, the efforts of these gifted musicians were devoted to gaining command of the established jazz styles and technical procedures, not to exploring fresh areas of expression. This led, however, to a gradual elimination of stylistic inconsistencies and to the integration of all aspects of performance that were the essential basis, in Czechoslovakia as elsewhere, for the partially successful bid for freedom from American models which took place during the 1960s.

Jazz Monthly, June 1970

Extending the Language:
four instances

Illustrating ways in which the expressive and technical resources of jazz are increased

James P. Johnson

Perhaps jazz was born in New Orleans, but New York soon was up to something different. One way of explaining the divergence would be to suggest that the influence of vocal blues on phrasing and instrumental timbre was crucial in the South, not in the North. During the early decades of this century New York was to a considerable extent a piano town, highly competitive in this as in other respects, and it is said that when Jelly Roll Morton passed through in 1911 his normally well-nourished ego received a considerable blow from the executive skills of the best local players. His transformation of ragtime into jazz was a matter of the blues, plus greater sophistication in the handling of contrasted themes and, later, of the small, collectively improvising band. For the New Yorkers it involved almost everything except the blues, but it happened mainly—or at any rate first—on the piano keyboard.

The example of ragtime and the possibility of improvisation were common to both North and South—also to the Middle West—yet the special point about the New Yorkers was their musical curiosity. James P. Johnson best illustrates how this operated on several levels at once. His imaginative, beautifully organised, but finally inappropriate accompaniments to—or rather duets with—Bessie Smith may demonstrate his failure to grasp the blues, yet this was essentially a creative misunderstanding in that it left him open to other influences of perhaps still earlier origin. As Dick Wellstood wrote, "James P. is the focal point. The rags, cotillions, mazurkas and all those other unknown phenomena came together in him and he made jazz out of them" (1). Unlike most of the other New York pianists, such as his pupil Fats Waller, or Willie 'the lion' Smith, Johnson, despite his wide-ranging interests, never lost contact with those country-dance fiddle-tunes, banjo music, hymns, marches, folksongs, etc. from mid-nineteenth century, as is confirmed by some of the piano solos, like *Mule walk, Blueberry rhyme* or *Arkansas blues*, which he recorded in late middle-age. At the other extreme, he is said to be the sole old-timer who, in 1947, had a word to say in favour of Dizzy Gillespie (2).

Of course, Johnson was luckier than most jazz musicians in his early background. Born in New Brunswick, N.J., probably on February 1st

1891, he initially learnt from his mother, and when the family moved to Jersey City, near New York, he continued with a local musician named Bruto Giannini. This man had considerably more vision than the average piano teacher, for he appreciated the uncommon bent of his pupil's exceptional ability. Johnson was allowed to go on with his stomps and rags—with the fingering corrected—but he was made to work intensively at scales, arpeggios, and all the other basics of a well-rounded technique. Giannini also taught him harmony and counterpoint, and, perhaps most important, he studied the classics of European keyboard literature. This latter was an interest he was able to pursue in New York, to which the family next moved. Johnson began appearing as a musician while still at school there, and performed in a wide variety of circumstances, sometimes in the lowest of dives, but he also attended orchestral concerts and piano recitals.

This balance of earthiness and sophistication remained characteristic, but the point of Giannini's four years of training at this stage of Johnson's career was that it equipped him to learn still more. Interviewed decades later (3), he was quite clear as to what he had got from each of the dominant Harlem pianists of an older generation such as Fred Bryant ("He invented the backward tenth. I used it and passed it on to Fats Waller") or Sam Gordon ("He played swift runs in thirds and sixths, broken chords, one-note tremolandos"). Johnson also had the taste, technique and knowledge of the classical repertoire to benefit from the European tradition's long harvest, and he mentions adapting procedures from Beethoven and Liszt in particular. The latter is the significant name because for Johnson and the other most advanced New York pianists, as for Liszt, Alkan, Chopin and other Romantic piano composers almost a century before, the point of virtuosity was not the chances it offered for display but that it was a catalyst, a means of extending the instrument's scope and hence their music's range of expression. The audience could be dazzled if it liked, yet what mattered to the pianists was bringing fresh resources—rather literally—into play. The Harlem keyboard men of Johnson's generation formed the first school of jazz virtuosos of whom we have real knowledge, and the exploratory drive was still active when, many years later, it led one of his contemporaries, Eubie Blake, to begin studying the Schillinger system of composition at the age of sixty-six.

It had been active much sooner in the piano rolls that Johnson, Blake and several others began to cut during 1917 and which are our earliest evidence of their work. This method of recording eliminates some of the most personal aspects of execution, but items such as *Baltimore buzz* convey Johnson's exultant joy in playing, a feeling which comes only from having conquered one's instrument (*cf* recordings by the young Hines, the young Gillespie, etc.). *Gypsy blues* or *Don't tell your monkey man* speak clearly, too, of his knowledge of pianistic resource, of his technique, and of an imagination which finds its most apt expression on the keyboard. These and several other rolls are almost incessantly inventive, and communicate not only instrumental mastery but a personal gaiety, even optimism, of which only the sourest intellectuals would disapprove.

Because of the better Harlem pianists' classical links it is not surprising that these pieces are fully worked-out fantasies on given melodies rather than jazz improvisations. The archetypal case, Johnson's rather later piano roll of excerpts from *Running Wild*, an all-Negro musical, is in direct descent from the kind of treatment nineteenth-century virtuosos gave to operatic melodies; the rhythms are different, but little else. Such items remain delightful to hear yet sound like a beginning, not an end, because the demands of a mode of expression centred on the piano, the types of resource and kinds of formal organisation that go with it, can be heard on these rolls, especially *Vamping Liza Jane* or *Railroad man*, supplanting the requirements of the original melody, which finally is dissolved in the texture. Sure enough, having broken with ragtime's static syncopations and rather formal expression of mood, as well as its emphasis on thematic melody, in favour of a more developed pianism and all it implied, many other things followed, not least the necessity of a smoother rhythmic flow.

We cannot be absolutely certain about such details with piano rolls, of course, but Johnson's first gramophone recording, *Harlem strut*, dating from 1921, though basically a piece of 2/4 ragtime, does have a tendency towards a 4/4 pulse. This is more apparent in *Carolina shout* and *Keep off the grass* done later that year, although here the flowing forward movement is by no means supplied by the left hand alone, each piece having various ternary patterns superimposed on the underlying 4/4 to offset any possibility of rhythmic squareness. This was eventually taken up by orchestral jazz, as in Don Redman's 1927 scores of *Whiteman stomp* (a piece composed by Waller) and *Tozo* for Fletcher Henderson. Other bands caught up later—e.g. Lloyd Hunter's *Sensational mood* of 1931—but Johnson and his friends were doing it in 1921. As Wellstood wrote, "He had an almost architectural way of handling rhythm, of placing pulses like building blocks, and a wonderfully subtle manner of allowing different rhythmic conceptions to exist simultaneously in both hands" (4). This is literally true, and in, say, *Keep off the grass* we find the beats of one two-bar unit grouped 3+3+2 in one hand against 3+2+3 in the other, and then these patterns reversed between the hands in the next two bars (5).

During the 1920s Johnson was extremely active in the world of Negro showbusiness and it is remarkable that he retained mastery of this sort of playing. In fact he did more, developing his compositional skill and executive control to the points shown in *Riffs* (1929) and *Jingles* (1930), which channel great rhythmic zest through airy, prancing trebles and resonantly-spaced basses, marking almost—though not quite—the summit of his achievement as a jazz pianist. So far as recordings are concerned, the peak came at a surprisingly later date with the magnificent group of solos he set down for the Blue Note and Signature labels during 1943, including *Carolina Balmoral, Blues for Fats, Caprice rag, Improvisations on Pinetop's boogie* and the items mentioned in the second paragraph. These performances, besides preserving the simple happiness of country-dance tunes within the lucid complexities of Harlem piano at its ripest, were an achievement in quite another sense for they came after the stroke Johnson suffered in 1940, from which he only recovered slowly, and which marked the start of the slow decline in his health that resulted in his death in 1955.

Despite the long-matured brilliance of this and much other music, however, Johnson remained a neglected figure, except among his fellow pianists. They had a just appreciation of his apparently inexhaustible inventive power and, in most cases, beautifully disciplined playing. We can savour these, too, on the several versions he recorded (on piano roll or disc) of each of his most famous pieces, where the thematic material is always varied in new ways, with chanting lyricism and spry elegance. Yet *Jazz Hot and Hybrid* (6) or *Jazzmen* (7), books which exerted a largely undeserved influence in their day, made not a single mention of him. Or consider two groups of recordings he cut in 1944, one of solos on Waller melodies, the other of compositions of his own accompanied by an inept drummer. Among the latter's more gross solecisms is that he plays straight through the recurring breaks of pieces such as *Over the bars*, thereby considerably diminishing their effect. It is typical of the misunderstandings to which Johnson has been subject that these ill-matched duets—or rather duels—have repeatedly been praised (8) at the expense of the sensitive, manifestly affectionate solo improvisations in memory of his recently-deceased pupil.

As if to console him, and arising directly, of course, out of the admiration of his fellow professionals, Johnson's influence was very considerable. It would not be quite true to say that his followers "constitute the elite of the jazz piano tradition" (5) because several highly significant figures like Earl Hines, Bud Powell, and bluesmen such as Jimmy Yancey were untouched by him. Yet one still could devote a whole essay to his formative rôle in the playing of others, and, aside from obviously related stylists like Willie 'the lion' Smith, Johnson's concern with resources hitherto untried in jazz had a marked, possibly crucial, effect on the attitudes of Duke Ellington and Art Tatum. Even Thelonious Monk, on one celebrated occasion, thought he sounded like Johnson, and if his two versions of the blues *Functional* be juxtaposed with the older man's two *Blue moods* pieces the idea appears less far-fetched. Waller might seem the obvious example of Johnson's influence, yet the similarities between these two are less revealing than the differences. Thus, remembering the attention he gave to the European classics, Johnson's harmony is rather disappointingly conventional, whereas on the very few occasions in the recording studio that Waller gave something like full rein to his talent he produced music of considerable harmonic interest, as in *Clothes line ballet* or *Beale Street blues*. Rhythmically, however, it is the younger man who is conservative, and, with a few exceptions like the 1923 *Snake hips* piano roll, which is in an even 4/4, his playing often has a rather old-fashioned 2/4 feeling, whereas Johnson's left-hand parts show far more variety and exorcise the rhythmic ghost of ragtime with a consistent four-to-the-bar. Pianistically they were quite different, too, with Johnson's delicacy, precision and grace answering Waller's power and warmth.

If this last comparison suggests greater subtlety on Johnson's part, that is correct. Items like *Scouting around* or *Crying for the Carolines* use the same type of folk material and draw on the same European tradition of virtuoso keyboard writing as did Louis Moreau Gottschalk (9), the New Orleans-born composer who attempted this sort of fusion far ahead of jazz. If Johnson's pieces have a more complex impact than *Le banjo* or *Bamboula* (subtitled *Danse des Negres*), if, too, they seem more personal statements than ragtime with its slightly mechanical cheerfulness—itself the reverse image of the nostalgia and insecurity of Stephen Foster's Negro dialect songs—it may be that in Johnson both the folk roots and the aspirations to cultural status went deeper.

Though he played an important rôle in freeing jazz from the ragtime influence, his attitudes remained in some respects closer to those of the rag composers than to those of jazz musicians. Although their music was descended in part from the sardonic parodies of the cakewalk, they wanted their formal, fully notated compositions to be considered as art, not entertainment. Hence Scott Joplin's attempt at opera with *Treemonisha,* hence Johnson's attempt with *The Organiser,* which had a libretto by Langston Hughes. Rare exceptions like Bix Beiderbecke aside, it was many years before jazzmen began to reflect the Harlem pianists' wide interest in non-jazz musics, but Johnson's attempts at large-scale composition were virtually inevitable. *Tone Poem,* completed in 1930, *Harlem Symphony,* which followed in 1932, Suite in Sonata Form on *St Louis blues* (1936) and the Jasmine Concerto for piano and orchestra all had a few performances and then were dropped by performers and audiences who were unprepared for the sort of fusion they attempted, whether successfully or otherwise. More accomplished composers than Johnson—such as the nineteenth-century Russians—met almost insoluble difficulties in matching folk material to symphonic processes, and we may doubt whether he, any more than Ellington, would be able to control long-duration forms. Perhaps his orchestral pieces, whatever their status, are best regarded as part of an intrinsically healthy movement to remove the divisions between 'serious' and 'popular' art. Their continuing unavailability in print or on disc must be regretted, however, for in our present state of enforced ignorance we shall always be uncertain of how Johnson fared (10).

Jazz Monthly, September 1959

Dizzy Gillespie

Gillespie's innovations long since passed into the lifeblood of jazz and it scarcely is necessary to discuss the elements of his style now. Yet although the extent of his influence cannot be questioned, his position in the music has for many years been quite different from what it was just after World War II, when bop made its first impact. For non-American listeners that impact was initially felt through the records he made, several with Charlie Parker, for obscure, long-defunct companies such as Guild or Musicraft in 1945-46. To have gone on listening to these for some thirty years has been a considerable enrichment because, although on first acquaintance they seemed to possess a rather contrived audacity, they have retained a power to delight, even astonish. Uneven in musical quality they certainly are, but all contain great moments, and it long ago became obvious that the finest of them are among the classics of recorded jazz, their value as unlikely to diminish in the future as it did in the past.

Many factors went into the making of postwar jazz: some were the creation of individuals and some were the result of a cross-fertilisation of ideas; some had been for years developing in the jazz of the 1930s, even of the late '20s, others had come from spontaneous insights. The early Gillespie records were the first attempt at a synthesis of all the playing and thinking which had gone on, but if by 1945 the key musicians were ready, the record company supervisors were not. It took them a while to grasp that something fresh had occurred, and so on many sessions boppers were confronted with players whose ideas had been completely formed in the 1930s. In view of the new music's deep roots this was not too damaging, but unquestionably these early performances, in terms of style, are less than completely integrated.

Melancholy baby, Cherokee and *On the Alamo*, recorded under the clarinetist Joe Marsala's name, are representative here, setting Gillespie in a tight, jivey late-swing framework. He sounds like a disciple of Roy Eldridge—not in the negative sense of a Johnny Letman, mechanically echoing the mannerisms, but as one who has divined further possibilities within that idiom and can see where they might lead. His continuity already is better than Eldridge's, his use of the upper register less illogical. *Blue 'n' boogie*, the first item recorded under Gillespie's own name, finds him in comparable circumstances but achieving more positive results. The underlying pulse is wrong, and his execution is less immaculate than it soon became, yet the lengthy trumpet solo, although loosely put together, includes features of melodic invention, rhythmic structure, harmonic thinking and tone-colour that were to remain characteristic. Everything else in the performance is made to sound redundant, and, the 1944 recordings of Parker with Tiny Grimes and Thelonious Monk's with Coleman Hawkins notwithstanding, this improvisation is the earliest fully-fledged statement that we have from a major postwar jazz musician.

Soon Gillespie recorded with a more apt personnel, including Parker and Clyde Hart, who pecks out the chord changes with discretion and sympathy, and was among the few pianists qualified for this sort of music in 1945. *Grooving high* and *Dizzy atmosphere* are typical of

89

the boppers' initially rather drastic renewal of the jazz repertoire, and are fertile ground for improvisation, their themes packed with musical incident yet enigmatically honed to bare essentials. Parker, indeed, is especially fluent, revealing a side of his musical personality not much represented on studio recordings: his tone has an airy, singing luminosity reminiscent of Benny Carter, and the alto saxophone solos on both these pieces are full of grace and elegance. This delicacy again characterised his work on the 1946 *Ornithology* session, and, to a lesser degree, the *Relaxing at Camarillo* date of the following year, but it was always rare.

Gillespie has two solos in *Grooving high* the first of which begins strikingly but collapses with a miscalculated descending phrase which leads into a bland guitar solo by Remo Palmieri. Later the tempo halves and he plays some beautifully shaped legato phrases that would then have been quite beyond any other trumpeter; this passage later provided the basis for Tadd Dameron's fine song *If you could see me now*. On the faster *Dizzy atmosphere* he takes a daring solo which conveys the essential spirit of the bop solo style and in itself is almost enough to explain the commanding position Gillespie held in the immediate postwar years. After the solos there is an attractive unison passage for trumpet and alto saxophone which flows into a deftly-truncated restatement of the theme—a neat formal touch.

The date which produced *Hot house* and *Salt peanuts* had a still better personnel, including Al Haig at the piano. Using the chord sequences of popular songs as the basis for new compositions was common during this period (though *not* an innovation, as so often claimed), and Dameron's *Hot house* is a superior instance of the practice, supplanting the usual AABA pattern of four eight-bar phrases with one of ABCA. Gillespie's solo here is effectively poised over Haig's responsive accompaniment, and, as on *One bass hit part 1*, contains definitive illustrations of the bop use of double-time. Parker digs deeper than at the previous date and shows himself well on course for his great *Koko* session, which took place a few months later and is dealt with on an earlier page.

Salt peanuts is a good, rather aggressive theme based on an octave-jump idea, and this arrangement, which includes some interesting harmonic touches, draws from the two-horn ensemble a fuller sound than usual. Parker seems less assured than before, yet Haig is good and Gillespie better. His entry could scarcely be more arresting, and emphasises as clearly as any moment on these recordings the absolute freshness of his imagination at this time: surely nobody else would then have dared to attempt this passage on the trumpet. The rest of his improvisation is played with equal conviction, but in another version of this piece, recorded soon after, some of the intensity is replaced with a sharper clarity of organisation.

Although Parker's work was uneven almost throughout 1945, there is no doubt of the added emotional depth he gave to these recordings, and Gillespie noticeably dominates more in his absence. Twelve months after the *Salt peanuts* date the trumpeter led a session on which—at last—all the participants were bop adepts. Sonny Stitt, who shared with Sonny Criss a reputation (which really belonged to John Jackson) of being the first man to emulate Parker's style, has a fair sixteen-bar solo in *Oop bop sh'bam* that is close to the master in tone yet far simpler in melodic and rhythmic concept. Its effect is completely obliterated, however, by Gillespie. The trumpeter did other fine things at this date, such as his solo on *That's Earl, brother* and his imaginative accompaniment to Alice Roberts's singing in *Handfulla gimme*, but on *Oop bop sh'bam* he plays with unrelenting intensity and perfect balance between detail and overall form that produce a masterpiece of jazz improvisation, worthy to stand beside Louis Armstrong's stop-time chorus on *Potato head blues* of almost exactly nineteen years before.

Despite the originality of their small combo work, to which almost equally powerful expression was given on several other titles in this series, including *Confirmation, Bebop* and *Shaw 'nuff*, the boppers were unable to establish a comparable orchestral idiom. In fact, due to its intimacy and relative complexity, bop, like New Orleans jazz, was inherently a music for small groups. The harmonic vocabulary, which scarcely was more advanced than Duke Ellington's of several years before, could easily have been written into band scores, but melodic and rhythmic subtleties derived from the leading soloists' improvisations could not. The linear shapes of the reed and brass scoring in Gillespie's earlier big bands, like that of Billy Eckstine which preceded them, did incorporate some new ideas, but included no innovations of ensemble texture comparable to those then being carried forward by Gil Evans with Claude Thornhill's band which are discussed elsewhere in this book. The boppers were able only to adapt their style to the big band rather than the converse.

Their best arranger was Gil Fuller, who, while possessing a good sense of traditional swing band style, and having an acute awareness of any large ensemble's requirements, managed to sacrifice fewer of the new ideas, to compromise less with the old. In fact, his scores, which are less subtle of mood and texture than Ellington's but more complex than Count Basie's, seem, in their use of the orchestra as a virtuoso instrument, to descend from Sy Oliver's work for Jimmy Lunceford. Marked differences arise because of Fuller's wider melodic, harmonic and rhythmic vocabularies, yet both men used their orchestras as vehicles for dazzling ensemble display, with sudden contrasts that, however aggressive, never descended to Kentonesque melodrama. Fuller's imagination, like Oliver's, was disciplined, in a sense almost conservative, and his scores are characterised by clarity of texture, an exceptional fullness of sound whether loud or soft. And yet if there are orchestral scores which at least partially embody the spirit of the little bands of the mid-1940s they are Gerald Wilson's *Grooving high*, Oscar Pettiford's *Something for you*, both of 1945, and Fuller's 1946 *Things to come*, an adaptation of the small combo *Bebop*. Unfortunately they were all played too fast in the recording studio to produce their complete effect, and Fuller got this conception over more successfully in *The scene changes*, which he recorded for the obscure Discovery label three years later.

On neither *Things to come* nor *One bass hit part 2* are Gillespie's solos at all happy (in fact he does better on Pettiford's *Something for you*). His inventive power is as evident as before, yet it is as if he had difficulty in shaping his material in relation to the heavier sounds and thicker textures of this setting—which is surprising in view of his prewar experience in swing bands. The above comments on the orthodox nature of his orchestra's library are borne out by a conventional statement of Dameron's excellent *Our delight* theme or by the saxophone writing in *One bass hit part 2*, but on the former, and also in *Ray's idea*, Gillespie responds to the themes' melodic substance with masterful solos that are better aligned with their accompaniment. On *Emanon*, basically a rather old-fashioned powerhouse blues, there are uncommonly forceful exchanges between leader and band, some agreeably pungent ensemble dissonance, a piano solo by John Lewis, and a striking passage for unaccompanied trumpet section. There seems no escaping the fact that in such relatively backward-looking pieces as this the boppers' attempts at orchestral jazz succeeded best.

It was also in 1946 that Gillespie made his first recordings with strings. These were of Jerome Kern melodies and remained unissued for many years because of objections made by that composer's widow to the allegedly bizarre treatment to which they were subjected. During 1950 he made another attempt and recorded eight miscellaneous titles which suggest that Mrs Kern may have been right, even if for the wrong reasons. Eddie South, on some delightful records made in Paris with Django Reinhardt during the late 1930s, proved that the violin is a fully viable jazz instrument, but this lead has never been followed up (least of all by the crudities of Stuff Smith). En masse, certainly, strings have been a consistent failure in this music, and it has been widely accepted that they cannot be employed in jazz due to their inherent sweetness. Nothing could be further from the truth. There is a large number of works by twentieth-century composers, such as Schoenberg's String Trio, Bartók's Quartets Nos. 4 and 5, Xenakis's *ST/4*, or Boulez's *Livre*, which prove that this whole family of instruments can yield sounds as invigorating, indeed as harsh, as any found in jazz. In short what is wrong with the use of strings on jazz dates is the incompetence of the arrangers employed, and never was this more so than with Gillespie's 1950 attempts, where they were only one of a number of apparently irreconcilable factors.

For *Swing low, sweet chariot* Johnny Richards wrote an absurd light-music introduction for the strings and then established the rhythm with—of all things in a Negro spiritual—Latin American percussion; a male voice choir sings not the rather sultry original melody but a commonplace new one, presumably also by Richards; Gillespie's trumpet solo has better continuity than we might expect in these circumstances, but a final touch of incongruity is provided by a return of the strings' introduction. On *Alone together* and *These are the things I love* the strings interrupt less often, and he manages a few dashing phrases in *Lullaby of the leaves*, but he never really sounds involved and it is impossible to understand his enthusiasm for this project, which was carried through at his instigation. *On the Alamo* typifies the whole enterprise, for although Gillespie blows with real power here, the trumpet passages are separated by interludes of quite offensive gentility from piano and strings—light music at its heaviest. If *Interlude in C*, a tasteless hodge-podge on a theme from Rachmaninoff's Piano Concerto No. 2, seems to have the thinnest string writing of all it may only be due to comparison with that composer's far richer alternative being unavoidable.

The virtually complete musical failure of these 1950 items with strings may seem unimportant until we recall that already the previous year, with his conventionally-instrumentated band, Gillespie had recorded such inanities as *You stole my wife, you horse-thief*. A random sampling of his small combo recordings from about this period tells the same tale, and shows an almost catastrophic decline from the master-pieces of just a few years before. *The champ*, an excellent theme, gives rise to a fine trombone solo from J. J. Johnson, but Gillespie merely reshuffles his mannerisms, and the other players are frankly ex-hibitionistic. *Tin tin deo* or *Birk's works*, also from 1951, are only negative in their restraint—despite some good moments from Milt Jackson's vibraharp on the latter—and *Stardust*, which features the trumpeter throughout, is distressingly pedestrian. The reunion session with Parker compelled Gillespie to make an altogether exceptional effort (e.g. his solos on take 2 of *Relaxing with Lee* or take 4 of *An oscar for Treadwell*), but the overall impression left by most of his records from this time is of an artist who no longer wishes to dominate, or even to control, his surroundings. And rarely did he ever again. Perhaps the reasons for this were psychological as much as artistic, but Gillespie's rarely swerving downward path from the classic small combo recor-dings he made during the immediate post war years was among the most saddening features of the jazz landscape in the 1950s (1).

Jazz Review, November 1959

David Mack and Serial Jazz

During 1965 a British musician called David Mack had a record issued bearing the familiar title of *New Directions* (1). With it he proved that it is possible to write *and improvise* jazz which, dispensing with tonal harmony as its structural determinant, uses twelve-tone serial tech-nique. And by employing it rigorously, Mack indicated a possible new path for jazz as surely as Ornette Coleman. To understand what he did three things are necessary. First, we must look over some fairly recent music history to see how and why serial technique, or dodecaphony, arose. Next, grasping its potentialities as an extension of the jazz language will be aided by comparing Mack's work with the less strict use of tone-rows on a number of other records. Finally, we must ask what further possibilities serial technique had for jazz, and contrast these with the rival path of development.

Harmony, while still an evolutionary force in European music, was an intrinsically developing language. It had an apparently innate tendency to enlarge its chordal vocabulary, admitting discords previously thought unacceptable. Because it extended over several centuries, this was not a steady growth—for example, Haydn and early Mozart are simpler than much Bach. Yet the overall procedure has been well described as the gradual 'emancipation of dissonance'. In practice this meant a rising degree of chromaticism. This infiltration went forward most quickly in the latter half of the nineteenth century and led to new melodic and harmonic relationships between the twelve notes of the chromatic scale which made it harder to relate them to a tonic, a key-note.

By the early years of our own century, composers employed an increasing number of chromatic chords and combinations of intervals only partially connected with diatonic harmony—for instance, chords built of fourths or from the whole-tone scale, mixtures of the tritone with other intervals, and so on. Thus were weakened the 'gravitational' pull towards the tonic and, consequently, the traditional relationships between chords which had for so long given Western music much of its cohesion. The result, finally, was atonality, and a possible consequence was loss of structural coherence. Of course, some people announced the imminent death of music, but the situation paralleled that around 1600 when the old system of church modes went out. Once again, new formal principles were needed.

These had to grow naturally, and have roots in the past. If the key system's waning power threatened formal incoherence, it was from the resultant equality of all twelve notes of the chromatic scale that new techniques would probably arise—and such proved the case. Because the suspension of tonality was a purposive and organic process, as the old system weakened its hold composers began, not always consciously, to introduce new elements to replace it. Basically what happened was a change from vertically-conceived devices of functional harmony to decisively linear ways of thought.

Two features should be noted: first the reintroduction of 'real' counterpoint displacing the harmonically-inspired polyphony of the classical and romantic periods, and, second, a more varied melodic construction. Both are complex matters, and this is not a place to discuss the renewed validity of the in some cases very old contrapuntal devices that Schoenberg and others revived. Sufficient to say that whereas in classical works they were inevitably modified by functional harmonic considerations, in the atonal music of the early years of this century they attempted to replace harmony with their own intrinsic form-giving qualities. Similarly, little can be said here on the rhythmic features of this music, except, obviously, that they paralleled the development of freer melody: as the emphasis on linear rather than harmonic construction increased, so greater rhythmic freedom became possible.

On melody itself, however, something must be said. Building on nineteenth-century practice. Schoenberg and others wrote melodies which, with their compound intervals, chromatic inflection, numerous passing notes and rhythmic decoration, increasingly used all twelve available notes. And to achieve both tension and variety within a highly detailed texture, they grew more reluctant to repeat notes or even to repeat one before the other eleven had sounded. Such melody was of a highly subjective expressiveness and resulted from a free association of musical ideas rather than their formally-patterned elaboration. It was a kind of aural expressionism whose disadvantage was the immense strain imposed on the imagination of the composer and upon the listener's powers of assimilation. For lucid musical structures more was needed than expanded techniques of melody-writing and counterpoint.

By now all twelve notes were utilised freely, greater formal control could only lay in their more consistently ordered use, and it is of this that serial methods consist. Twelve-tone technique can be employed in ways ranging from very simple to exceedingly complex. It covers invention and development of material and overall structural control. Within its bounds are possible an apparently endless variety of personal styles, just as in the tonal system.

After extensive preliminary sketching, the dodecaphonic composer sets all twelve notes in a particular, chosen order, this being known as the tone-row. This row, or series, is the basis of the whole composition, rotating in the background just as the triad permeates tonal music. The note-order, once decided, is regarded as fixed and is repeated in every strand of the work's texture, its continued presence ensuring the superior unity characteristic of serial music.

While keeping its integral structure, the row may be used in many forms. It can be reversed and both the original and retrograde forms inverted. These four shapes may be transposed to start on any of the twelve chromatic steps, the row thus being available in forty-eight forms. This may seem unmusical, even mechanical, but while the note-order is set by one form or other of the row, there is limitless scope for imagination in time-values, rhythm, tone-colour. Twelve-note technique also permits a greater variety of vertical combinations than tonal harmony. Again, this is not the place to particularise, but a study of appropriate dodecaphonic scores would show that this method has limitless potential. Seen from an historical viewpoint, David Mack's jazz was simply another demonstration of this.

It could scarcely be emphasised too strongly that the above is a highly simplified account of the steps that led to the decline of tonality, for other factors were at work. Also ignored are the precedents for serial methods to be found in the works of pre-dodecaphonic composers such as Reger. Further, the description of twelve-tone technique itself could not be more superficial. It is hoped, even so, that the foregoing gives some indication of why and how the new structural method arose (2).

Once American Negro musicians had adopted European harmony, many aspects of jazz development were pre-set. As Hindemith says, "with harmony it seems to go as with the tree of the knowledge of good and evil: once you have tasted its fruits you have lost your innocent approach" (3). The nature of our harmonic system is such, that is, that jazz was committed to a growing chordal vocabulary and consequent increase of melodic richness. Indeed, so far as harmony is concerned, jazz has, in a very condensed way, paralleled several centuries of European development in as many decades. Obviously, such haste meant that much had to be omitted. Jazz might be termed 'root-position music'. That is, it has not made great use of the enriching effects of chordal inversions that are so striking a feature of good European music. Perhaps it is the task of such players as Bill Evans to explore the jazz potentialities of this large area of harmony.

At all events, jazz reached chromatic harmony quickly—in the 1930s, not the following decade. The most ignorant criticism levelled at the boppers was that they imported 'alien' and 'European' chords into jazz. In fact, most of the chromaticisation of jazz harmony was carried out by virtuoso soloists of the swing period. The harmonic sophistication of Coleman Hawkins's finest ballads may be equalled by Charlie Parker, but it is not surpassed either by him or any of the 1940s generation. And Art Tatum, of course, is unequalled in all jazz for his mastery of chromatic harmony.

Having reached full chromaticism—within the already noted limits of jazz harmony—history shows that we should expect signs of tonal dissolution. They duly appeared in Thelonious Monk's late-1940s work, the most obvious device being his perhaps over-frequent use of whole-tone scales. Here the absence of semitones undermines the key-defining effect of diatonic scales with their mixture of tones and semitones. It had earlier been used, in different, more complex, ways yet for the same purpose, by Debussy and Schoenberg. Note also Monk's fondness for minor seconds and minor ninths—the latter often appearing when we might expect octaves and thus reminiscent of the serialists' avoidance of octave-doubling. His general melodic practice is most revealingly heard in company with more conventional musicians with whom he has recorded, such as Clark Terry. On the *In Orbit* LP Terry's favourite interval appears, significantly, to be the third, while Monk responds with much spidery chromaticism. Also relevant are the tonally-indefinite introduction to *Evidence*, and Monk's celebration of the tritone in *Skippy*. Most drastic is his superimposition of motives in *Evidence* and *Mysterioso*, and this is worth comparing with the endings to Duke Ellington's *Hot and bothered* and Mal Waldron's *Vibrations* where in each case the pairs of combined themes 'fit' in the most academic sense, whereas Monk plays one motive against the other without apparent regard for the tonal consequences. This is because key-feeling is no longer so important; Monk still thought tonally, of course, but he showed that atonality was not far off.

It was with the work of Cecil Taylor in the 1950s that jazz properly reached atonality. This pianist said he thought tonally, but on even his first LP—*Jazz Advance*—there are passages to which it would be hard to ascribe key centres. It is symbolic of the haste with which jazz rushed through European harmonic resources that the less satisfactory aspects of Taylor's work are a particularly good illustration of the dangers of free atonality mentioned above. Conventional melodic units—two- and four-bar phrases—rely on the cadential impulse of traditional harmony and therefore tend to disappear from atonal thinking. Having arisen out of tonality, twelve- and thirty-two-bar choruses are naturally based on the idea of regular melodic periods, and, while these were challenged by the assymetry of some bop phrasing, it is in the atonal context that they really lose their point. By rejecting tonality we also weaken, if not lose, the repeating chorus as a meaningful basis for construction, leaving the improvisor with little, formally, to guide him. Something must replace it.

Several of Taylor's recordings illustrate the formlessness and apparent lack of direction that can so easily result, both early ones like *You'd be so nice to come home to* and later examples such as *D trad, that's what*. A related difficulty is the rôle of the bass in atonal jazz. On many Taylor discs it is hard for the ear to connect the tonal lines played by the bassist with the atonal extemporisation above. This produces an effect of unreality, for often the notes sound neither right nor wrong. The same happens on other recordings wherein harmonic considerations are treated very freely. For instance, on Sonny Rollins's *Freedom suite* there are passages where it is hard to feel that the bass part has much harmonic significance, even though the music is tonal. Such adventures show us jazz risking structural incoherence, then, just as European music had about half a century earlier. Once again new formal principles were needed, and it was no surprise to find American jazzmen in the 1950s beginning to record experiments with the twelve-tone method. And just as the basic ideas of serial technique had been hit upon by at least two other men besides Schoenberg, so these later ventures were made independently of each other.

A good example of primitive jazz serialism is Miles Davis's *All blues*. Here, instead of a chord sequence, the improvisations are based on a series of five scales, that is, five selections of notes from the twelve available. Davis constructed fragmentary tone-rows which replace harmony in giving the music coherence. A similar case is *Tragedy* by Don Ellis. Basic here are four note-clusters rather than scales. Again the main point is desertion of tonal harmony, for construction of these clusters is not affected by traditional harmonic unities, and they act, in an elementary way, as incomplete tone-rows. Ellis's sleeve note is worth quoting; "The four note-clusters are numbered. The soloist may change from one to another at will, indicating his change to the rest of the group by holding up one, two, three or four fingers. The bass plays on the cluster basically—as if it were a conventional chord—sticking close to the main tones of the cluster, but having freedom in his choice of passing notes. The soloist, too, may go in or out of the 'harmony' guided solely by his ear".

Max Roach's *The man from South Africa* uses the same device less satisfactorily. Here theme statements are conventionally harmonised but solos are based on clusters of harmonically unrelated notes. The trouble with such tone-clusters is that, being only selections from the twelve available notes, some tones are emphasised at the expense of others and a residual key-feeling results. As Ellis says, "After playing on these clusters for a while they become 'tonal' to the ear and you hear melodic ideas that can be close to the sound of the cluster or further away, so it is actually like improvising on slow-motion chords". In Roach's case this is heightened by tonal piano chords and the use of ostinatos, which, again by emphasising particular notes, give a tonal bias. It is not suggested that music is good or bad according to whether it is tonal, atonal or serial, but pieces such as *Tragedy* or *The man from South Africa*, by attempting to replace tonality with an ineffective dilution of twelve-tone devices while, in the Roach, hanging on to conventional harmony in theme statements, with ostinatos, etc., reveal the divided aims and inconsistent techniques characteristic of transitional works. One of the main points of dodecaphonic methods, remember, is the equality of all twelve notes, which normally replaces key-feeling while ensuring unity by other means.

On looking at the actual use of twelve-tone techniques in jazz we find as many approaches as there are examples—an expected illustration of the diversity which serial methods allow. Ellis's *Improvisational suite No. 1* employs its row only as a point of departure for an unusually varied collective extemporisation. No attempt is made to develop the row along customary twelve-note lines. As Gunther Schuller writes in the sleeve note: "The row is used as the basis for a kind of musical 'free association'. The tones (pitches) of the row and the specific order in which they are organised are guide posts which the improvisor uses in a free manner". Free and in-tempo sections alternate, the former are atonal and the latter relatively tonal, Ellis's free employment of the row accommodating all this.

Such music, with its mixture of tonality, atonality and free dodecaphony, should not be confused with the transitional inconsistencies of *Tragedy* and *The man from South Africa* because in the *Suite* the new method is unequivocally accepted even if nothing like full advantage is taken of it. Strict use of a series is found in Shorty Rogers's *Three on a row*, an elementary academic exercise. Here again we have a mixture of old and new for the row is heard twelve times, at a variety of tempos, the statements linked by conventional harmonic passages. With this piece it is possible to sense for the first time something of the unity imparted by twelve-tone methods.

A further stage is marked by Schuller's *Abstraction*, a work attempting to reconcile the extremes of early-1960s jazz with something like the extremes of pre-aleatoric straight music: Ornette Coleman and a rather Webernian application of serial technique. Schuller saw parallels between Coleman's playing and twelve-note music and tried to isolate and emphasise them here. His main points were that the alto saxophonist's choice of notes, not primarily determined by harmonic considerations, might operate well against an atonal dodecaphonic background; also that both musics tend towards a comparable non-thematic continuity, outwardly fragmentary but inwardly cohesive.

Abstraction is in ABA[1] form: B is an unaccompanied cadenza by Coleman, A is the composed material, and A[1] is its exact retrograde; Coleman also plays during parts of both A and A[1]. However reasonable the composer's ideas may seem, they appear questionable in practice. This is because the parallels between free and serial music do not go very deep. Coleman's line sounds foreign to the serial context, the shared lack of key notwithstanding. One feels that he might equally well improvise against a performance of, say, Webern's Quartet Op. 28. The result would be 'interesting', but not a unified piece. Lest this comparison be thought unfair, it should be noted that Schuller's contribution was fully composed before Coleman heard it and began to extemporise. Had it been practicable to work out details in the recording studio in something like the Ellington manner, Schuller modifying his part in accordance with Coleman's improvising and vice versa, the result might have been different.

If free and dodecaphonic music will hardly mesh together, it is still possible, despite what was said above on confused transitional works, to use serial technique along with conventional harmony. This is because the former grew out of the latter whereas free and serial musics are based on different assumptions. The proviso is that the musician concerned must have achieved both maturity of expression and real technical control: uncertainty of aim is fatal. He must accept both techniques for what they are, at least to begin with, and seek to make one enhance the other, rather than dilute both.

Remembering the musical intelligence he showed with *Israel*, it is not surprising to find John Carisi bringing this off. His beautiful *Moon taj* and *Angkor Wat* are not strictly dodecaphonic, yet the firm structural control that is felt despite lush colours and richly-variegated instrumental texture works through the twelve-note rather than the traditional elements present. Carisi's amalgam of serial technique, harmony and virtuoso orchestration produces a unique kind of twelve-note impressionism, and, the Eastern inspiration notwithstanding, there are no self-conscious orientalisms. Reconciling tonal harmony with dodecaphonic method in so hastily developing a music as jazz inevitably exacted a price, and there is little extemporisation. This appears, however, close to the "twelve-tone music filled with Ravelian flavour" which Dimitri Mitropoulos hoped for (4).

Nearly all the above instances of serial jazz contain good music, but their limitations should not be missed. Carisi has said there is no point in making a religion of pure improvisation as this can lead to its own rigidities, and what counts is the overall result. This is obviously true, yet jazz developments have usually been concerned with preserving, in fact enriching, extemporisation, not limiting it. If twelve-tone technique is fully viable within jazz one may reasonably insist on improvisation being retained. But in Rogers there is none at all, with Schuller it occurs but is not properly related to its surroundings, and in Carisi it is restricted.

On none of these records is there even an attempt at extemporisation with a twelve-note series used strictly, and some people incautiously dismissed this as impossible. But recent history suggests that dodecaphonic methods yield best results when adopted wholeheartedly, as we might expect. Art usually thrives on limitation rather than in the seductive freedom of total licence: the benefit of aesthetic and technical discipline is that it compels the imagination to work harder. Partial attempts at serial jazz of the sort discussed so far, while necessary, were unlikely to produce a main stream. But a jazz making full use of twelve-note methods would offer scope for a wide range of emotional expression and technical development. Such music would be liberated from what George Russell called "the chord prison" (5) and improvisation, while having new paths to travel, would be brought into closer union with ensemble composition, the whole within a wider variety of forms. With just one LP David Mack showed this was possible.

New Directions was recorded in 1964 with Shake Keane (trumpet and flugelhorn), Ralph Bruce (soprano saxophone), Al Baum (alto saxophone), Gordon Lewin (tenor saxophone and clarinet), Jim Easton (baritone saxophone), Don Lowes (piano), Coleridge Goode (bass), Joe Gibbons and Eric Allen (percussion). All the compositions, written in 1958, are by Mack, who also directed.

While ensembles are to the fore on several tracks, there is serial improvisation in all the dodecaphonic items. On *Ralph's mead* Bruce and Keane are heard quite briefly, though what they play accords strictly with the score's note-row. And Keane's serial improvisation aside, ensembles again predominate on *Johnnie's door*. *Cameo* includes longer solos, by trumpet and clarinet, and in *Chiquita moderne* Mack combines jazz and Latin idioms while serial principles are maintained, again including in Keane's solo. To cap this, he managed to introduce ostinatos which do not weaken the prevailing atonality because of the strength of the overall twelve-tone organisation.

But *Tonette* may be the most remarkable track. This includes a passage of subdued collective extemporisation which still adheres to the row! It must be obvious that a high standard of musicianship is necessary to produce dodecaphonic solos at all, but to bring off collective improvisation at this early stage was extraordinary. Also on this item, Keane plays a free-form extemporisation—adhering, that is, to neither row nor chords—against a serial background. This parallels the Schuller/Coleman *Abstraction,* and if Mack's combination of free and twelve-note jazz is more convincing it probably is because it is briefer, a small section of a work rather than its whole point.

Mack's remaining dodecaphonic piece was *Half-tone poem*, the record's most gentle track. Here he concentrated on mellow sounds which he felt had been neglected in much serial writing, and it is particularly delightful to hear Keane's flugelhorn riding over the murmuring saxes. An advantage of twelve-tone methods is that they almost compel careful attention to all details, and *New Directions* is one of those rare jazz discs—along with certain items by George Russell and Gil Evans—where the listener can afford to let his ear dwell on every single sound.

His achievement was that he created a music which, while remaining jazz, dispenses with tonal harmony and is based on the fullest use (so far as the ordering of pitches is concerned) of serial methods. His bandsmen were able to improvise, if not at great length, and because of the employment of note-rows, their solos are in every bar closely related to the composed material, the tone-row of each piece binding together the whole performance—which swings in an almost old-fashioned way. And in Mack's pieces one is no longer aware of the seemingly inescapable string-of-choruses format that is so tiresome a feature of all but the greatest jazz records (which, admittedly, transcend it).

However, one would have liked to hear more extended twelve-note improvisations. And it would have been interesting to know whether Mack could have produced longer compositions with more varied formal resources, could have used more ensemble counterpoint, and a more astringent chordal vocabulary. Needless to say, he was never given the chance. But still he had surpassed the inconclusive American experiments and proved that thoroughgoing dodecaphonic jazz was possible.

In essence all this represented the continuing influence of the European tradition on jazz and was thus a 'conservative' development. If there is an argument against it this is that twelve-tone technique did not arise in jazz quite so naturally and inevitably as in European music. With Europe there were few other alternatives, while in jazz far more could have been done with tonal harmony. Yet jazzmen no longer occupy an enclosed world: the more intelligent among them cannot be blamed for awareness of newer resources, or for using them. We may never hear 'blowing dates' based on tone-rows instead of the blues and *I got rhythm*, but if dodecaphonic methods had been incorporated into the main stream of jazz this would probably have been effected largely by improvisation. Jazz and serial technique would eventually have altered each other, but in the process the latter might have become, so far as jazz was concerned, chiefly an extemporisor's tool.

Yet the exploration could have had many forms. To take a random example, Skalkottas's later music illustrates the kind of procedure that might have appeared in jazz, and, like Carisi's pieces, shows how, if need be, contact with tonality may be retained. In this Greek composer's works, while tone-rows are used and tonality in the traditional sense is absent, a tonal centre is sometimes established by frequent emphasis and repetition. (There is a trace of this in Ellis's very freely tonal *Imitation*.) And on occasion, even in violently dissonant and uncompromisingly atonal pieces, Skalkottas maintains a sort of tonal residue by employing strongly diatonic melodies and treating them in every way possible to subvert their tonality. (There is more than a hint of this in Cecil Taylor's *This nearly was mine*.)

As emphasised, one of the greatest advantages of twelve-tone technique is its unifying capacity. It is a hard saying for jazz, but in art unity is an aspect of quality, and it is here that a collective music so often must fail. Dodecaphonic methods carry no guarantee of quality, but the sort of coherence imposed by serial procedures might have lessened the kind of anticlimax produced when, say, an Ory follows an Armstrong on *Savoy blues* or a Davis follows a Parker in *Now's the time*.

It was suggested above that there were two solutions to jazz problems in the 1960s, and the alternative to serial technique was, of course, Ornette Coleman's innovations. Linking Mack and Coleman does not imply equal stature. The former's work could have been done by another similar minor figure, whereas Coleman may be the most original player jazz ever had. Armstrong and Parker did not 'change the direction of jazz' because, as noted, during what we may call its harmonic period, its chief technical moves were pre-set. Rather did they enable it to travel faster: their effect was developmental, not revolutionary.

But Coleman indicated a new direction, potentially the most vital move in the music's history. His work was 'radical' in offering a shift from European technical assumptions, perhaps towards new ways of musical thought altogether. Coleman's music virtually bypassed harmony in favour of a free modality; it also abandoned equal temperament tuning, which had been a consequence of harmony and its fixed intervals. If this appears merely negative, we should recall George Russell's theory that jazz has always been a linear—that is, scalar, modal, non-harmonic—music, and this is why it rushed through chordal resources so quickly, as an interlude or preliminary (5).

Free and twelve-tone jazz would often have surface similarities. Both are mainly linear in their thought, and it was noted above that chorus-structure and regular phrase-lengths dissolve in non-tonal contexts. Both types of jazz would therefore have much asymmetrical phrasing and discontinuous melody, and bar-lines would mean little. Discontinuity and asymmetry were anticipated in bop, and the possible lack of a regular pulse was foreshadowed by Monk's solo ballads, which 'let in the silence', by several vintages of Giuffre's trio recordings, and by others. Such music might have led to the athematicism discussed by André Hodeir in his remarkable essay on Monk (6), this, too, being heralded not only by Coleman's *Free jazz* but by more conservative performances such as the Parker *Bird's nest*. As Hodeir says, continuity and symmetry of musical discourse were partially destroyed by Debussy, Schoenberg, Webern, and decisively replaced by asymmetry and discontinuity in Boulez, Stockhausen and others. Were this reflected in jazz it would not be so much a sign that it continued to parallel the European tradition but that, musically, it had at last reached the twentieth century.

The different basic assumptions of free and serial jazz are partly clarified when we consider the former's suggested oriental affinities, although even here the music follows a partial European precedent and one is reminded of a number of works such as Mahler's *Das Lied von der Erde* with its oriental melismata in the last movement. It cannot be too strongly emphasised that all European music, and jazz, is of extreme rhythmic simplicity compared with many oriental musics, but free jazz did seem to link up with Eastern ideas in its attitude to time.

All significant Western music—including most jazz—embodies a European, post-Renaissance, concept of time, and, consequently, of

the necessity of form. Most jazz, like other Western music, has a beginning, middle and end. But to complain that a John Coltrane performance such as *Chasing the 'trane* is too long is probably to apply in-
correct criteria. It seems to stop when its force is spent, not when a
particular set of formal requirements has been met; it appears unconcerned with overall design, hoping to make its effect in other ways.
The same is true of seemingly quite different jazz such as Romeo
Nelson's *Head rag hop* piano blues, which, with its incessant bass and
directionless pentatonic doodlings high above, could easily have
stopped sooner or gone on longer. In view of Russell's theory, it is
interesting that our 'normal' ideas of form should be ignored in the
primitive and sophisticated extremes of jazz. In twelve-note jazz, of
course, the European time-concept would remain, and this indicates
its 'conservatism'. Indeed, the vital divergence in basic assumptions
between this and free jazz may be their different attitudes towards
time, and, consequently, their different views of the nature and meaning of musical form.

Despite this divergence, both free and dodecaphonic jazz might
have presented us with music which had no themes, few regular
phrases and no harmony. Some early post-Coleman jazz, such as LPs
by Giuseppi Logan, Byron Allen and others, did lack apparent form,
and serial jazz, with its firm structural control, appeared, for 'normal'
Western ears, to have the advantage here. There was no apparent
reason, however, why free jazz should not in due course have
developed entirely new formal procedures of its own which might well
have owed little to European, let alone oriental, ideas.

It is useless to speculate about these, but it should be noted that
structural methods dependent neither on harmony nor on twelve-tone
technique are entirely possible. Random samples are Debussy's great
conception of the rôle of the quality of sound itself in determining form,
and the technique of 'metrical modulation' found in the works of the
American composer Elliott Carter. Aside from the structural question,
it might be asked, in view of the surface similarities between free and
dodecaphonic jazz, what was so wrong about works like Schuller's
Abstraction, which tried to reconcile the two? Had further such works
appeared, it is true, remembering Sidney Finkelstein's valuable point
about jazz being a mixture of languages (7), that both free and serial
camps might in them have learnt from each other. Yet the real potentialities of free jazz were almost certainly unlike those of other music.

Following Coleman's subsequent unwillingness to provide
leadership (like Armstrong after about 1930 or Parker after around

1950—despite their continuing refinement of earlier achievements), and following Albert Ayler's death in 1970, these potentialities have remained largely unrealised. If free jazz had been harnessed with established techniques developed in other areas of music it might in any case have missed its finest qualities. This contrasts sharply with earlier jazz, which so readily, and of necessity, absorbed resources from outside, and is the best single indication of how new the new jazz of the early 1960s actually was.

Jazz Monthly, October 1965

Two Pieces on Ornette Coleman

I

Not many decades ago, the aesthetic and technical assumptions that had shaped European music for several centuries were regarded as fixed. Early music was seen as inept striving towards classical ideals, of historical interest only, and music of other cultures was patronised as the concern solely of anthropologists. Such arrogance could not last, and its breakdown was heralded, as significant movements usually are, by a few isolated individuals. Following Debussy's concern with Balinese music, several artists like Picasso and Epstein became interested in sculpture from Africa and elsewhere. As André Brassai has written, "The totems of the Negro and the Polynesian, the Aztec and the pre-Columbian symbols, Etruscan and Hittite gods, Indian fetishes, all these have conquered the West . . . Unknown or despised at the beginning of the century, today they have entered the museums of fine art. . . . At first they were atrocities, then curiosities, then objects of research . . . now transformed into masterpieces. . . . The primitive hand seems able to bypass the control of the conscious mind and express emotions directly" (1). By "primitive" he means untaught, and of this more later.

Quite apart from the aroused curiosity of musicians, painters and sculptors, technology was beginning to shrink the effective size of the planet, and one result was an interaction of cultures that will surely continue for a long time. Such fusions must involve many losses as well as gains, but Charles Ives, probably the most original musician America has produced, once wrote, "The time is coming, but not in our lifetime, when music will develop possibilities inconceivable now, a language so transcendent that its heights and depths will be common to all mankind" (2).

So long as a tradition remains isolated there is little scope for outright rejection of its tenets, even though they be subject to constant slow modification. But once opportunities arise to compare its procedures with those of other cultures, which offer alternative arrangements of intellect and emotion, then fundamental questions begin to get asked. A musician can nowadays be led to this in several ways. For instance, he can hear on the gramophone a wider range of music than his forebears can have dreamt to exist—can be influenced by a far greater variety of attitudes to sound and its expressive potentialities. A larger perspective brings its own difficulties, and too great a choice of paths can be almost as inhibiting as rigid academicism. But, in view of the diversity of materials and methods which had become available by the 1960s, it was to be expected that young jazz musicians would question established ideas to an extent not possible for earlier generations.

It is against this background that the seemingly complete breakdown of conventions in the more extreme new jazz of that time and since—the music of Albert Ayler, Pharoah Sanders and others—must be heard. The growth of an art is a reconciliation between its internal evolutionary strength and its external opportunities, and it would obviously be misleading to explain it, as some social theorists do, solely in materialistic terms. It is possible that the new developments to which Ornette Coleman's work gave rise, besides being part of a larger cultural pattern, might also be truer to the real nature of jazz than most of what had gone before. Certainly we ought to see these changes not as a breakdown, but as an end to insularity.

Jazz has long been considered a hybrid, an historical accident, and the European basis of many of its elements is clear. The harmonic and consequently the melodic vocabularies stem from the old world, and, whatever may be said about the special skills of jazz players, the rhythmic approach has been more European than anything else. Yet, as noted on an earlier page, jazz rushed superficially through several centuries of European resource in a few decades. Why?

There have always been other elements in jazz that have aligned badly with its extensive European borrowing, and these are assumed to be—picturesque phrase—'African survivals'. But are they? The so-called 'blues scale', with its pentatonic modality, occurs in folksong from several parts of the world and is not exclusive to Africa, still less to American Negro music. Microtones also, though supposedly a unique feature of the blues, are found in many other widely dispersed folk traditions. However, despite fanciful theorising based on a convenient ignorance of such matters, some of the originality of jazz as a musical language has been due to the ways the 'foreign' elements have affected jazzmen's handling of European resources. An obvious example is the virtual transformation of instruments: the trumpet in the hands of a Bubber Miley, the clarinet in Jimmy Giuffre's later music, the saxophone as played by Gato Barbieri are scarcely recognisable as the instruments we hear in symphony orchestra and dance band.

The persistence of such factors implies that jazz, while inconceivable without its European borrowings, was only partially committed to that tradition. One sign of this, as noted in another context, is a lack of concern with form that becomes apparent at the stylistic extremes of jazz, and contradicts the implications of the carefully planned endeavours of more 'central' figures like Duke Ellington or Thelonious Monk. The structural shapes of the former's *Concerto for Cootie* or the latter's *Evidence* are clearly perceptible, yet an unaccompanied field holler such as Vera Hall's *Wild ox moan* or Coleman's two alto saxophone improvisations on *The ark* could just as easily have gone on far longer or stopped much sooner. As Coleman said, "In a certain sense there really is no start or finish to any of my compositions" (3). It seems unlikely that the significance of this is to be explained solely in terms of 'survivals' from a now-remote African past, still less in the light of a hasty reinterpretation of borrowings, however extensive, from European musical practice. Is the hybrid phase of jazz merely a preliminary to the emergence of its real qualities?

It must be indicative of the ill-defined position of jazz that it has always been necessary to discuss it in terms of other musics, yet a useful parallel can be drawn between its position in the early 1960s and that of certain aspects of European music about half a century before. Schoenberg's answer to the tonal crisis was briefly outlined in the previous essay, but Debussy had another and quite different solution. Whereas in the former composer's atonal (but pre-serial) music, or in the earlier work of jazz atonalists such as Cecil Taylor, the form-building effect of harmonic progression is still residually present, in Debussy's more extreme pieces it is not. Briefly, he came to regard each chord as an entity in itself, without functional relationship with other chords. Logic and order did not therefore depart from his music but asserted themselves in other ways as he turned to melismatic and ostinato devices reminiscent of certain medieval music and, perhaps more significantly, of the orient.

For our purposes, Debussy's contributions may be simplified under two headings—his interest in non-European techniques, and his attitude to sound. Both these found echoes in music beyond the scope of this volume, but the earliest composer fully to grasp their meaning was Edgard Varèse. Even if he handled them in startlingly new ways, Debussy's basic materials were still determined by French musical tradition. Varèse, however, saw in the older man's abandoning of traditional harmonic relationships and concern with what until then would have been dismissed as 'exotic' techniques not only the end of formalised stylisation of musical material, but also of the strict division between music and non-musical sound. In his own words, Varèse "began to think of sound as a living matter to be moulded, free from arbitrary restrictions" (4). The working out of this in Varèse's own pieces, in those of such different composers as Cage or Stockhausen, and in electronic works, cannot be gone into here, yet the extreme diversity of this music and of much that has followed shows that belief in a stylised, purely 'musical' language has long since been discredited.

Now this kind of freedom in the handling of sound has always, up to a point, been at home in jazz, as the onamatopoeics of *Liberation suite* by Charlie Haden, Coleman's ex-bassist, the variety of sounds Eric Dolphy conjured from his bass clarinet, or Sun Ra from his entire ensemble show. But these are comparatively recent examples from the 1960s which in an earlier decade would have been at least partially inhibited by conventions borrowed by jazz from older European music. That they are no longer so is due to Ornette Coleman. He sensed that no more could be done with European techniques in a jazz context, especially harmony with the restricting effect it had (even after Charlie Parker, even after Art Tatum) on melodic, and, less directly, on rhythmic choice. So he bypassed that whole complex, and the musicians who followed him saw this and the hints of his fiercely vocalised tone and abandonment of equal-temperament tuning as marking an end to traditional restrictions on musical material. In effect, Coleman freed the non-European and non-African elements that had always been present in jazz, allowing them a larger part in shaping the new music.

What was next heard in jazz was an investigation of the expressive possibilities of sound untrammelled by preconceived musical stylisation, European or otherwise. This sometimes became a mere hedonistic play with noise, for when there is so much freedom discipline ceases to be a luxury. In fact a new sort of formal control, of a kind impossible even a few years before, did tentatively emerge. The structural ordering of the LP-long *Complete communion* and *Symphony for improvisors* led by Don Cherry, Coleman's former trumpeter, follows no models to be found outside jazz yet is formally satisfying as is little earlier jazz—even when on a much shorter time-scale. That Coleman's methods worked equally well over a short distance is shown by such passages as Haden's excellent but little-known bass solo on Keith Jarrett's *Lisbon stomp*.

Of course, as the historian A. F. Pollard said, revolutions often prove to be high jumps rather than long jumps, and when the tumult dies it is found that we have come to earth closer to our starting-point than was imagined. Not that revolution and innovation ever were the same thing, as Stravinsky reminds us (5). It is no surprise that, at least so far as his alto saxophone improvisations were concerned, Coleman eventually took up a less extreme position. But that was not the end of the story.

Jazz Monthly, June 1966

II

Following his classic quartet sessions for the Atlantic label, which permanently established his reputation, Coleman's Blue Note recordings confirmed his greatness as a jazz improvisor. But if this music is set beside what can only be called his attempts at non-jazz composition, a dichotomy in his output is revealed which is disturbing. On an LP such as the Blue Note *New York is Now!* the richness and vitality of Coleman's inspiration is staggering. There are no really new developments, yet, while his means of organising long solos remain stable, the kind of freedom in tempo as well as of tempo demonstrated in, say, *Clergyman's dream* recorded at the historic Croydon concert (6), has gone several degrees further in his beautiful *Garden of souls* improvisation.

From this viewpoint it is instructive to hear Coleman with Elvin Jones on the latter piece, for this drummer was largely responsible for initiating the switch of emphasis away from regular time-keeping which became associated with the jazz that stemmed from Coleman's own innovations, and the latter has none of the trouble certain others experienced with Jones's fluid rhythmic structures.

The linear fragmentation that had long been part of Coleman's way of playing, and is partly a consequence of his method of juxtaposing outwardly dissimilar shapes—part of his small legacy from bop—is likewise taken several stages further in *Broad way blues*. Perhaps this is best heard as a condensation of the slightly Cageian use of silence on the Croydon performance actually named *Silence,* a point underlined by Jones's and the bassist Jimmy Garrison's almost tentative support here. The thematic motive of *Broad way blues*, incidentally, is of a startling triteness whose satirical intent seems confirmed by the extraordinarily imaginative transformations it undergoes during the alto solo.

Bill Evans, the pianist, once suggested that "the person who sees furthest into the future is likely to be the person who sees furthest into the past" (7), and the sort of jazz heard on the above titles is best considered as a return to—or a discovery of—the music's basic essentials. Yet how is this apparently fundamentalist jazz of the 1960s to be reconciled with the character of *We now interrupt for a commercial*, the wild complexity of whose collectively improvised textures Coleman seems bent on emphasising by means of Mel Fuhrman's bland tv-announcer voice, which surrealistically breaks through the performance at several points? No matter how densely packed its lines become, this track is always dominated by the leader's violin, and maybe its wildness is just the point. If this piece is compared with other Coleman violin items such as *Snowflakes and sunshine, Bells and chimes* or the Croydon *Falling stars,* it will be found that his treatment of this instrument has not changed, has never 'developed', and perhaps it was not meant to.

Charles Mingus's astonishing bass work on the *Money Jungle* LP with Ellington and Max Roach provided an obvious precedent for a freer use of stringed instruments in jazz, but a more direct lead for Coleman's venture may have come from Haden's strangely desolate solos, both arco, as in *Peace*, and pizzicato, as in *Focus on sanity*. The bass solo by Steve Swallow in Paul Bley's *Violin* echoes the multi-voiced aspect of Coleman's alto saxophone playing, and the duet between Henry Grimes and Gary Peacock on Ayler's *Prophet* is also relevant. Something close to Coleman's actual violin tone is found in Grimes's playing on his own disc, *The Call*, and especially in Joe Friedmann's cello solos on Charles Tyler's *Strange uhuru, Three spirits* and *Black mysticism*. Closer still to home are the resources deployed by David

Izenzon, Coleman's one-time bassist, on the Croydon *Sadness*, which seem, probably misleadingly, to result from a slowing-down of his leader's method. However, if the sound Coleman draws from his violin is not unique, what he does with it is new to jazz and contradicts the attitudes explicit in his saxophone improvisations.

Despite their rejection of so many received Western ideas, especially about musical structure, Coleman's alto solos still conform to the 'modern' European, that is post-Renaissance, concept of art as expressing the unique vision of an individual creator who imposes his personal order on the confusion of everyday experience. But his violin improvisations are more radical. In them he sounds less civilised, more complex, the showers of notes, matted in dense, frantic textures, seem to well up with little conscious supervision. Because the player intervenes at key points to shape the solo only in a very general way, this music, like certain compositions by two other great American musicians, Charles Ives and John Cage, appears to mirror life's flux rather than subject it to a personal and therefore arbitrary order. It is worth recalling here Cage's quoting with approval an orchestral player who said of Ives's Symphony No. 4, after a rehearsal, "It doesn't resemble music as much as it resembles life" (8). Such music's incorporation of the impermanence, the endless transformations, the accidents of life itself, also remind us of Pierre Restany's description of the work of the motion-sculptor Jean Tinguely as "a passionate adventure of the real ... seen in itself and not through the prism of conceptual or imaginative transcription" (9).

Certainly Coleman's violin playing may represent an indeterminacy as drastic as Cage's, even if far cruder in its operation, and we should note the latter's comment that "the whole idea of chance operations is that the field of awareness that's now open to us is so big that if we're not careful we'll just go to certain points in it, points with which we're already familiar. By using chance operations we can get to points with which we're unfamiliar. But that basic desire may be missing in people who use chance because they think it's easy" (9). In fact it is very hard, and the way Coleman plays the violin in no way resembles automatic writing—as has unsurprisingly been suggested. Anybody who has attempted really free improvisation, especially as a member of a group, will know how readily one falls back on stock responses, above all on the muscular habits acquired through years spent with an instrument. Speaking of a crucial stage in his development, Marchel Duchamp said, "I didn't get completely free of that prison of tradition, but I tried to, consciously. I unlearned to draw. The point was to forget *with my hand*" (9). This relates to André Brassai's comment, quoted on an earlier page, about the power of the untutored hand "to bypass the control of the conscious mind and express emotions directly" (1).

Coleman has the advantage that he never learnt the violin academically, and he has a better chance of playing, as he says, "without memory" (10) on it than on his alto saxophone. His long professional experience with the latter instrument has made him highly conscious of the jazz tradition with its stockpile of stereotyped phrases, whereas the quite different tactics he adopts on the violin allow him to get closer to the goal of playing—as Duchamp wanted to draw—as if tradition did not exist. The main stream of jazz in the 1960s was typified by Coleman's saxophone improvisations and marked a discovery of the real potentialities of that music, but his violin playing reached still further beyond the articulated frontiers of knowledge towards a still more basic level of musical utterance.

One problem that we as listeners have is the lack of any detectable link between the violin and the saxophone musics. Perhaps, with *Falling stars, Bells and chimes* or *We now interrupt for a commercial*, the chaos is in the ears of the beholder, who feels his own kind of order threatened, but the expression of these violin pieces is 'level', not subject to the calculated diversity we have, through our experience of music from the late-eighteenth century to the present (including jazz), come to regard as normal. Despite this, because of the plethora of detail, these items, like some facets of the jazz which has followed Coleman, have an almost rococo aspect, and are best regarded, in H. R. Hitchcock's words, as "atactonic—avoiding structural expression" (11).

This does not help us, though, with our next problem, which is the lack of any resemblance, let alone any internal relationship, between the way Coleman plays his violin and the manner in which he writes for string instruments in formal compositions such as *Dedication to poets and writers, Space flight* or *Saints and soldiers*. If the saxophone and violin improvisations represent different paths back to the roots of jazz and to the fundamentals of musical expression respectively, how are we to take these completely written-out works for string quartet? Each has a certain character of its own, if only with regard to texture and tempo rather than in terms of musical thought, and *Dedication* has a slightly wider range of gesture than the later pieces. But all are limply static in their total effect. All are written, too, in a sort of garrulous heterophony that flows on and on, never arriving at points of climax or resolution, the idiom being, very approximately, an inept compromise between simplified Berg and coarsened Webern.

If only because of its avowed indeterminacy, *Sounds and forms* for wind quintet might seem more relevant to the aims of Coleman's improvisations, especially those on the violin. This piece has been recorded twice, but comparison of the two versions leads only to negative conclusions, and although the polyphonic textures reflect jazz collective improvisation it is only in the sense that several things are usually going on at once. Coleman has said he aimed to write "for the wind instruments so as to allow them to create a new piece every time the composition is performed" (12), but, even with quite different teams of musicians on the two recordings, this does not happen. The sole new feature of the more recent version is the trumpet links which the composer improvises between its ten movements, but, again, neither in their musical material nor in their level of expressivity do these relate perceptibly to what the quintet plays.

Its composer may speak of "a new piece every time", but whatever indeterminate procedures are written into the *Sounds and forms* score do not work, and he does not appear to have grasped that the demands and consequences peculiar to this kind of activity do not parallel those implicit in a jazz solo's indeterminacy. It is no use Coleman saying this piece is "a combination of diatonic and atonal intervals that creates a form out of a sound and a sound out of a form in which the five instruments blend not by coming together but by moving in opposing directions" (13), because a) all music creates forms out of sounds and vice versa, b) there is no such thing as an atonal interval, c) the instruments do not move "in opposing directions", except on the melodic plane.

Even more than the string pieces, this music drifts on steadily, departing from nowhere and arriving nowhere: when there is no change of emphasis there is no scope for expression. These ten movements do not even have the homely stiffness of a motto in pokerwork, or the jerky authenticity of a home movie. The expressive force of Coleman's jazz underlines the absence of links between the formally composed and spontaneous segments of his output, just as the latter falls into two apparently unrelated parts, the problematic music for violin and the magnificent improvisations of the only alto saxophonist worthy of sharing a sentence with Charlie Parker (14).

Jazz Monthly, February 1969

Improving the Form:
four cases

*Attempts at giving jazz a more varied
formal dimension*

Tadd Dameron's *Fontainebleau*

Dameron should have been one of the most prominent jazz composers, arrangers and bandleaders in the immediate postwar years for he was certainly among the most gifted. He lacked technical slickness, and that was surely a disadvantage in the busy world of the record makers, but nearly everything he wrote was modestly yet firmly individual. The melodic style, warm but fresh, was the most distinctive single aspect of Dameron's work, yet his orchestration for small and medium-sized groups was instantly recognisable, too. Confining himself mainly to conventional instrumentations, and never seeking really unusual sounds, his textures are almost always striking.

The concise inventiveness of many of his themes, such as *Ladybird, Cool breeze, Stay on it, Jahbero, Our delight, The squirrel, Half step down, please, Symphonette, Hot house* and *Good bait*, won them classic status in the jazz of the 1940s, and they gave rise to remarkable improvisations by Charlie Parker, Dizzy Gillespie, Fats Navarro and others. Navarro was, indeed, the finest interpreter the composer ever found, and they recorded together often during those years. Following the great trumpeter's premature death in 1950, Dameron's career appeared to lose its impetus, and from then until his own demise in 1965 little was salvaged except bits and pieces. Malcolm Lowry (1) compares an artist to a fireman rescuing valuables from a burning house, that house being the work of art, unscathed, intact in the mind which conceived it, but which the artist has had to set on fire before he can exteriorise it. What he finishes with—the 'completed work'—is a small heap of salvaged objects. This will scarcely serve for the greatest works of art, but it would be hard to better as an image of the last decade and a half of Dameron's life.

He had the more gifted jazzman's usual ambition to break out of the straitjacket of repeating twelve- and thirty-two-bar choruses, and wrote an extended piece called *Soulphony* for Gillespie to play at Carnegie Hall. This has sunk without a trace, but he made further attempts, and the most convincing is *Fontainebleau,* which he first recorded in 1956 (2). It tries to suggest, rather than directly portray, the palace of that name (described in the sleeve note of the original

American issue as "where the Bourbons used to cavourt"!) and the surrounding forest.

According to Dameron, the quite simple formal plan has three parts. The first, *Le fôret*, opens with a brooding introductory theme that is heard first on the string bass, then on bass doubled with baritone saxophone, then on the remaining horns—trumpet, trombone, alto and tenor saxophones. This leads to the main theme of the section, and of the whole work, stated by Kinny Dorham's trumpet. It is a flowing, lyrical melody characteristic of the composer, and, though perhaps unsuitable for large-scale development, is entirely suitable for its limited use here. This theme is extended in a written-out (not improvised) alto saxophone solo played most expressively by Sahib Shihab, and by the ensemble. A transitional piano solo from Dameron himself leads to *Les cygnes*.

This opens with a brief ensemble that manages to suggest the main *Forêt* theme without direct statement, and then a baritone saxophone ostinato bridges to the *Cygnes* theme, the other principal idea of *Fontainebleau*. It is announced on baritone saxophone and trombone accompanied from above with another ostinato by alto and tenor saxophones. As this is developed, trumpet and alto interject motives derived from the main *Forêt* theme.

Transition from *Les cygnes* to *L'adieu* is ill-defined and the third section introduces no fresh material. It begins with another ensemble suggesting the chief *Forêt* theme, followed by the baritone saxophone ostinato that earlier appeared at the beginning of *Les cygnes*. Over this a modification of the *Cygnes* theme itself is given out by alto and tenor saxophones, and it resolves, still supported with the baritone ostinato, to the introductory *Forêt* theme on alto, then on both alto and tenor. This, too, is in modified form—almost jaunty compared with its sombre initial appearance. Restatements of this motive, by trumpet, then by alto and tenor saxophones, alternate with two further ensembles, the last of which brings *Fontainebleau* to a close.

It is typical of Dameron to proceed by suggestion rather than direct statement, but his thematic cross-references from one section to another help to produce a satisfyingly tight structure. And the listener's interest is sustained by real melodic invention. As usual, the orchestration is effective, and recalls a comment by Dexter Gordon (3), made after playing some Dameron scores, that every line—all the subsidiary parts—had melodic significance, not just the top one. In fact variety is achieved here with diversified themes and the melodic extensions arising from them, by line, that is, not colour. Colour and texture have their place, however, and the composer gets a notable effect by introducing two of his themes—the *Forêt* introduction and *Les cygnes*—in low register and then transposing them to high on their reappearances. Similarly, the baritone saxophone ostinato is succeeded by an alto and tenor one in *Les cygnes*.

These changes, allied to the slowly quickening tempo, produce a feeling of increasing brightness as the work moves from its brooding start to an affirmative conclusion. The weaknesses, as noted, are the vague demarcation between *Les cygnes* and *L'adieu*, and the fact that the latter, because it introduces no material of its own, does not constitute a truly independent third section: another theme was needed, and it is hard to believe that Dameron would have found it difficult to think of one.

Fontainebleau leaves no room for improvisation, but this performance is considerably aided by Dorham's trumpeting, by Sahib Shihab's alto and Cecil Payne's baritone saxophone, and by Shadow Wilson's drumming. The ensemble playing is scarcely in the highest class, yet a more cleanly executed reading by a larger group which the composer recorded in 1962 (4) has a rather unpleasant routine-session glibness which robs the piece of some of its character. Dameron often complained about the poor quality of the performances his work received, and insisted that he was poorly represented on records, but Dorham & Co. showed a proper understanding of his pithy yet relaxed music (5).

Jazz Review, February 1960

Reflections on some of Duke Ellington's longer works

Once Ellington's bandsmen, particularly his trumpeter, Bubber Miley, had aroused his interest in the potentialities of jazz and he decided "to forget all about the sweet music" (1), he, like certain others, was not slow to feel dissatisfaction with the cellular structure of jazz. The best of his recordings from the 1920s, even when leaning heavily on Miley's thematic inspiration, reach towards an overall unity which, if as yet musically inferior to what Jelly Roll Morton had already achieved, still aimed at transcending the repeating chord cycles to an extent that was almost certainly beyond the older man's ambitions.

This could only lead to attempts at getting outside the cellular form altogether and at producing something that was not only longer but organically larger. Ellington's first move, on records at least, was his 1931 *Creole rhapsody*, which exists in two versions of fairly unequal merit. The second of these, originally filling both sides of a twelve-inch 78 r.p.m. disc, was condemned by Constant Lambert (2), and the jazz community, always profoundly grateful for any attention given to their music by any straight musician, responded with a devout belief in the superiority of the earlier version, which took up both sides of a ten-inch 78. Yet, as A. J. Bishop's detailed analysis demonstrates (3), Lambert was quite wrong in saying that the later recording owed its increased length to the mere addition of padding. On the contrary, the twelve-inch recording, with its varied tempos and more effective climax, shows that the composer was quick to learn from his initial mistakes. Even so, while making considerable improvements in detail with his expanded score, Ellington left the piece nearly as unsatisfactory as before in just the area where he had wanted to innovate, that of form. This was because, in trying to do without a set chord sequence repeating through the work, he denied himself a convention upon which he depended more than he realised, and this in turn because he had nothing with which to replace it. *Creole rhapsody*, in both versions, consists of a number of fragments which, however attractive in themselves, are not related in any organic way but are merely strung together. This occasionally produces arresting contrasts, yet the piece is at its weakest when Ellington, having got stuck, throws in bridging piano solos almost literally to make ends meet. He apparently realised this, and his next long piece, *Reminiscing in tempo*, of 1935, which originally took four ten-inch 78 r.p.m. sides, marks a reaction that, like most reactions, went too far in the opposite direction. Here there is unity at the expense of adequate diversity, too much time and space being occupied with many-hued but still insufficiently varied statements of the thematic material. Thus it shows little more skill than its predecessor in long-term musical planning (4).

At this point it must be asked whether Ellington really understood the magnitude, or even the nature, of the task undertaken in such works. During the course of some observations on *Black, brown and beige*, a later and considerably longer piece, the composer Robert Crowley suggested that Ellington indeed "lacked the knowledge and experience necessary for victory. Unity in a large work, organic transition, apt proportions, variety and strategic placement of climaxes—the skill to secure these is not congenital, as are a good ear and melodic inventiveness. This compositional skill has to be learned, by most of us through patient and wisely-directed study. Even the genius has to learn it, if only subconsciously, via absorption from the works that embody its principles" (5). These are, of course, the masterpieces of eighteenth- to twentieth-century European orchestral and chamber music—works that were of scant interest to jazz musicians of Ellington's generation, especially in their formative years.

It must also be recognised that he in any case had little opportunity of acquiring the skills to which Crowley refers. Committed to decades of one-night stands with his band, having to cope with many commercial pressures in order to keep that band together, his development, in brief, stunted by jazz having unhealthily close links with the popular entertainment industry, it is not surprising that Ellington's technique, evolved solely by experiment with his band (6), had major weaknesses. Nor is it unexpected that these should be most apparent in would-be large works, as, of necessity, these impose the greatest strain on any composer's resources. If there is no need to discuss all of his later attempts here it is because they nearly all reveal the same lack of organic development, are usually improvisatory in by no means the best sense, and proceed arbitrarily from one point to another without that proper sense of direction which signifies overall structural control in any idiom.

Though Ellington may not have been altogether aware of the kind of technique required to shape his ideas into convincingly sustained wholes, the frequent use of suite format in his later years may be taken as a tacit acknowledgement of his limitations. Here, as in his short and less ambitious pieces, the actual thematic ideas often are brilliant, as are his use of instrumental colour and, on a small scale, of harmony; the melodic invention, also, scarcely ever falters. Yet these qualities do not always preclude disjointed results, and an instructive example is Dance No. 1 of the *Liberian suite*, which falls into two completely unrelated halves. An out-of-tempo section lasting about two minutes is followed by a dialogue between tenor saxophone and full ensemble, and while each makes perfect sense in itself—the former being one of the most imaginative passages of its kind Ellington ever wrote—their juxtaposition is quite incongruous. Dance No. 2 presents a still worse case. It begins with another dialogue, a series of forceful exchanges between clarinet and band, that is broken off by a vibraharp entry so banal as to make one laugh out loud.

The rest of that movement is worthless, but it happens that the whole *Liberian suite* benefits from an exceptionally clean performance, the band apparently having had a better chance to become acquainted with the music than often was the case with Ellington's longer pieces. This never really helps the music, however, and it is hard not to feel that the vibraharp's entry marks the point at which inspiration ran out. Dance No. 3 is well-dressed *kitsch*, and the two remaining movements, despite some effective playing by individual bandsmen, never attain the level of Dance No. 1, or even of the first section of No. 2.

' A trouble with the suite format is that while it relieves the composer of long-term architectural problems it imposes a need for stylistic consistency over several deliberately contrasted movements. Except in the *Newport suite*, at once his least enterprising and least interesting work in several parts, Ellington scarcely ever maintained this. Despite the ambition which drove him to produce one large composition after another, this failure implies a lack of creative confidence that sometimes is evident in his smaller-scale activities. An example is the appalling 1956 re-recording of *Koko*, his 1940 masterpiece which in its original form stands as one of the classics of recorded jazz but whose essential qualities are destroyed in the later version. Lesser men do this, too, of course, as is shown by Woody Herman's wholly inferior 1958 re-recording of Ralph Burns's 1946-47 *Summer sequence*, but a complicating factor in Ellington's case was that there was always a vociferous public ready to applaud his worst excesses of self-destruction. An instance is the 1956 Newport Festival rape and murder of *Crescendo and diminuendo in blue* that was unctuously praised as "a reminder of what jazz was like before the cool boys ripped out its heart" (7). Such unqualified acceptance of even his poorest efforts is unlikely to foster the self-criticism which is an essential part of every real composer's equipment.

Further, many isolated movements of the suites are musically successful not because of their compositional virtues but because they are vehicles for interplay between the ensemble and an individual performer whose prominence secures at least continuity. Probably Ellington's best achievement in this regard is *Hiawatha* from *The beautiful indians*. Here the relation between soloist and band is constantly shifting, and although the former usually carries the main thread, the lead is occasionally seized by the brass. Al Sears's line is considerably diversified, ranging from conventional legato tenor saxophone phrases to groups of detached, sharply accentuated notes; brass and tenor sometimes pursue simultaneous, contrapuntal lines or fill in between each other's phrases; one moment the soloist is isolated high above the ensemble, the next his is only the most prominent thread in a complex texture. It is unfortunate that the richness and variety of this movement is followed by the anticlimax of *Minnehaha*, a vehicle for Kay Davis's vocalise that is expressive of nothing beyond a naïve love of prettiness for its own sake.

So far as maintaining stylistic consistency throughout the 'Shakespearian impressions' of *Such sweet thunder* is concerned, Ellington courted trouble by writing no less than a dozen movements. These range from the inconsequential *Circle of fourths*, which sounds as if it were thrown off in the recording studio at the last moment, to some of his finest inspirations. A descendant, so to speak, of the *Coloratura* movement of *The perfume suite, Madness in great ones* puts Cat Anderson's high-note trumpet virtuosity to acutely expressive use with something like the power of genius. And *Sonnet for Caesar* has a nobility that is indeed rare in jazz.

Another artistically successful individual movement is *The happy-go-lucky local*, which, as a result of subsequent independent recordings, has led an existence separate from the rest of the quickly forgotten *Deep South suite*. It ranks with the original versions of *Crescendo and diminuendo in blue* and *Harlem* as one of Ellington's most convincing extended pieces. Like *Madness in great ones, The happy-go-lucky local* is a remarkable inspiration, though a description—long, isolated alto saxophone notes, insistently harsh brass chords, Anderson again almost shrieking above the rest of the band, etc.—would make it seem another string of disjointed effects. In reality these coalesce into a unified design which defies analysis—in contrast with *Overture to a jam session* from the same year, which, despite its clearly defined formal shape, leaves an impression of discontinuity. Music does not often summon up visual images in the minds of genuinely musical listeners, yet few can there be for whom *The happy-go-lucky local* would not evoke a rather inefficient locomotive making its way across some hot and dusty plain in the American South. As usual, perfection is denied us, and the entry of Jimmy Hamilton's antiseptic clarinet dissipates the atmosphere with a completeness that is almost as disconcerting as the promptness with which it is restored the moment he stops. However, this unfortunate episode cannot rob

The happy-go-lucky local of its status as the supreme musical train piece, surpassing not only Ellington's own earlier *Lightning* and *Daybreak express* but also the attempts of straight composers such as Villa-Lobos (*Little train of the Caipira*) or even Honegger (*Pacific 231*).

Nothing could be more different to the musical stupidity of the 1956 Newport version of *Crescendo and diminuendo in blue* than the original recording, made in 1937. As with *Harlem* and *The happy-go-lucky local*, Ellington introduces a concept from outside, as it were, to help impart unity, and in this case it is the seemingly quite mechanical idea of a rise and fall in volume. Yet mechanical it is not, for instead merely of piling on more instruments and then taking them off, he devised a musical argument wherein the volume's rise and fall is integral to the development of the material. Considering that basically the piece is just a series of ensemble blues choruses, the compositional achievement here is a considerable one.

So it is in *Harlem*, where the unifying idea is that of evoking various facets of life in the Negro quarter of New York City. This justifies the frankly sectional structure, on pictorial, if not on strictly musical, grounds, and it is unsurprising that Ellington never equalled this piece later on a comparable time-scale.

While *The happy-go-lucky local*, *Crescendo and diminuendo in blue* and *Harlem* all offer slightly different solutions to the formal problem, there are important respects in which they are similar, above all their virtual elimination of individual improvisation. The exception is *The Happy-go-lucky local's* clarinet solo, but, even allowing for Hamilton's characterless playing, it is significant that this detracts from the impact of the work. It appears that Ellington could only make a success of these items by rejecting improvisation, and this is regrettable for one of his greatest achievements with his shorter pieces was the fusing of composition and improvising.

Again, the unifying ideas he employed were not new, and in no way derived from the substance or especial qualities of jazz. This applies to many other long jazz works, from Charles Mingus's *Pithecanthropus erectus* to *The comedy* by the Modern Jazz Quartet. As implied by the above mention of Honegger and Villa-Lobos, the underlying concept in all these cases is that of the symphonic poem, which arose in nineteenth-century Europe. The onamatopoeics of *Pithecanthropus erectus* may be set beside those of Beethoven's Pastoral Symphony, *Harlem's* attempt to portray moods and places linked with those of Strauss's *Aus Italien*, *The comedy's* character studies compared with those of Liszt's

Faust Symphony. Obviously such confrontations will not be to the advantage of the jazz pieces, and it has to be asked whether jazz is compatible with large-scale composition except on terms of such compromise that even improvising has to be eliminated. The question seems acute if we recall the absence of improvisation from other long pieces such as Tadd Dameron's *Fontainebleau* and its inconclusive rôle in Mingus's *Black saint and sinner lady*.

Naturally, more than one view has been taken on the potential of jazz for significant growth, and it is worth quoting Robert Crowley again: "More often now than in Ellington's youth, [the jazz musician] has had fine teaching on his instrument and 'knows his chords', but he has no real skill in counterpoint and knows nothing of musical history". As a result, if he finds himself "at about twenty-two, with the urge to do something 'bigger' than arranging or 'getting away' on the chords of popular tunes", he may, "if he has the intelligence and humility ... settle down to the arduous work of acquiring all the traditional compositional skills ... When this happens, recent history shows, he is probably lost to jazz, his experience in which will prove to be only a handicap. His mature music will be concert music in the contemporary international idiom" (5). It may be added that the career of Mel Powell, ex-Benny Goodman pianist, ex-Hindemith pupil, is a perfect illustration of this process (8).

In view of the Europeanisation of jazz almost from the outset, it would be idle to deny the relevance of Crowley's remarks. Ellington's leaning to the concept of the nineteenth-century symphonic poem may, indeed, have represented an unconscious recognition of the above principles. Yet this brings us full circle because in addition to having sacrificed improvisation in payment for his few successes in writing 'important' works, Ellington, as we saw, did not really know how to make his musical language work on any considerable scale. One trouble, certainly, was his adherence to the strictly conventional instrumentation of the large dance band because this had evolved for more mundane purposes than playing long and aesthetically ambitious jazz compositions; it is significant that, even in his early days with Claude Thornhill, Gil Evans adopted a notably more flexible instrumentation. A few pieces like Gunther Schuller's *Variants on a theme of John Lewis (Django)*, André Hodeir's *Osymetrios I* and *II* (on Monk's *Mysterioso*) or Lalo Schiffrin's *Tunisian fantasy*, a set of variations on *Night in Tunisia*, show it is possible to use a short jazz piece as the basis of something that is larger, not just longer, and Ellington occasionally did this himself, as with his 1952 expansion of *The mooche* (which includes plenty of improvisation).

But it is surely more relevant to the future of jazz that a number of extremely diverse works occupying whole LPs, such as George Russell's six-movement *Jazz in the space age* and Ornette Coleman's thirty-six-minute *Free jazz,* have been achieved which form perfectly coherent wholes without external, quasi-pictorial aids to unity. They do so on their own terms, which is to say that the music's shape arises out of its language.

It is somewhat ironic to reflect that despite for several decades having a reputation as a bold experimenter well ahead of the field, Ellington never brought off this on a like scale, partly because of his conservative attitude towards the language of jazz. (The incorporation of modal improvisation into the comparatively short movements of the *Far-Eastern suite* came too late to effect a major shift in the attitude of a composer then in his late 60s.) Ellington's best short pieces, such as the 1940 *Koko* or *Dusk*, are big music masterfully concentrated on a small scale, his long works are mostly small music weakly spread on a large scale. To be an art's major miniaturist, however, is still to be something very considerable, particularly when most practitioners of that art are extremely minor miniaturists (9).

Jazz Monthly, January 1964

Some Jelly Roll Morton piano solos

A critic once ended a review of Morton's very extensive series of recordings for the Library of Congress (1) with the phrase "blessed are those who cannot wail [improvise], for they shall inherit Jelly Roll Morton" (2). He also described the first jazz intellectual as of no more importance as a composer than, among others, Lil Hardin or Gordon Jenkins, and said his approach was that of codifying improvisation into "predetermined, predictable and controlled structures". If they have no other value, such opinions at least indicate the persistent confusion over the composer's rôle in jazz.

One legitimate difficulty has been that whereas we have had many improvisors of quality, jazz composers, in the full meaning of that term, have been few, and so there has been less opportunity of forming apt criteria. Of course, many jazz musicians have written excellent pieces, such as *Chant of the weed* by Don Redman or *Israel* by John Carisi, but those who have expressed themselves chiefly, and best, through composition have been rare. Apart from Morton, the names are: Duke Ellington, Thelonious Monk, Tadd Dameron, John Lewis, Charles Mingus and George Russell.

Yet to speak merely of expression through composing here is to mislead, for, however firmly they may control their modest structures, these men have usually employed the improvisation of their bandsmen as a basic, often as the most important, element in those structures. It is just this interpenetration of composing and improvisation, rarely the same in any two pieces, which creates a part of the critic's problem. Yet it is difficult, whether we try Morton's *Doctor Jazz*, Ellington's *Harlem airshaft*, Monk's *Criss cross*, Dameron's *Lyonia*, Lewis's *Three windows*, Mingus's *East coasting* or Russell's *Knights of the steamtable*, to hear the flexible and extremely diverse ensembles as a crutch for poor soloing of the sort implied by the opening paragraph's quotation. Indeed, far from improvisation being codified and stereotyped, its impact is heightened in such cases by the context in which the composer has placed it. This is demonstrated in reverse by the fact that, for example, Barney Bigard counted for very little once he left the Ellington band, that Clarence Shaw nowhere else made the impression he did on Mingus's records, that Milt Jackson's most characteristic statements were made in company with Lewis and Monk.

Differences between Mingus and Monk, between Ellington and Dameron, are obvious enough, yet what links these men, behind all the divergences of period, style and method, is that, at least when working on short time-scales, they consistently tried to balance improvisation with the overall demands of form, collective discipline with individual freedom, in short to unify the divided aims of most jazz bands. Although more outwardly diversified results may have been obtained by younger men, Morton's achievements in this sphere are musically as impressive as any; and he was first.

His chief legacy is the group of band recordings made by the Red Hot Peppers during 1926-30, for certain of which the 1923-24 piano solos provided instructive preliminary studies. A knowledge of the reminiscences and performances he recorded for the Library of Congress in 1938 is essential, however, because although there can be no guarantee that Morton's memory was always correct, or that his recreations of earlier musicians' styles are necessarily authentic, they do shed new light on his own work. One reason for this is that the three-minute duration of a ten-inch 78 r.p.m. disc, inside which he had always had to confine himself before, no longer applied, and he was able to give a fuller account of his improvisatory powers.

Particularly impressive in this respect are *Creepy feeling* and *The pearls*, the latter being his finest version of one of his best compositions. It has three themes that genuinely belong together yet which are effectively contrasted. Sets of three themes are common in his pieces, of course, and these performances suggest that whenever possible he liked to develop each. It is probable that on some 78 r.p.m. versions made during the 1920s he raised tempos so as to get everything essential in, but here the pace is more relaxed and *The pearls* is only one item which gains from this.

King Porter stomp is another instance of the freer approach adopted at the Library of Congress sessions in that the rather deliberate presentation of each theme followed on earlier recordings is abandoned in favour of improvising on the composition as a whole, not just on its third theme. The rhythmic momentum of the latter choruses is striking here, though it is a pity Morton did not achieve this without increasing the tempo so markedly.

The twelve-bar blues and thirty-two-bar popular song usually have led soloists to improvise on the chords and abandon the original melodies, but Morton, with groups of three distinctly characterised themes, had material richer in developmental potential to start with. His remarkable account of *Kansas City stomps* is an instructive example of his powers of improvising and formal organisation working together with probably little conscious separation between them. The published sheet music is in an $AABBCC^1$ pattern, but Morton treats these themes cyclically in rondo form wherein A, instead of merely being repeated, is subject to a fresh improvisation each time: $AA^1BB^1A^2CC^1A^3$. This is really three interlocking sets of variations, but their performance, which is notable for its rhythmic invention, shown by the use of syncopation and polyrhythm, and, for the period with which Morton is associated, slightly unusual touches of harmony, unites them into an indivisible whole. That is because while the basic formal plan may well have been preconceived, it is carried through with what surely was spontaneous invention. (It should not be imagined, however, that this degree of structural coherence is all that uncommon in jazz, or that it is confined to the work of the few jazz composers. For instance, an analysis of Jimmy Yancey's *State Street special* reveals a similar formal shape (3).)

Morton leaned more heavily on improvisation in these Library of Congress recordings than he might have thought advisable on a band session, yet the concepts of thematic variation and contrast that were at the heart of his method are always in evidence. *Hyena stomp*, which is unusual for him in having only a single theme (derived from one section of *King Porter stomp*), is a clear illustration of this. After contrasting presentations of the theme in the first two sixteen-bar choruses there follow six variations, each flowing logically out of and into its neighbours yet each based on an idea derived from the theme and with a marked character of its own. This piece deserves to be more widely known because it is a remarkable instance of his imaginative fertility in developing a single motive. And it is here, too, that we can best observe one of the several links between Morton and Thelonious Monk, for the latter also had a highly developed skill in conjuring a whole solo out of one brief idea, as his 1954 recording of *Locomotive* well shows (4).

Jungle blues is again unusual, being a deliberately old-fashioned performance based on a simple repeating riff. It seems unlikely in this case that Morton had a very precise formal pattern in mind at the outset, but he elaborates the riff into three separate themes. Plenty of other examples of his skill in spontaneous structural control may be found on these recordings, such as *Mama'nita* or *Pep*, both of which are superior to earlier versions. The three choruses improvised on the second theme of the latter, for instance, show Morton's rhythmic invention well placed at the service of formal requirements (5).

Jazz Monthly, September 1962

Gil Evans

There has always been cool jazz. Far from being a new development of the 1950s, this vein of expression, wherein the improvisor 'distances' himself from the musical material, goes back almost to the beginning. The clarinetists Leon Roppolo of the New Orleans Rhythm Kings and Johnny O'Donnell of the Georgians, two bands that recorded in 1922, both avoided the conventions of 'hot' playing, as did other prominent jazzmen of that decade like Bix Beiderbecke and his associate Frankie Trumbauer. Much recorded by the New York school of the late 1920s follows a similar approach to expression, and this is true of several prominent figures of the 1930s such as Benny Carter, Teddy Wilson, and particularly Lester Young, whose links with the official 'cool' movement are acknowledged. The free jazz of the 1960s, also, had its 'cool' exponents like John Tchicai and John Carter.

The comparatively reticent expression of such players was at a disadvantage in the early years, when jazz was heard mainly in noisy dancehalls and cabarets, and attempts at an orchestral extension of their work suffered for a related reason. The large bands of Fletcher Henderson, Jimmy Lunceford and many others spent most of their days touring, and this imposed various kinds of standardisation, not least upon instrumentation: a leader playing one-night stands, perhaps with long distances to travel between them, could scarcely appear with a different personnel, repertoire and instrumentation at each. Despite their undoubted—if somewhat overrated—contribution to jazz, the swing bands, once established, stood in the way of further orchestral developments. These could only resume when the bands came off the road and orchestral jazz was created by ad hoc groups assembled mainly, if not exclusively, for recording purposes. Such conditions allowed far more varied instrumentation than hitherto, a wider choice of repertoire—which no longer had to be orientated to a dancing public, and the application of more diverse techniques of writing. Missing from much of this later music is that feeling of integration which can only be achieved when a group of men play the same repertoire together over a long period, but in compensation the studio players' superior executive skills allowed more adventurous scores to be attempted.

As usual when such changes occur, the shift of emphasis had begun earlier than is generally assumed, and in an unexpected place. At first,

Claude Thornhill's band had sounded rather like that of Glenn Miller (!), but he showed it was possible, with fairly discreet additions to a conventional dance band instrumentation, like french horn and tuba, and with devices such as having the reed section play without vibrato, to produce a strikingly fresh sound. This change, however, was not merely for the sake of novelty, which would be of little musical interest, but was a step towards expressing modes of feeling different from, perhaps even opposed to, those of the swing bands. *Snowfall*, a rather static composition of Thornhill's, confirms this, but, although he always insisted it was the leader who created this sound, it was Gil Evans who knew what to do with it. As Evans said, the sound "hung like a cloud" (1), which implies extreme relaxation; upon this background he imposed movement, and part of the exceptional effect of the best Thornhill recordings arises from an ambiguity between the energy of the music's gesture and the passivity of its basic tonal quality.

This is perhaps most evident in *The old castle* (2), originally a fairly simple keyboard piece by Mussorgsky, which in Evans's hands tells of a world rich and strange, full of subtle, elusive feelings; indeed, Steve Lacy, who played a later vintage of Evans's music, said "Sometimes, when things jelled, I felt true moments of ecstacy, and recently a friend of mine who worked with the Thornhill band in the 1940s when Gil was principal writer said that some nights the sound of the band around him moved him to tears" (3). It is remarkable that this was done with what fundamentally was still a dance band instrumentation, yet Evans's work, like many seemingly radical departures, had a sound traditional basis, and he took certain cues from Duke Ellington, whose *Koko* he appositely quotes in Thornhill's *Arab dance*. As André Hodeir said (4), as far as scoring for a conventionally-instrumentated swing band was concerned, Ellington was so far ahead of his contemporaries that for many years there was no question of the underlying principles of his writing influencing them. When Evans began orchestrating along basically similar lines (though always with greater and more varied flexibility) it was not surprising, therefore, that the fact went unrecognised.

In his finest Thornhill scores, Evans, instead of blankly contrasting the brass and reed sections like Henderson in his arrangements for Benny Goodman in the 1930s, blends them in an almost infinite variety of ways. With such pieces as his evocative treatment of *La paloma* we find the craft of dance band arranging transformed virtually into an art of recomposition, for Evans quite drastically re-orders the components of each piece. In some cases, such as the extremely original writing behind and after the expressionless singing on *Sorta kinda*, the result almost seems a deliberate mockery of swing band conventions, so considerably does it improve on the standardised scoring which then prevailed in most other places.

That standardisation reached such a point that we normally listen to swing records—and Henderson's band is a good example—only for the improvised solos, not for the ensemble scoring. But the orchestral idiom Evans worked out with Thornhill is of such distinction that the opposite is the case, and although the ensemble writing on, say, the performances of Charlie Parker themes is amazingly inventive and quite unlike anything else being done in the 1940s, the soloists, with the exceptions of the guitarist Barry Galbraith on *Anthropology* and *Donna Lee* and the trumpeter Red Rodney in *Yardbird suite*, contribute nothing that is relevant. The best 'improvising' on these pieces, and on *Robbins nest* (despite an allusion to Kreisler's *Caprice Viennois*), occurs in Evans's orchestral passages, where he comments on the themes more creatively than any of the bandsmen, playing 'on' the ensemble just as a composer would. These sections are, indeed, a remarkable anticipation of George Russell's later assertions that "a jazz writer is an improvisor, too" (5), and that the finest jazz composition "might even sound more intuitive than a purely improvised solo" (6). The point is underlined by comparing Evans's account of *Yardbird suite* with the bland arrangement of this piece Gerry Mulligan wrote for Gene Krupa, but Evans's best Thornhill moments come with the long *Donna Lee* introduction and the still more remarkable coda, which condenses some of the introductory material with real daring. Russell also said that a jazz composer might "write an idea that will sound so improvised it might influence improvisors to play something they have never played before" (6). This is exactly what happened, though not inside the Thornhill band with its generally inadequate soloists.

Inevitably, many jazz musicians became interested in what Evans was doing, and prominent among them was Miles Davis, then a member of Parker's Quintet. Except in a few slow pieces like *Embraceable you* or *Don't blame me*, where he managed quite satisfactory improvisations, this trumpeter found the hectic complexity and furious aggression of bop uncongenial, and it is not surprising he was attracted to that music's opposite in the jazz of the late 1940s. Eventually he decided, in Evans's words, that "he wanted to play his idiom with that kind of sound" (1), and the result was a band which, if it fulfilled scarcely any public engagements, made three historic recording sessions for the Capitol label in 1949 and '50. The story of that band and those sessions has been told many times and need not be repeated here, although it is useful to have Evans's confirmation that "the idea of Miles's band . . . came from Claude's band in the sound sense. Miles liked some of what Gerry [Mulligan] and I had written" (1). In the course of discussions between Davis, Evans, Mulligan, John Lewis and others it was decided that what they needed was a medium-sized group that besides having the cool, restrained Thornhill sound would combine chamber music intimacy with much of the variety of texture possible to a full jazz orchestra. The instrumentation was: trumpet, trombone, french horn, tuba, alto and baritone saxophones, piano, bass, percussion, and, again according to Evans, this choice was decided by its being "the smallest number of instruments that could get the sound and still express all the harmonies Thornhill used" (1). Although subject to various changes, the personnel was selected with care so as to ensure all participants were sympathetic to the musical aims of this unusual enterprise. That the leaders were not completely clear about those objectives, however, was shown by the fact that they considered giving their alto chair to the highly unsuitable Sonny Stitt (7), a Parker disciple, instead of to the far more apt Lee Konitz, who did in fact get it. The final choices were, indeed, excellent, and the music had a unity which must always be rare in jazz.

Nearly all the studio performances will repay detailed study, and they were supplemented years later by the appearance on an obscure Italian label (8) of recordings of 1948 broadcasts from the Royal Roost, where the band played briefly in New York; luckily, these include items not done for Capitol, such as Lewis's *S'il vous plaît*, Evans's *Why do I love you?*, alternative versions of his *Moondreams*, etc. The group's musical approach has been subject to repeated analysis because it represented the first viable alternative to bop, although, still following the Thornhill precedent, its importance lay in an ensemble style, not solo playing. Several of the pieces—*Move, Venus de Milo, Budo*—were mainly vehicles for improvisation, yet it was more significant that the sounds of all instruments were fused in a texture whose parts moved with a supple fluidity that contrasted with the hard, bright, darting lines of bop. The harmonic vocabulary was quite advanced for the jazz of that time, but the constantly shifting pastel sounds were chiefly the result of orchestration which took some of Evans's procedures with the Thornhill band to their logical conclusion. With trombone, baritone saxophone and tuba, the instrumentation might seem to place undue emphasis on the bottom register, yet, although this obviously does account for the repertoire's dark tone, the absence of a tenor saxophone's rich voice helps to keep the characteristic veiled textures from becoming too cloudy. Further, so far as one can tell without seeing the scores, the most dissonant note in any chord is usually given to the french horn, the softest-voiced of the wind instruments present, and this helped deflect the music's astringency, contributed to the air of remoteness and mystery which it retains even in the most obviously 'exciting' up-tempo moments.

Undoubtedly the most original piece the band recorded was John Carisi's *Israel*, a modal blues which stands high among the recorded classics of jazz. But Evans's contributions run it close, and in *Moondreams* the very brevity of the solo passages, by Konitz and Mulligan, emphasise that this is an essentially orchestral conception, in fact a study of slow-moving harmonies crossed with subtle changes of texture. Its sonorous gravity is relieved by a passage wherein the horns ascend and then peel off, leaving Konitz sustaining a high, thin note which contrasts almost dramatically with the full, deep chords that soon engulf it. In the quiet final sequence, against long-sustained harmonies, the horns play odd, disjointed little fragments of phrases which create a pointilliste effect. This passage, which is more effective in the broadcast versions than on the studio recording, is reminiscent of the fragmentary brass phrases under high tremolo strings in Variation II of Strauss's *Don Quixote* or of the tiny oboe and clarinet phrases snickering around the brass in Variation IV. Strauss also provides a precedent for the melodic independence of Evans's tuba writing, although the climate of feeling the latter projects is far more rarefied in this case, the final vibrant stillness of *Moondreams* suggesting it to be the ensemble's tribute to their exemplar, Claude Thornhill.

It can scarcely need adding that this score is no mere 'arrangement' of a 'song', but is in the tradition of 'compositions for band', like Beiderbecke's *Krazy kat* or Thelonious Monk's original version of *Epistrophy*. All the pieces Davis recorded at these sessions, in fact, are set out as continually developing entities (note the skilfully varied thematic recapitulation of *Move*), and Evans's other main contribution, *Boplicity*, is in this respect among the most interesting.

Of all these themes, this seems most perfectly suited to the ensemble's rich yet unadorned sonority, and its atmosphere of trancelike relaxed intensity is somehow heightened by the way at the close of the opening chorus the melody flows on into the first bar of the next, so that Mulligan's baritone saxophone passage starts only in the second bar—a small but delightful metrical surprise. Also noteworthy is the bridge of this second chorus. The first half consists of six bars instead of the expected four and the two main voices start an octave apart before spiralling off into counterpoint; the second half is of four bars and Davis's trumpet most tellingly alludes to the preceding phrase; the final eight bars of this chorus present an interesting variant of the main thematic phrase. The last chorus offers still more variety, with each eight-bar segment treated differently. The first is an exceptionally fine duet between Davis and the ensemble, while in the second he is accompanied only by the rhythm section; the third is a piano solo by Lewis, and the gradually diminishing tonal weight of these twenty-four bars is balanced by the final eight bars' restatement of the chief thematic phrase—which at the same time answers the variant that occupied the same place in the preceding chorus.

If *Why do I love you?* is a far less perfect score this is because it has to accommodate Kenny Hagood's singing, but the final chorus still consists of a strikingly oblique restatement of—or rather allusion to—the original melody, another of Evans's written 'improvisations'.

Even if this music's commercial failure was unavoidable—and the band's library included several more excellent pieces unmentioned above, such as Lewis's *Rouge*, Mulligan's *Rocker* and George Wallington's *Godchild*—it still might have been expected, in view of its wealth of new resources, to affect other jazzmen. This it scarcely did at all. Echoes may be caught on the J. J. Johnson date of several years later which recorded Lewis's *Sketch 1*, but as this had Lewis at the piano, and as both he and the trombonist had been in the Capitol group, this may be considered a direct descendant. A similar comment obviously applies to the Mulligan 1951 session which used two baritone saxophones, and to his later Tentet recordings. Almost the only examples of indirect influence are a few virtually forgotten Shorty Rogers pieces such as *Wail of two cities* and *Baklava bridge*, and some Hal McKusick items discussed on another page. The jazz community, in fact, turned aside, as so often, from an area of potentially major growth, and the error was confirmed by the jazz press of that time, which disliked the Capitol titles because of their refusal to sink into some convenient pigeonhole. Altogether, people began to forget about Gil Evans: his brilliance had been made obvious, but several years passed before anyone was reminded of the fact.

Not that Evans was concerned. True, he did little recording work, but that was because he refused to write for less than the musicians' union standard fee—a trait unlikely to endear him to the artist and repertoire departments of certain companies. But he scored music for radio and tv, for nightclub acts and for what was left of vaudeville. Such records as he did arrange were mainly backgrounds for rather obscure singers like Marcy Lutes, Helen Merrill and Lucy Reed, though he did write a subtly evanescent, hauntingly memorable recomposition of *You go to my head* for Teddy Charles's *Tentet* LP, and, later still, *Blues for Pablo* and *Jambangle* for Hal McKusick. For the rest, Evans, a self-taught musician—though he insists that "everybody who ever gave me a moment of beauty, significance, excitement has been a teacher" (9)—filled gaps in his education, "reading music history, biographies of composers, articles on criticism, and listening to records" (1). There were other reasons for his relative non-participation in jazz at that time. As he said, "I have a kind of direction of my own ... my interest in jazz, pop and sound in various combinations has dictated what I would do at various times. At different times, one of the three has been stronger" (1). Such an attitude would obviously prevent Evans from being a member of any self-conscious and organised movement in music for any length of time, and it may be added that he has never been overly concerned with the 'importance' of his writing, as a lot of it has been done not so much as personal expression as in pursuance of further knowledge through learning in a practical way.

One is not surprised to find, therefore, that he writes slowly through a conscientious desire to avoid clichés: "I have more craft and speed than I sometimes want to admit. I want to avoid getting into a rut. I can't keep doing the same thing over and over. I'm not a craftsman in the same sense as a lot of writers I hear who do commercial and jazz work. They have a wonderful ability with the details of their craft. The details are all authentic, but, when it's over, you realise that the whole is less than the sum of the parts" (1). Because his writing is so individual, Evans has always found it necessary to rehearse his scores personally, and desirable to work with musicians of his own choosing. Mulligan comments on this: "Gil is the one arranger I've played who can really notate a thing the way a soloist would blow [play] it. . . . For example, the down-beats don't always fall on the down-beats in a solo, and he makes a note of that. It makes for a more complicated notation, but, because what he writes is melodic and makes sense, it's not hard to play. The notation makes the parts look harder than they are, but Gil can work with a band, can sing to them what he wants, and he gets it out of them" (1). It remains as difficult, however, to obtain an exact description of Evans's rehearsal and recording processes as it was of Ellington's. "No, no, it's more mysterious than that" protested Steve Lacy when, talking to him in London during the mid-1960s, the present writer probed with a series of technical questions. "You get so carried away by the feeling of his music that you lose sight of the details" (10). In a sort of confirmation of this, Mulligan said that what attracted Charlie Parker to Evans's music was the exploratory stance it adopted. Later he wanted to play some of Evans's scores but, says the latter, "by the time he was ready to use me I wasn't ready to write for him. I was going through another period of learning by then" (1)

Fortunately, he was ready for some more jazz by 1957, when Miles Davis decided to make an orchestral LP. Considering the lyrical fragility of the trumpeter's best work up till then, *Miles Ahead* may have seemed an unproductive idea, but what he wanted was to explore further the lines opened up by the Capitol sessions, especially as nobody else had troubled. *Boplicity*, in particular, had already demonstrated the perfect understanding between Davis and Evans, and the latter's collaboration was clearly essential. They decided to record ten pieces: John Carisi's *Springsville, The maids of Cadiz* by Delibes, Dave Brubeck's *The Duke, My ship* by Kurt Weill, Davis's *Miles ahead, Blues for Pablo* by Evans, Ahmad Jamal's *New rhumba, The meaning of the blues* by Bobby Troup, J. J. Johnson's *Lament* and a rather inconsequential Spina/Elliott standard called *I don't wanna be kissed*. Evans scored these as a series of miniature concertos for Davis, but fused them together in a continuous aural fresco whose connective resonance and authority gain strength with each addition. It sometimes is hard to isolate where one piece ends and another starts, but this principle of merging performances, discovered apparently during work on *Miles Ahead*, was taken further on subsequent LPs, eventually leading to a fusing of all other elements in his music.

Evans devised an interesting extension of the Capitol sessions' instrumentation, a telling variant of that used by Thornhill: apart from Davis, who played flugelhorn, there were five trumpets, three tenor trombones, bass trombone, two french horns, tuba, two clarinets doubling flutes, bass clarinet, alto saxophone, string bass and percussion. These are treated largely as a body of individual players, and the chords are composed of the most varied tone-colours, which are dealt with according to their natural intensity, some being allowed greater prominence than others. In this respect one is reminded of Schoenberg's *Funf Orchesterstücke* Op. 16, especially No. 2, and it indicates the development of Evans's musical language that whereas *Moondreams* is reminiscent of aspects of Richard Strauss, here one thinks of Schoenberg. *Miles Ahead* has received so much attention elsewhere (11) that comment on separate movements is unnecessary, though the scoring's effect is often that of light imprisoned in a bright mineral cave, its refinement such that at times the music flickers deliciously between existence and non-existence. No matter how involved the textures, though, it always is possible to discover unifying factors as an altogether remarkable ear is in control, ruthlessly—and almost completely—eliminating clichés. Complaints that these Davis/Evans collaborations produced unrhythmic music were due to faulty hearing, and the widely quoted metaphorical description of the textures as "port and velvet" (12) is inept. Despite its richness, the orchestral fabric is constantly on the move, horizontally and vertically; it is unfortunate that some listeners cannot hear music's pulse unless it is stated as a series of loud bangs. The introverted mood of several panels in the *Miles Ahead* fresco had been anticipated by Ellington pieces such as *Blue serge*, and the underlying clarity of Evans's constructions is revealed by setting this version of *Blues for Pablo* beside the one earlier recorded by a Hal McKusick small group. Both preserve the same relationships between themes, tempos, degrees of textural density, etc., and form an amusing comment on the notion that Evans provided Davis merely with vague impressionistic backgrounds.

In fact, and even though one may object to the show business mentality which lies behind the phrase, he had made the most remarkable comeback in jazz history. Soon his imitators were demonstrating how inimitable his methods were, some of the worst examples being Ernie Wilkins's scores for the *Map of Jimmy Cleveland* LP (13) and certain Bill Matthieu pieces for Stan Kenton's band, especially *Willow weep for me*, *The meaning of the blues* (both with Rolf Ericson assuming the Miles Davis rôle) and *Django* (14). All these simply fit together various elements learnt—by rote, as it were—from Evans, whereas his scores are developing musical organisms which establish and proceed from premises of their own.

Further collaborations with Davis followed. Some, like the *Quiet Nights* disc, exposed the partnership's weaknesses, and Evans's boring re-write of the first movement of Rodrigo's *Concierto de Aranjuez* was a strange miscalculation. So, too, was the bogus flamenco of *Saeta* and *Solea*, although these were solo vehicles for Davis in which Evans had little part. The last three items are on the *Sketches of Spain* LP, but an altogether finer expression of Evans's taste for Iberian music is *Lotus land*, a track on the *Guitar Forms* record that he made with Kenny Burrell (15). However, before either *Quiet Nights* or *Sketches of Spain* came *Porgy and Bess*, which contains, at least in potential, the finest music Davis and Evans recorded together.

Of course, in its original form Gershwin's opera takes up an entire evening, but the excerpts Evans and Davis selected are put together in such a way as to summarise the drama's several aspects. They show, also, that the original music has deeper roots than Gershwin's detractors concede—deeper, perhaps, than he himself knew. On certain items, such as *Prayer* or *My man's gone now*, occurs some of the most eloquent playing Davis ever recorded, and though Evans frequently sets dark, massed sonorities against the trumpeter's passionate self-communing, there is some exquisite scoring, too, as in *Fishermen, strawberry and devil crab* or *Here comes the honey man*. Hear, also, Davis's re-reading of *It ain't necessarily so*, whose meaningful obliqueness is set off by staccato french horn chords—Evans for once using a conventional device.

Although the *Porgy and Bess* LP contains magnificent jazz—and one plays some tracks over and over, as if to savour a rare essence—the performances left even more to be desired than those of *Miles Ahead*. One cannot be sure about such things without seeing the scores (and it is a perpetual handicap to the proper musicological study of jazz that scores are *never* obtainable), but one of the musicians who played on the *Porgy and Bess* dates shortly afterwards said the following in a private communication to the present writer:

"The crux of the matter is that Gil, on both sets of dates, did not rehearse carefully enough, as is evident already on *Miles Ahead*. I believe this is mostly the result of the unfortunate conditions under which American recording is done. It is too costly for any project of more than average difficulty to be done well, unless the music in question is rehearsed before the date (which is illegal according to union rules), or has been previously performed.

"Under these, to say the least, less than ideal circumstances, both Miles and Gil have a too relaxed attitude about accomplishing the tasks they set themselves. In pieces which are scored as sensitively and as intricately as Gil's, it's a shame to let the performances cancel out half of their effectiveness. Many details of scoring simply could not be—or at least were not—touched upon in the sessions I was on. Some things were left undone which *I* would not have let go.

"But, as I've indicated, the blame lies more with the conditions than the people. And I suppose one could say that it is remarkable that both LPs are as good as they are. If Gil were a better conductor it would also help: he sometimes confused the players. On the other hand, he is quite patient—perhaps too much so for his own good—and very pleasant to work for. Whatever excellence these recordings possess I would attribute (aside from Gil's own magnificent scores, of course) primarily to the supreme abilities of some of the leading players, like Ernie Royal [trumpet], Bill Barber [tuba], the very fine reed men (on all manner of flutes and bass clarinets), and in general the respect which all of us, despite what I've said above, have for Gil Evans."

Such problems were considerable, yet Evans solved them with alacrity—indeed as soon as he began making records under his own name instead of in partnership with Davis. One or two items on his first, *Gil Evans plus Ten* (16), such as *Remember* or *Nobody's heart*, may appear to continue the line of ballad scores he wrote for Thornhill, as if he were recapitulating before going on to something new, but in fact the material ranged from *Ella Speed*, associated with the folksinger Huddie Leadbetter, to Tadd Dameron's *If you could see me now*. A commitment to the present is enriched by a sense of the past, and this marked the beginning of a personal reassessment of the jazz repertoire, and from his next record, *New Bottle Old Wine*, onwards Evans turned his back on non-jazz themes. The latter disc conducts a miniature history of jazz, running from W. C. Handy's *St Louis blues* to *Bird feathers* by Charlie Parker, but Evans makes all eight compositions his own while paradoxically preserving their original extremely diverse characters; by a further paradox, he appears to give his chief soloist complete freedom while clearly remaining in control of every bar. That soloist is 'Cannonball' Adderley, a minor disciple of Parker, and so this LP gives a hint of what might have happened if Evans had been able to work with the great altoist himself. In the event, several others, including the trombonist Frank Rehak in *Strutting with some barbeque* and Chuck Wayne, the guitarist, on *Lester leaps in*, outclass Adderley, and Evans's writing provides so stimulating and enriching a commentary as almost to swamp them all.

Certainly it is untrue to assert, as some writers have, that he needs a soloist to focus his processes around. In *St Louis blues*, though Adderley appears to hold the centre of the stage, the shifting, tirelessly inventive background is of such fascination, what with Evans's characteristic reshaping of the themes, his alterations to the harmony, and such details as the independent guitar or tuba lines, that the listener soon finds himself attending not to the soloist but to the 'accompaniment'. And in *King Porter stomp*, also, how much further Evans goes in such matters than, say, Henderson in his arrangement of this piece for Goodman's band: to speak of variations on the themes would be too formal a description of a process so free, and here again we have written 'improvisations' in exactly the sense that George Russell meant (6). The same is true of all the other tracks, which teem with interest and range from the quietly luminous sensitivity of Fats Waller's *Willow tree* to the violent assertion of Dizzy Gillespie's *Manteca*, whose virtuoso brass writing the players throw off with such apparently casual ferocity.

On Evans's next LP, *Great Jazz Standards*, the soloists got closer to holding their own. Johnny Coles has a beautiful trumpet solo in Bix Beiderbecke's *Davenport blues*, as does Steve Lacy, on soprano saxophone, in Monk's *Straight, no chaser*. Yet Budd Johnson does better still, his rounded clarinet phrases contrasting with the abrupt whole-tone lines of Don Redman's *Chant of the weed*, the solid 4/4 of his tenor saxophone solo on Evans's *Theme* being excellently set off by complex brass figures. To how much better advantage does Johnson appear in these surroundings, or on Evans's *Out of the Cool* record, than in the dreary 'mainstream' sessions (17) which usually are this neglected musician's lot! Evans can use these and other soloists in pieces which are far removed from their normal style or period—e.g. Coles on *Davenport blues*—without any incongruity because the material is so transformed, the vision so strong as to unify everything. His orchestration of *Straight, no chaser* is far more to the point, though also far more elaborate, particularly the final ensemble, than previous attempts, by Hall Overton and others (18), to score Monk themes, and throughout this LP the level of invention, yet again, is amazingly high, above all in the lengthy and very searching treatment of John Lewis's *Django*. Hear, too, the ensemble textures in *Ballad of the sad young men*—massive yet without any hint of inflexibility. It is the same on the next record, *Out of the Cool*, which contains, for example, a hypnotically prolonged

Where flamingoes fly, whose acute melancholy is etherealised, dissolved. Such pieces well accord with Claude Levi-Strauss's view of music as "a machine for the suppression of time" (19), and embody a more authentically modern sensibility than a lot of more overtly dissonant jazz.

From this point on there is a striking loosening-up of Evans's music, comparable only to that undergone by George Russell's work after he began to make his Sextet discs for the Riverside label. Consider, for instance, the much freer treatment of the background riff in *Summertime* on the *Svengali* LP in comparison with the earlier version on the *Porgy and Bess* disc. No longer is Evans concerned with mathematical symmetry or balanced repetition, but rather, it seems, with a reflection of the mysterious complexity of the forms of nature, in particular nature's love of analogy instead of repetition. The lyrical tenor saxophone 'solos' by Wayne Shorter in *Barbara story* on *The Individualism of Gil Evans* two-LP set or by Billy Harper in the Ampex *General assembly* are only single threads in textures which now defy both description and analysis; the music is a seamless web in which lines cross and re-cross, glowing, opalescent colours come and go in inexhaustible combinations. Hear, for example, the magically woven fabric of *Hotel me* on the *Individualism* set, the exquisite beauty of even the tiniest details of the Ampex *Proclamation*. On these later recordings identification between the music and the individual performers is so complete that, especially in deep, multi-voiced ensembles like those of *Concorde*, it is impossible to guess where writing stops and improvisation begins. There is an extraordinary reconciliation, or rather a shifting balance between freedom and control whose philosophical implications go beyond jazz, beyond music.

At this stage each Evans record is 'untypical' because he sets himself different objectives every time. But despite this constant renewal, there are still lines of continuity. Thus Joe Beck, guitarist on the Ampex date, occupies a position midway between horns and rhythm section like that of Ray Crawford in *Out of the Cool* or Barry Galbraith on the Russell/McKusick LPs. In fact this music increasingly happens on several levels at once, recalling the multiplicity of events in Charles Ives's works. For instance on *Las Vegas tango*, a gravely serene piece from the *Individualism* set, things happen close up, in sharp focus, others take place in the middle distance, some murmur far away on the horizon, and the exactness of Evans's aural imagination is such that we can hear it all, every note, every vibration, carrying significance. Yet one gains the impression that he feels music, like other forms of truth, should never be immediately understood, that there should always remain some further element to be revealed. Note the gradual, almost reluctant, disclosure of the melodies of *La nevada* and *Bilbao song*, or the way the theme of *Joy spring* is not heard until right at the end.

These endings, many of which fade, like beautiful sunsets, as we look at them, in turn suggest by their very inconclusiveness that Evans, again like Ives, has an Emersonian dislike of the spiritual inactivity which comes from the belief that one possesses a truth in its final form. It is tempting to think that in achieving the lyrical resignation of *Flute song* or the alert tranquillity of *Barbara story* Evans uses sounds rather as Mallarmé uses words—as mirrors that focus light from a hundred different angles on to his precise meaning. But they remain symbols of meaning rather than the meaning itself, and much is left to the imagination. If the listener is unwilling, or, worse still, unable, to exercise this faculty then he will soon be left behind (20).

Jazz Monthly, December 1958 and February 1960

INTERLUDE II

A Review of Sidney Finkelstein's *Jazz: a People's Music*

When calling music dated we usually speak perjoratively. Yet the best is as dated as the worst. Every bar of Mozart spells the second half of the eighteenth-century; we cannot imagine Stockhausen's music belonging to any but our own time. And so, obviously, in jazz it is impossible to think of King Oliver's records being made today; Albert Ayler would not have played in the 1930s quite as he did in the '60s. If music speaks—and not always favourably—of its own place and time so must the criticism which seeks to interpret it. Our response to a work of art should be conditioned by a knowledge of its creator's aims, but we ought also to be aware of the prevailing conventions of his period. And when reading old criticism we must keep in mind the state of knowledge and the climates of opinion current when it was written. Finkelstein's *Jazz: a People's Music* (1) is very much a book of the 1940s. Yet just as the finest music transcends its period so the minute corpus of good jazz criticism retains its power to illuminate. Though only a few of them can be mentioned here, Finkelstein's basic propositions are as relevant now as on first publication in 1948, and will remain so.

He said the book "aimed at breaking down barriers" and this is the key to its position as the first mature statement of jazz criticism: ahead of anyone else, Finkelstein saw this music as a continuous process wherein each part related coherently to all other parts. This is not a view that has ever been favoured by the jazz audience for vast quantities of time and ink have been expended on splitting the music into rigid, mutually-exclusive categories and on insisting that only one or other of these divisions really is jazz at all. Certain commentators have, indeed, been able to inspire in their readers a credulity towards such dogma that would be the envy of an African witch doctor, and so when settled ideas are challenged the concerted howls of indignation are well organised. Yet jazz obstinately remains in one piece, and any of its phases can only be understood fully in relation to the whole, our perceptions being aided by an aesthetic and technical continuity which runs in both directions. Thus appreciation of Art Blakey's drumming with Thelonious Monk is helped by knowledge of Baby Dodds's work on the Bunk Johnson American Music recordings; the significance of the harmonic waywardness of New York stride pianists like Willie 'the lion' Smith is unlikely to be grasped without awareness of the later working-out of these tendencies in Art Tatum. All such links are part of an evolution which

"is far from having achieved its full goals. The intricate problems being tackled by jazz musicians today have to be mastered under adverse conditions ... but music, like history, has a movement which can be checked but not turned back. It was inevitable that in the change from a folk and communal music to a highly individual music qualities should be lost as well as gained. Silly theories have been spun out of the loss, with anguished cries of 'decadence', 'European influences', 'degeneration', 'commercialisation'; the latter term being used to characterise ... all jazz using new materials. ... Modern jazz has made rich additions to our culture. It has provided an expression of feelings which could not be encompassed within New Orleans music."

It need scarcely be added that the 'cool' jazz of the 1950s which followed bop and the free jazz of the 1960s which followed hard bop further extended the emotional spectrum. To see this enrichment as a 'dilution' is merely perverse:

"Jazz can be defined, but only in terms of a flexible, growing art which changes as the conditions under which it is performed change, and because thinking individuals arise who, responding to fresh needs, add something new to something old. The 'something new' is to be judged ... by whether it is a genuine addition to the music, to its human content, technique and expressive breadth. When it is, the result is 'real jazz' precisely because it is different, and because experiment and change are in the essence of jazz".

From which the apparently rather elementary point follows that the seeds of present developments can always be found in the past. However, Finkelstein was the first writer on jazz to make this clear, reminding us that Louis Armstrong's "solo work parallels much of the modern saxophone solo style. His chords do not move into the harmonic extremes of bop, yet the method he used was basic to bop". The author observed this same forward movement in Ellington, also, pointing out that he replaced

"The over-sweet, harmonically confined Tin Pan Alley ballad with a chromatic and sinuously moving melodic line; and he made this kind of line the basis for a number of band compositions. Frequently [it] will combine with the blues to produce a polytonal music . . . of which *Cottontail* is a remarkable example. *Koko* is another . . . using definite modulations and polytonal passages, with the music always lucid and under control. These performances lead directly into bop".

In fact the best application of Finkelstein's evolutionary stance is the latter part of his penultimate chapter, a summary of events as swing changed into bop. This is one of the few genuinely brilliant passages of jazz criticism to be found, not least for the way it keeps every relevant musical factor in just perspective. The author appears to have understood, and so close to the events, many factors whose significance was only seen by the rest of us years later. An instance is his describing Charlie Parker as "almost wholly a blues performer"; that seemed a nonsensical observation in 1948, though obvious enough now.

Perhaps the jazz atmosphere of the 1940s is most evident in Finkelstein's spirited defences of major figures like Armstrong and Ellington. It may now seem improbable that such advocacy was needed, yet the climate of intolerance in those days was such that many outstanding achievements were subject to constant belittlement. Had they been merely polemical the author's defences would hold no interest now, but he countered jazz commentary that was about as firmly rooted in observation and experience as a medieval map of the world with some of the most perceptive appreciations of the leading figures thus far to appear. The most extreme statement of the case against Armstrong was made by Rudi Blesh in *Shining Trumpets* (2). As Finkelstein said,

[Blesh] "laments that Armstrong did not integrate his 'genius' with the 'music' and the 'destiny of his race', thereby failing in his task of filling 'the overwhelming and immemorial need of his own race to find a Moses to lead it out of Egypt'. Such statements betray ignorance. First, 'race' itself is an unscientific and meaningless term. The Negro people of America, in ancestry and physiology, are not a race. There is no special and limited 'music' of the Negro people.

148

They have a right to know and use all music, making it their own, as they took over whatever music they needed in the past. The Negro people are not waiting for a 'Moses' to lead them out of 'Egypt'. They are putting up a collective struggle for the right to live as free human beings on equal terms with anybody else. The causes of discrimination and the special exploitation Negroes suffer are not such as could have been changed by Armstrong playing New Orleans music instead of popular songs with large bands. Certainly his early records are among the most beautiful pieces of music-making in which he ever took part. But had he continued playing *Dippermouth blues* and *Gully low* for the rest of his life with small combinations it is hard to see how this would have abolished segregation or the poll-tax. The end of such a course would probably have been starvation."

But the author is not an uncritical fan pretending that Homer never once nodded: unlike a certain kind of apologist he does not insult us by pretending there is no real difference between *Wild man blues* and *Hello, Dolly*. Aware of the conditions that inhibit jazz formally while forcing it to an excessive stylistic diversity, he describes Armstrong records like *That's my home* as "a genuine musical triumph", but points out that

"They arise out of a fierce struggle . . . to give the material a distinc-
tion it lacks in the original. . . . When to this strain is added the constant drive for novelty made necessary by the position of a successful entertainer in the big-time musical world; the lack of time for serious musical thinking which this new material and its problems require; the insecurity of a bandsman's career, and the unwholesome conditions surrounding the jazz performer's life; the night clubs, long hours, liquor and narcotics that become oc-cupational diseases of jazz . . . it is obvious that the strain must become overpowering . . . solos inevitably begin to sound much like previous ones, the tunes they are based on being in themselves so poor. The performer begins to lead a double musical life, and it is especially the least creative that is put on records. Armstrong might have become a much greater musician than he now is."

Still more enlightening are the book's comments on Bix Beiderbecke, Frank Teschemacher and several others, and this further illustrates Finkelstein's independence. He ignores, for instance, the time-honoured nonsense about the former's keyboard music sounding 'like

Debussy' and explains the real point of those fugitive yet significant little pieces:

> "Bix's piano writing is a further stage of his development, outlining another path that has become important to jazz. Handling the popular tunes meant handling the diatonic major-minor chords and key relationships implicit in them . . . to give his music freshness [he] began playing about with the chords themselves, expanding them into sevenths and ninths, adding chromatic notes, raising or lowering the tones of traditional 'sweet' chords, with the eventual result that the popular tunes themselves vanished from the scene, the musician creating an original music out of their harmonic idiom. The blues re-enter, although greatly transformed. This is the character of *In a mist* and some of the other Bix piano fragments. It hints at the piano playing of Monk, Erroll Garner, and in fact much of bop."

When *Jazz: a People's Music* first appeared such writing had few precedents (3), and as the book had such limited distribution and has been for so long unobtainable it is worth giving another example of Finkelstein's analytical ability. For instance on Teschemacher:

> "His clarinet timbre was reedy, with a deliberate avoidance of vibrato or any hint of sweetness. He developed the blue note into a solo and ensemble style, leaning heavily on off-pitch notes. These are not handled in the tantilising New Orleans manner of sliding on and off the pitch, or worrying at a single note, but are struck solidly. In the ensembles he does not spin a line of decorative figures over a trumpet lead, but, instead, strikes a blue note on the beat to give each chord a blue feeling, or else spins a series of short, staccato phrases which give a feeling of being in another key from the melodic lead. His solo melodic line wanders into strange keys without preparing the listener's ear. Instead, they tantilise the ear with a feeling of being harmonically lost, but always return 'home' in a satisfactory way."

Among much else, Finkelstein conducts an excellent discussion of the nature of jazz melody, which he considers to be inherently two-voiced, this being an aspect of the mixture of musical languages from which jazz grew, and which has determined so many of its special characteristics:

"The ensembles of the Oliver Creole Band records, with Johnny Dodds playing against the cornet lines of Oliver and Armstrong, are particularly beautiful examples, as are many of Sidney Bechet's final ensembles against a trumpet player of the calibre of Tommy Ladnier, Muggsy Spanier, Bill Davison and Max Kaminsky. . . . In many New Orleans and Ellington performances it is impossible to tell where one 'variation' ends and another begins. The same characteristic occurs in bop. Monk's *Round about midnight*, for example, is built on the twelve-bar antiphonal blues pattern in which can be traced the statement and answer, the downward and upward curve of the blues melody, although it is hidden in an elaborate harmonic and instrumental texture. If we study the antiphonal character of the blues melodic line, we see that it carries over into the hot solo itself. This may seem paradoxical, but if we examine the many great blues solos of jazz, such as those of Armstrong, Dodds and Bechet, we will find two contrasting melodic lines laid down within the same solo, as if the one instrument were playing both the melodic lead and the accompaniment or decoration. Armstrong and Dodds, in *Wild man blues* or *Gully low*, provide fine examples, as do also Dodds's *Lonesome blues* solo, Armstrong's *Melancholy blues, West End blues* and *Basin Street blues*. Lester Young's solos are often of this character, using the low, honking notes of the tenor sax to lay down the contrasting bass melodic line. J. C. Higginbotham built up a similar brilliant solo style on the trombone, taking over many of Armstrong's trumpet figures."

Finkelstein was surely correct in arguing that the antiphonal nature of jazz melody is the secret of collective improvisation—which is perhaps the most singular achievement of this music. The finest spontaneous ensembles are not merely an unrelated playing together, in the manner, say, of the average Eddie Condon performance, but are a subtle interplay of statement and answer. Certainly the best 'post-New Orleans' music of Oliver and Jelly Roll Morton confirms this, as, in quite different ways, do the American Music recordings of Wooden Joe Nicholas and Bunk Johnson, and several later developments such as the close-knit teamwork of John Coltrane's Quartet with Elvin Jones.

This review has been as full of quotations as the Prince of Denmark, but that must be apt when paying tribute to the writer on one's chosen subject to whom one perhaps owes most. As implied above, many jazz commentators are so incompetent that they can only be judged by the amount of harm they do, and, amid all the divided counsel of the postwar jazz world, Finkelstein was the first, and for several years the only, critic to offer the sort of coherent view of this music that encouraged systematic study. But for the chance discovery of *Jazz: a People's Music* in a dark corner of an obscure bookshop, at least one listener's concern with jazz might never have become the lifetime interest that it in fact did.

Jazz Monthly, January 1965

Individual Voices:
five examples

Contrasting means and modes of expression, used towards different ends

Martial Solal

What first attracted me to Solal's music were dismissals of it as 'not jazz'. It may appear too easy a paradox, yet almost the best advice that one can offer to people who want to find out about jazz is to attend to those whose work is supposedly 'not jazz'. Besides their music often being of high quality in itself, it may offer a rethinking of jazz essentials and even, in a few cases, indicate a new direction for the art. Thus each considerable stylistic change in Duke Ellington's output was greeted by his followers as a betrayal of what had gone before, as a subsidence into 'not jazz'. But, as Edmund Wilson says, "It is likely to be one of the signs of the career of a great artist that each of his successive works should prove for his admirers as well as for his critics not at all what they had been expecting, and cause them to raise cries of falling-off" (1). Later musicians were able to go one better than Ellington, and the work of Lester Young, Charlie Parker and Ornette Coleman among others was proclaimed as 'not jazz' almost from the moment they appeared.

Sure enough, Solal proved to be among the best jazz pianists. Like Django Reinhardt, the guitarist, he is not merely outstanding among European players but within the whole context of the music. This is no place for a biography, yet it should be noted that Solal was born at Algiers in 1927, made his first attempts at jazz during 1940, and reached Paris in 1950. The first record the present writer encountered was *Kenny Clarke plays André Hodeir* (2), on which musical interest is largely divided between the scores and Solal's contributions. He is prominently featured and takes long, strikingly imaginative solos, *Bemsha swing* containing one of the best. However, Solal is a natural jazz musician and besides fitting into the sophisticated compositional climate of Hodeir's writing he could, in 1957, take a perceptive and sympathetic rôle in some recordings with Sidney Bechet (3). Impressive is the way Solal is able to simplify his harmony to accommodate the older man (4) yet still produce ingenuities like the reharmonisations of that repeated-note figure in *It don't mean a thing*.

Solal has a very fine keyboard technique — that is, skill in employing his instrument, which is not the same thing as facility, which is what all too many pianists have. Solal possesses that kind of agility, too, as it happens, but he uses it instead of being used by it. He composes, as well, all the material on some of his LPs being his own.

An outstanding early record was *Jazz à Gaveau* (5), which finds him with Guy Pedersen on bass and Daniel Humair at the drums. Perhaps *Aigu-marine* is the best track, a contemplative yet searchingly disciplined piece, although *Dermaplastic* particularly well illustrates the way that Solal's improvised variations grow naturally out of the theme. Likewise in *Jordu* seemingly unimportant changes made during the theme statement—linear paraphrases and decorations, rhythmic alterations—foreshadow what and how he will improvise later. And it is no surprise that the variations are thematic, using elements of Duke Jordan's melody in a way reminiscent of Sonny Rollins, even of Thelonious Monk. Relevant also here is the manner in *Gavotte à Gaveau* that melodic fragments are gradually shaped into a convincing overall structure.

The musical point with which Solal alternates two tempos both in *Gavotte à Gaveau* and in *Nos smoking* directs attention to a later and more consistent LP called *The Martial Solal Trio* (6). *Le beau Danube bleu* is notable for his darting treble lines, always informed with melodic purpose, but more remarkable are the interplay between the three instruments and that the frequent changes of tempo and texture always seem natural. Gilbert Rovère is now the bassist, Charles Bellonzi the drummer, and as they are making what essentially is ensemble music with Solal it is fortunate the recording balance places them well forward. *A San Francisco sans Francis*, another of the pianist's punning titles, underlines the collective nature of their work as does the extremely inventive dialogue between keyboard and percussion on *Green Dolphin Street*. Note the clever thematic restatement on this latter track.

My old flame is valuable for its functional use of double-timing, for the manner in which its final piano cadenza avoids rhetoric, and for the way Solal appears, as in *Jordu*, to use the shape of the original melody as a framework even when he ventures far from its actual notes. Finally, on this LP, a joke: *Four brothers*, Jimmy Giuffre's display piece for the Woody Herman saxophone section, played on the harpsichord. This admirably good-humoured performance shows, despite substantial recorded evidence to the contrary from Meade Lux Lewis, Erroll Garner and several others, that this instrument does have a jazz potential. Its chief musical point, however, is a series of breaks leading to a deft caricature of the sort of cadenza found in some of J. S. Bach's toccatas.

The harpsichord is one thing, electric organs are another. On one side of a third LP, *Son 66* (7), Solal, alas, plays the latter instrument and sounds as bad on it as everyone else. He has a very personal sense of time which survives on the harpsichord but not on the organ; his piano touch is most individual, too, but this, of course, survives with neither organ nor harpsichord. Still, Solal's *Mercredi 13* suggests that one day somebody besides Stockhausen (8) might do something with the electronic marvel.

Luckily, the other side of the *Son 66* disc is quite different, containing four of Solal's most adventurous performances. *Morceau de cantal* has a drone bass, like Jordan's *Scotch blues*, yet, as if to emphasise that this is no limitation, Solal's treatment of the piece is as insistently varied as that of *Le beau Danube bleu*. Recording techniques have a rôle in the remaining tracks, and on *Archiduke* steep changes of volume are electronically produced while in *Forêt cinghalaise* a pre-recorded accompaniment and Solal's improvisation over it are alternately but irregularly faded in and out. *Leloir est cher* has an unusual cymbal solo with distant bass and keyboard support, a dialogue between piano and bass with both—for once—recorded at the same strength, and a further exhange wherein drums and bass alternate with unaccompanied piano. It is as if the material is examined from a number of different angles while constantly being rearranged, but the real point is that all these ingenuities are used for expressive and firmly musical ends. As in *Conversations with Myself*, Bill Evans's set of multi-recorded piano improvisations (9), the jazzman is in charge, not the engineer. Not surprisingly, a lot of this music—and some of that on Solal's earlier discs—seems fragmentary at first, but, as with Art Tatum, continued listening reveals an underlying unity.

Jazz Monthly, October 1967

Miff Mole's Okeh Recordings

Time passes so quickly that the so-called New York school of the late 1920s has now been out of fashion for several decades. The received unfavourable opinion on their considerable body of work has repeatedly been confirmed by application of inappropriate criteria, derived from other jazz which had different aims. Yet non-conformists who compare Gunther Schuller's dismissal of supposedly "commercial performances geared to a thriving mass market requiring a consumers' product" (1) with Red Nichols's comment that "the principal aim was to turn out something which met the approval of your fellow musicians right there in the recording studio" (2) may wonder if the truth is not more complex. In fact, this was music for music's sake, and, to an extent then uncommon in jazz, was unequivocally intended for listening.

The best recordings of Nichols, Mole, Eddie Lang and their companions show us musicians working hard at sophistication, as some jazzmen always have, ever since the days of the ragtime composers. Essentially this meant the absorption from other traditions of techniques fresh to jazz, and was important for two reasons. First, jazz, with a relatively short continuous tradition behind it, needed further resources to enable growth—at least until the 1960s, when Ornette Coleman led an attempted rejection of this music's steadily accumulated European borrowings. Second, as the world effectively gets smaller its musics may fuse. As is remarked on an earlier page, that would entail many losses as well as gains, yet, while conservative refinement of existing materials can produce beguilingly polished results, more disturbing astringent and asymmetrical elements cannot be ignored, and in a shrinking world assimilation of the exotic may not only be unavoidable but actually a rule of life. Some of the transformations of acquired materials and methods which have taken place in jazz might to that extent be prophetic.

Not surprisingly, the New York musicians, like the West Coast group of about thirty years later, sometimes got their pieces overcrowded with incident, as items such as Nichols's *That's no bargain* or *Washboard blues* (1926) show. And this was a perfectly honourable weakness, scarcely to be avoided in the development of a new style, as is confirmed by several early Duke Ellington records such as *Georgia grind* (1926). Such attempts at sophistication were further confused by the fact that all these musicians were still shaking off the notably tenacious influence of ragtime. This can be heard not only in the New Yorkers' recordings but on such diverse items as Charlie Creath's *Market Street stomp* (1925), Bennie Moten's *Kansas City breakdown* (1928) or in Ellington's piano work in *Deacon jazz* (1924). The increasing rhythmic flexibility of Mole's trombone parts throughout his 1927-30 sessions for the Okeh company (3), though clearly forecast by his earlier playing with Ladd's Black Aces—e.g. *Muscle shoals blues* (1922)—further illustrates this, and points to a third factor, that leading performers were amplifying their instruments' jazz capabilities.

Mole was one of several trombonists who, in Burnett James's words, freed that instrument from its earlier "moronic and fatuous antics" (4), although the detailed fluency of, say, his *Honolulu blues* solo was approached by few of them during the 1920s. A further example of his striking mobility is the *Shimme-sha-wabble* he recorded with Frank Teschemacher, although his dates yield many other surprises, like the balanced three-part counterpoint between Nichols, Jimmy Dorsey (on clarinet) and himself in *Davenport blues*, which is not the sort of thing at which the New Yorkers were supposed to be any good. Although this music no doubt was organised according to Mole's ideas, he never dominates unduly, and other voices were allowed their say, often appearing in a better light than elsewhere. On *Davenport blues*, for instance, Dorsey's alto saxophone solo, making thoughtful use of the main thematic phrase, is preferable to the my-next-trick-is-impossible jugglery in which his virtuosity often tempts him to indulge on other sessions, and this feeling is confirmed by his shapely improvisation on, of all things, *A hot time in the old town tonight*. Mole's recordings benefitted from the explorations in which he participated under Nichols's leadership, but his own dates were more relaxed, less insistently probing.

It is hard to decide how justified Nichols was in saying (2) that rather than copying Bix Beiderbecke, they both derived inspiration from the same sources, for this is not explicit enough. There are obvious links between Beiderbecke and the New Yorkers, such as the bass saxophone breaks in Mole's *Feeling no pain*, which recall the Bix and his Gang recordings, or the touch of *klangfarbenmelodie* in this piece's thematic recapitulation, duly echoed at the beginning of Beiderbecke's later *Wa-da-da* (and at the end of Louis Armstrong's *Two deuces*).

Far more significant, in terms of the growth of jazz as a musical language, is the advanced harmony common to both groups of players, not only in written ensembles but in the soloists' tendency to use the upper intervals of chords—ninths, elevenths, even thirteenths—with a fair amount of chromatic alteration. Twenty years later people who had never attended properly to Beiderbecke, the New Yorkers, or to the more adventurous jazzmen of the swing period imagined this to be an innovation of bop. Relevant listening here includes Mole's *Feeling no pain, Imagination* plus Beiderbecke's *Humpty Dumpty* and *Krazy kat*, which, along with the carefully ordered rising intensity of *Clarinet marmalade*, give a fuller idea of his aims, of his search for overall formal coherence, than the admittedly intense poetic beauty of his *I'm coming, Virginia* or *Riverboat shuffle* solos.

Nimble and angular, *Feeling no pain* is most appealing, and this, like *Humpty Dumpty* and *Imagination*, was composed and scored by Fud Livingston, a musician whose striking contributions to 1920s' jazz have never been properly studied. In the last-named piece, recurring thematic phrases and contrasting improvisations cohere in a pattern that is satisfying yet significantly new. Indeed, the New Yorkers' links with Beiderbecke must not be exaggerated, for the ensembles of *Imagination* or *Feeling no pain* are considerably more original than those of the earlier Bix and his Gang titles. Beiderbecke may have felt that his sometimes rather conservative choice of repertoire offered the most secure basis for daring advances in other directions, but his version of, say, *At the jazz band ball* (1927) is still modelled on the Original Dixieland Jazz Band's recordings (1917-19), however much more imagination it displays.

Mole's treatment of such material was different, as his rather sardonic reading of *Original Dixieland one-step* shows. This is made to sound light and airy, emphasis being achieved by understatement, although, as on *Hurricane*, there is a taut sequence of solos, each so concentrated as to appear complete in itself yet leading irresistibly into the next. Pee Wee Russell and Mole are outstanding in *Original Dixieland one-step*, but it is the maligned Nichols, his trumpet solos dancing yet oblique, who fares best on *Honolulu blues* and *My gal Sal*. The influence of Jimmy Noone on Dorsey's clarinet playing is apparent in *After you've gone* and particularly *Moaning low*; notable also is the freedom of Phil Napoleon's thrusting trumpet accents on *Navy blues*, clearly taking advantage of Armstrong's contemporary innovations. Pleasing, too, is the dialogue between Lang's guitar and the ensemble in *Some sweet day*, and his combination of sensitivity and robustness on *Hurricane*. Mole's *Crazy blues* solo is an especially well-rounded statement, also, and there is an impressive degree of light and shade in his solo on *I've got a feeling I'm falling*, one of Fats Waller's best songs, which, like the one on *Moaning low*, is full of unexpected linear inflections. Further evidence of his extension of the trombone's powers in this music are the sober gaiety he achieves in *Davenport blues* and his pointed intricacy on *Navy blues*. Other fine sequences include Russell's clarinet solo in *Feeling no pain*, Leo McConville's sweeping trumpet contributions to *That's a-plenty*, and the telling use of Livingston's clarinet against the brass on *You took advantage of me*.

Inevitably these are paid for with less successful passages, such as the later ensemble intensifications of *Moaning low*, which are not so original as the opening clarinet and trombone solos. And it is true that when faced with something like *A hot time in the old town tonight* the Molers—to mention at last the preposterous name the trombonist gave his recording bands—occasionally resorted to caricature. Note here, for example, the heavily sedate ensemble, blandly contrasting with the inane opening verbal dialogue, or the tuba's grotesque melody statement, recalling all too vividly a similar moment in King Oliver's *Frankie and Johnny*. Smith Ballew's epicene singing on *Navy blues* and *Lucky little devil* is a reminder that unisex was no invention of the 1960s, but the jaunty treatment accorded *You made me love you*, in direct contravention of the lyric's doleful reproaches, is less discouraging. In any case the lapses ought not to worry us unduly. Rather than a fully developed ensemble style, Mole offered a group of brilliant improvisors whose best music is quite undimmed by several decades' neglect.

Jazz Monthly, January 1973

Serge Chaloff

Jazzmen are notorious for having tastes quite different from those of their admirers, and Charlie Parker's high regard for Roy Rogers (1) or Miles Davis's for Ahmad Jamal (2) are well known. What is important, however, is not the sheer incongruity of such affinities but what the musician makes of them. Louis Armstrong claimed (3) that his extension of the jazz trumpet's upper range was stimulated by one B. A. Rolfe, a now-forgotten vaudeville player of the 1920s, and it is said that in many of his recordings Johnny Dodds was trying to imitate a then-famous eccentric clarinetist named Boyd Senter. Though it may take place largely at an unconscious level, such influences must undergo drastic transformation. Indeed, while every musician, creative or otherwise, starts by following examples provided by his elders, the extent to which he outgrows these is one measure of his final achievement.

The case of Chaloff, who, like most significant jazzmen of his generation, was influenced by Parker, is of interest here. Many players, such as the alto saxophonist Sonny Stitt, or even the more original Art Pepper, took such facets of Parker's music as accorded with their own temperaments and used them as bases for independent advances. Yet even after following their own paths for some years their work still contained echoes of Parker, rather as the solos of Henry Allen or Jonah Jones continued to reflect Armstrong. This is not an adverse criticism of these men, but it must be noted that some musicians, Chaloff among them, absorb their influences more quickly than others.

Chaloff was aided in this task of integration by having begun, using Jack Washington and Harry Carney of respectively the Count Basie and Duke Ellington bands as models, to formulate a personal approach before hearing Parker. His partial overlaying of the former influences by the latter is first apparent in the negative sense that he did not on his early records utilise the baritone saxophone's complete resources. This was the price he paid, at that stage, for the freedom of movement which his exceptional technique gave him. Chaloff's rigorous melodic construction and extensive harmonic vocabulary are aspects of his style towards which he obviously was helped by Parker, yet he stands closer to that great musician in the intensely emotional cast of certain recordings he made during the 1950s than in any specific technical procedures.

His solos on Woody Herman's 1947 *Four brothers* or *Keen and peachy* are too brief to give much idea of his powers, but contributions to Ralph Burns's *Dial-logue* and *Blue Serge* (1946), to Red Rodney's *Elevation* and *Fine and dandy* (1947), and especially to his own *Gabardine and Serge, Pumpernickel, A bar a second* and *Serge's urge* (also 1947) demonstrate his remarkable ease of movement, fullness and consistency of tone, and, most important, his ready linear invention. Chaloff spoke of *Bopscotch* and *Chickasaw* (1949) as his favourites among the early records and these show an advance in rhythmic control over the previous items; in the latter he has no trouble in relating quite intricate phrases to the beat, and on *The most*, from the same date, he shows extraordinary agility, at least equalling the fluency of Al Cohn, the band's tenor saxophonist.

Following his initial discs with Boyd Raeburn and George Auld, Chaloff's time in the studios was divided between Herman's band and ad hoc sessions like the above. By the end of the decade, though, ill-health forced his virtual retirement, and in the early 1950s his recording dates, or other engagements, were few. It was not until 1954 that he began recording again, in Boston, his home town, and with a not altogether suitable personnel.

Like many others, Chaloff absorbed the harmonic aspects of bop more readily than the rhythmic, and the influences of Carney and Washington continued to affect the rhythmic disposition of his music. Thus swing-style players like the bassist Jimmy Woode and the drummer Buzzy Drootin were quite adequate to his needs. However, Russ Freeman at the piano and Boots Mussulli on alto saxophone appear especially unsympathetic to the subjective character of Chaloff's later work. Mussulli is one of those numerous highly accomplished craftsmen able to fit themselves into almost any musical circumstances yet who have little to offer beyond their competence: it is obvious that Chaloff is in no way extended by the chase passage with him in *All I do is dream of you*.

What is arresting about the leader's playing, however, is that despite a lengthy period of inactivity it embodied such considerable advances on his earlier music. Illness must often have prevented regular practice yet his technique is actually better, and on the ultra-rapid *Love is just around the corner* he moves with greater freedom than ever, and is now bringing the baritone saxophone's full resources into play. One sign of this is that his solos have become more sharply assertive, as his first sixteen bars on *Zdot* or the unexpected twists of his line in *Love is just around the corner* show. Perhaps more important is his concern with tonal variation and the use of dynamics, particularly on *Easy Street*, by far this session's outstanding piece. This is exclusively a feature for Chaloff, and he takes it at a tempo that would be dangerously slow for many players; while not quite perfect in organisation or development, this solo, like his *Body and soul* of the following year, is very moving for its suggestion of a dreamlike inner landscape of haunting loneliness. His illness in fact was heroin addiction, and the desolation of this music, partly foreshadowed by his 1946 *Nocturne* with Sonny Berman, seems akin, among other things, to the later novels of Anna Kavan, which are marked by a similar affliction, particularly *Ice* (4), with its unending flight across a freezing world.

Later in 1954 Chaloff led a nonet drawn largely from Herb Pomeroy's band. While providing some contrast with the previous date, this setting is hardly more sympathetic, for he clearly needed the intimacy of small ensembles. True, the large band atmosphere prevails only on *Salute to Tiny* and *Eenie meenie minor mode*, but it is noticeable that Chaloff does not respond well in his solos on these items. Both are effective compositions, however, especially the former, which is by Pomeroy and aptly recalls Tiny Kahn's own writing. Better from Chaloff's viewpoint is *The fable of Mabel*, an amusing piece by Dick Twardzik that has moments of good scoring and includes a baritone solo notable for a telling use of tonal distortions. Better still is *Let's jump*, recorded with a smaller unit. Significantly this contains Chaloff's finest improvising of the date, an excellent passage of sustained invention. Twardzik's playing is the other striking feature of this occasion: he is handicapped by a poor instrument, yet his curious timing and sometimes unpredictable ideas suggest that his premature death in 1955 robbed us of a valuable contribution to piano jazz.

On the quartet session of March 1956 the ballads are tender and searching, and if none quite matches *Easy Street* there are still ample signs of Chaloff's further advances. The fast *Goof and I* and *All the things you are* reveal still greater technical assurance and an even fuller stream—almost a flood—of characteristic invention, the latter being one of his very best up-tempo solos. Of at least equal import is the role of tonal contrasts and dynamics. Chaloff is not concerned with the former merely to provide external colour to his lines, but works through different intensities of tone which on, say, *Thanks for the memory* help implement the expressive force of his ideas. Such tonal variation has always been part of jazz performing techniques and there are many precedents which stop our regarding this aspect of Chaloff's music as an innovation. But it is uncommon among members of his generation, and looks forward, if rather mildly, to the use of such devices by Albert Ayler and others in the 1960s.

Again, on some tracks, especially *I've got the world on a string*, abrupt changes of volume have a part, hard to define yet still positive, in the construction of his solos. Variety of phrase-length is more apparent, also, and there are several instances here of Chaloff's skill in paraphrasing melodies: the original line of *Thanks for the memory* is never stated but at the close of the performance its shape is hinted at with real subtlety. There is much sensitivity in *Stairway to the stars*, with every departure from the melody having an expressive rather than merely decorative purpose, and altogether this is the most rewarding set of performances recorded under Chaloff's name. It is difficult to imagine the baritone saxophone better played by him, or as well by anybody else, and it is singularly unfortunate that his small yet at one time seemingly quite secure reputation was obliterated by the more easily acceptable offerings of lesser men. During those few years when he resumed his career, Chaloff was demonstrably making steady progress in forging a mode of expression independent of any one stylistic school or even period. Maybe that precisely was his mistake so far as it concerned the pigeonhole-minded jazz public, which usually likes its idols to be comfortably small and plainly labelled. Despite this, at the time of Chaloff's death in 1957, at thirty-three, his most fruitful years appeared to lie ahead (5).

Jazz Monthly, May 1963

The *Spirituals to Swing* Concerts

The *Spirituals to Swing* concerts were put on at Carnegie Hall in New York just prior to the Christmases of 1938 and '39. The widest possible variety of artists contributed, and John Hammond's object in putting, for example, a primitive blues-shouter like Sonny Terry and a then avant gardist such as Lester Young on the same platform must have been at least partly educative. When Count Basie's band does *One o'clock jump* all they play is a few of the ensemble riffs, but the audience recognises them and applauds strongly. These people were swing fans, no doubt typical of their time, and the idea was to show them that this big band music they were so enthusiastic about, and thought so new, was just the latest episode in a quite diverse tradition. To hear, say, an advanced player like Charlie Christian on the same evening as the New Orleans Feetwarmers was to glimpse a perspective that until then had been available only to a few specialist record collectors.

Of course, the lesson was never taken in, and most jazz listeners, like so many jazz musicians, still do not know where their music came from or what its history has been. And on listening to the recordings made at these concerts (1) we gain an idea of why. The Golden Gate Quartet sing Negro religious songs most efficiently, yet contrast them with the flexibility and rhythmic adventure of Mitchell's Christian Singers and their efforts immediately appear unspontaneous, fatally simplified. The fact remains that the Golden Gates' slickness drew far more applause. In the no-man's-land where jazz works out its existence between more clearly identifiable forms, the bowdlerisers always have an advantage. This, obviously, is because dilutions are easier to absorb than the more concentrated article: twenty years after these programmes the blowsy romanticism of a Dave Brubeck was a more readily marketable product than the sternly realistic art of a Bud Powell, and it is always thus.

Not that much adulteration went on at these concerts. True, *Cavalcade of boogie* by Meade Lux Lewis, Albert Ammons and Pete Johnson is merely a string of flashy piano blues choruses, the treble figurations meaning little when divorced from interplay with left-hand ostinatos that are here obliterated by redundant bass and drums. But Joe Turner's *It's alright, baby* accompanied by Pete Johnson may be the finest of the several duets they recorded together, the anonimity of the playing for once completely transformed by the dark power of that ringing voice. Sonny Terry's *Mountain blues* is fascinating also, stunted harmonica phrases and his outlandish falsetto voice coalescing into strange patterns of rhythm, colour, melody. Years later, pieces like this replaced in the affections of the blues public the sort of music represented by Ida Cox's *'Fore day creep*, so Terry's presence, and Bill Broonzy's, too, at these events was prophetic as well as historically revelatory.

A one-time accompanist of singers like Ida Cox, James P. Johnson sounds, in his *Mule walk* and *Carolina shout* piano solos, as if he were merely running through something that no longer meant a lot to him, just to oblige (though his Blue Note and other recordings of a few years later contradict this impression). Nor does Basie sound the most willing of soloists: on *I ain't got nobody* he conservatively cuts back to echoes of Earl Hines and Fats Waller, his formative influences, there being few signs here of the organising of note-lengths, attacks, intensities, changes of keyboard register, of 'irrational' time-values and use of 'melodic silence' which make his best studio-recorded solos so remarkable. Nor does his band get to do much. *Blues with Lips* has a medium tempo that is exactly right for 'Lips' Page, whose trumpeting is featured; and this sounds like where Harry James got the ideas for his *Woo woo* and *Boo woo* recordings. *Rhythm man* is a powerhouse affair whose mannered scoring, presumably by Jimmy Mundy, reflects few of the virtues of what for a short while ranked as one of the greatest jazz ensembles of the time. Yet passages of *Lady, be good* give some idea of the impact it must have registered in person; and it is exciting to hear the fiery trumpeting of Harry Edison without all the clichés he acquired during the 1950s.

On the contrary, the New Orleans Feetwarmers sound less vivid than in the studio recordings they had made several years before. Sidney Bechet—not long out of the Southern Tailoring Shop, Harlem—is genuinely creative, though, on both clarinet and soprano saxophone, and it is interesting how his trumpeter, Tommy Ladnier, uses rhythmic devices similar to Louis Armstrong's to rather different ends. Jo Jones lightly takes the rise out of an older style of drumming here, but does so with humour and understanding; this should be compared with the patronising attitude evident in some of Gene Krupa's playing on the recordings of Benny Goodman's 1938 Carnegie Hall concert. And speaking of concerts, it is amusing that despite all the strictures about their supposedly inhibiting effect on jazz many of the performances here are much less formal than their studio-recorded equivalents. Those by Goodman's Sextet are a clear example of this, and there is fine vibraharp by Lionel Hampton on *Memories of you* and *Flying home*, outstanding guitar from Christian in *Honeysuckle rose* (alias *Gone with what draft?* alias *Gilly*).

Christian and Lester Young produce music of rare beauty on these recordings, and nobody who understands how jazz constantly grows and changes, no one who in particular has grasped how 1940s bop grew out of 1930s swing, will need to be told why it is instructive, and moving also, to hear this pair side by side. Two great jazz musicians—and if the guitarist appears slightly the lesser it is because his rôle was partly a transitional one. Christian's best moments here come in the least suitable frame, the raggedly jammed *Lady, be good*. His long, flowing lines—a shifting interplay of blues riffs and freer melodic ideas—clearly derive from Young but go beyond him rhythmically and harmonically, and so melodically. Hearing them together, as on *Good morning, blues* or *Way down yonder in New Orleans*, we can tell what was added to the common practice of swing and what was changed, and we almost can see Charlie Parker waiting in the wings. *Paging the Devil* has lovely solos, and *Mortgage stomp* is a sort of preliminary study for Young's *Lester leaps in*, one of the authentic masterpieces of recorded jazz. It is, of course, instructive to compare Young on this *Lady, be good* and on his 1936 studio version; his later work has been persistently underrated, yet his imagination was never more active than in those years. This is confirmed by his clarinet solo in *Blues with Helen*, surely one of the most affecting to be found in jazz (2).

Jazz Monthly, November 1967

Lennie Niehaus

It was unfortunate Niehaus first became widely known as a result of the tours he undertook in the mid-1950s with Stan Kenton's band, for the records he was then producing under his own name made it obvious he had nothing in common with that master of unintentionally comic bombast. The second thing to be learnt from them was that Niehaus had little to learn about playing the alto saxophone. His ease and fluency conveyed a feeling of relaxation and security that is always rare, and his attack and swing were almost equally striking. But the most notable single feature of the twenty-six performances considered here is the consistency of his inventive power in improvisation. He never seems at a loss for a good melodic idea, and, though his phrasing is concise and pre-eminently logical, an element of the unexpected is never absent.

In some ways, Niehaus's first LP (1), with a quintet instrumentation, remains the most informative of his abilities as a soloist. The scored passages are generally brief, and, apart from a few meandering contributions from Jack Montrose and Bob Gordon on tenor and baritone saxophones respectively, the leader fills all available solo space with notable effect. His consistency makes it hard to single out any performance as exceptional, though the quick-fire *Whose blues?* is a reminder that real spontaneity is less a matter of technical command than of a steady flow of ideas. Almost as impressive in this respect are *Prime rib*, with its double-time phrases, and the breaks of *You stepped out of a dream*.

Niehaus wrote the arrangements for all the recordings dealt with here, and these show a nicely understated skill, nearly always being shorn of unnecessary gesture. As his was a musical family he began his studies early and thus had a better chance of acquiring sound theoretical knowledge than many jazzmen. This places an agreeable variety of writing techniques at his disposal, but he is aware of the dangers of over-elaboration in the modest circumstances of small combo jazz. On the sleeve of his second LP (2) he writes, "With the more intellectual and academic approach there is a tendency for . . . work to become contrived and esoteric. It must be remembered that most modern jazz compositions written during the past few years are no more 'modern' than things Bartók, Berg, Schoenberg and others wrote twenty or thirty years ago." Such a viewpoint is healthy, first because it is historically and technically realistic, and second because it is a corrective to the attitude of many jazzmen who in the past have imagined themselves to be daring iconoclasts while purveying what actually was simple and conservative music.

On the octet performances of his second LP Niehaus still occupies most of the solo space and is fully able to justify this. His arrangements are similar in general style to many others being written on the West Coast at that time, and what individual character they possess is due more to certain technical details than to an overall new approach. Such features most often arise from his concern with unity, and he is fond of deriving introductions, bridge passages and codas from the theme, or part of it, whenever possible. Instances are *Night life, Have you met Miss Jones?* and *Circling the blues*; also typical of Niehaus is the way the introduction of *The night we called it a day* recurs in sequential form to effect a modulation.

The first batch of octet scores have a pleasingly full texture, with the themes announced mainly in block chords. By the jazz standards of his time, Niehaus had a quite extensive, though in no way personal, harmonic vocabulary, so these parallel chords often are interesting, and are effectively distributed over the ensemble. The result, however, could easily have been a rather too consistent harmonic richness, so he occasionally scores a passage for the horns without the rhythm section, as in *How about you?*, or has the drums only supply interjections, as on *Figure eight*. He has many similar procedures to ensure variety, such as the bridge of *Night life*, first played in block chords then scored contrapuntally on its return. Another example is the first section of the coda to *Just the way you look tonight*, where each horn plays a separate line based on a different part of the theme; the result is of considerable harmonic and contrapuntal interest, and one regrets this passage only being four bars long. Even drum solos are made to further the development of the piece, as in *Just the way you look tonight*, where, with piano and bass silent, the percussionist for a while alternates bars with the front line. There is a similar episode on *Seaside*.

Such devices, though, are very far from exhausting the scope of an ensemble of trumpet, valve-trombone, alto, tenor and baritone saxophones, piano, bass and drums, and Niehaus appears to have been conscious of the almost unrelieved homophony of the above scores. In his third LP (3) there is a certain amount of sectional differentiation, though not enough. Alto saxophone and trombone contrast tellingly with the full band on *Cooling it*, as do alto and tenor in *Bunko*, yet such antiphony is infrequent, and counterpoint mainly conspicuous by its absence. On his fifth record (4), for sextet, however, Niehaus included well-paced duets between alto and tenor saxophones and trumpet and baritone saxophone in *Thou swell*, and *Three of a kind* has an adroit fugal introduction and coda. There are effective dialogues between soloist and ensemble here, also, particularly on *Belle of the ball*, and some imaginative scored backgrounds to solos, for example in *As long as I live*, where, behind the leader, the other horns state the theme in fragmented form.

In solo Niehaus is as good as before, although the only other improvisations of real merit on these recordings are by the pianist Lou Levy in the first octet disc and by Stu Williamson on both trumpet and valve trombone in the sextet LP. Indeed, the assurance and conviction of the latter's work on the former instrument in *Thou swell*, *I wished on the Moon*, *Knee deep* and *As long as I live* mark it as being among his best on record. Bill Perkins, on tenor saxophone, is also heard to pleasing, if rather nonchalant, effect in *Three of a kind* and *As long as I live*. The gulf (in terms of invention) between the leader and several of his other bandsmen, however, is rather clearly shown by the chase passages of *Whose blues?* and *Rick's tricks*, and even more by the long series of twelve- and twenty-four-bar solos in *Circling the blues*.

The point is confirmed in a different way by Niehaus's success with slow ballads, particularly *The night we called it a day* and *Our love is here to stay* on the octet records. Best, however, is the quintet *Day by day*, which begins and ends with some exceptionally subtle harmonic writing that creates a feeling of remoteness which is at once quite contrary to the original melody's banality and exactly appropriate to Niehaus's very sensitive improvisation. This can stand beside Jimmy Giuffre's beautiful *Lotus bud* recorded with Shorty Rogers or Art Pepper's *Jazz chorale* recorded with John Graas. The same side of Niehaus's musical personality is also reflected in two compositions, *Night life* and *Debbie*, slow lyrical pieces of some melodic distinction. Also attractive are *Take it from me*, which has a forty-bar chorus instead of the usual thirty-two, and *Elbow room*, a blues with a bridge.

Writing like this and playing of the quality heard on *Whose blues?* or *Day by day*, while not suggesting Niehaus to be other than an entirely minor figure, did show perfectly explicit promise of further growth. Despite a few excellent later recordings, such as his striking versions of Perkins's *Little girl blues* and Benny Golson's *Four eleven west* (5), that promise was not really fulfilled, eventually he stopped making LPs, and, finally, dropped out of sight. Presumably Niehaus must be regarded as another casualty of the hostile circumstances in which jazz has always found itself.

Jazz Monthly, March 1958

Cross-Influences:
three directions

Combinations of jazz techniques with those of other musics

Improvisations for Jazz Band and Symphony Orchestra
by Mátyás Seiber and John Dankworth

Stravinsky once described jazz as "a different fraternity altogether, a wholly different kind of music making" (1), and, providing they did not think about it too hard, most people who are acquainted both with straight music and with jazz would agree. Yet despite some few possible, though dubious, traces of West African musical practice early on, the Europeanisation of jazz, as noted in previous chapters, is obvious. In fact, jazz, at least until the 1960s, resorted again and again to Europe, using its borrowings as a catalyst aiding growth. The jazz community is lazily inclined to dismiss such pieces as Teo Macero's *24+ 18+* (2) or Don Ellis's *Improvisational suite No. 1* (3) as 'pretentious', yet they are part of a continuing process of absorption, of transformation.

Naturally, the compliment has been returned, and occasionally to disturbing effect. One such instance is the Blues movement of Ravel's Violin Sonata—a sardonic comment indeed on that idiom. More interesting, however, are the cases where there is in effect a dialogue between two different views of musical structure like that which runs through the Ornette Coleman/Gunther Schuller *Abstraction* (4) involving the variational procedures of free jazz and of serial technique. A comparable, though slightly earlier endeavour of this kind was *Improvisations for jazz band and symphony orchestra* jointly written by Mátyás Seiber, the highly accomplished expatriate Hungarian composer then resident in this country and John Dankworth, a well-known English bandleader. Whereas in *Abstraction,* or even in Shapero's *On green mountain* or Babbitt's *All set*, which are discussed elsewhere in this book, the straight composer wrote and the jazzmen played, in *Improvisations* an approximately equal amount of writing was done by the representatives of each world, and the jazz band and the symphony orchestra play roughly equal lengths of time separately and together. The work is in one movement and everything derives from the same paragraph of thematic material; it is planned so that the potentialities of band and orchestra, and the different techniques of development open to them, are exploited systematically.

The main thematic material is, in fact, a four-bar phrase by Dankworth. This is announced at the outset by the orchestra and is developed along normal symphonic lines by Seiber. He makes it asymmetrical and treats it contrapuntally, passing it from one section of the orchestra to another. This theme is then taken over by the band in a somewhat regressive swing band ensemble passage whose block chords admittedly provide contrast with the counterpoint of the opening section. This was written by Dankworth with the addition of a few orchestral interpolations by Seiber. Next, Seiber develops a secondary idea of Dankworth's, this time employing both groups, and although the thread of the musical argument is skilfully maintained, the texture of this passage is rather muddy and the Dankworth brass, here and in similar places, dominated rather more, one feels, than Seiber calculated. The first scheduled improvisation is a trumpet solo. Commencing with a break, this is based on the main theme as announced by the band on its first appearance, and is followed by a bridge passage scored for the orchestra by Seiber and based on the main theme as given by the orchestra in the beginning. The section to which this leads is the most remarkable in the whole work, and the one in which the two idioms come most fruitfully into contact.

This is the solo alto saxophone improvisation, and it is not based—as would be the case in an ordinary jazz performance—on the chords that supported the theme, but on a new sequence Seiber scored for the orchestra. It consists of chords all of which contain four pitches and each group of three chords contains all twelve available notes. Each chord has a different instrumentation, appears in a different register, and has a different time value.

By now the music has acquired a definite atonal flavour which is strengthened in the next section. This commences with a brief episode for the percussion of both groups leading to pizzicato strings playing a canonic ostinato in three parts that is based on a twelve-note row. This ostinato is three bars long and the canonic entries are at two-bar intervals so the three parts are continually overlapping in different ways, with consequent changing patterns of accentuation. Above this atonal background four jazz soloists—trumpet, trombone, alto and tenor saxophones—enter one by one for a collective improvisation. This part of the work is brought to an end by Seiber, using a bitonally harmonised three-note motive that is subjected to a number of syncopated modifications by both groups and leads to a powerful climax.

Next comes a quiet twelve-bar blues that contrasts quite effectively with the complexity of the foregoing sections. Here the band is accompanied by the orchestra and all the music was written by Dankworth. The final section of the work to some extent mirrors the episodes that preceded the blues. First Seiber recapitulates the opening theme, this is followed by a contrasting section for the band, by Dankworth, that has a function similar to that of a cadenza in a classical solo concerto, ending with a solo by the jazz percussionist. The finale is an elaboration of the section that came immediately before the blues, based on the three-note motive. It is handled by Seiber, who uses both groups to build another large climax.

The *Improvisations* had their première in London during 1959 at a concert given by the London Philharmonic Orchestra under the American conductor William Steinberg—augmented, of course, by Dankworth's band. Though quite well received, it was inevitably overshadowed by the main item on the programme, Stravinsky's *Threni*. True, it is a minor piece beside such works as Seiber's magnificent *Ulysses*, rather as *Abstraction* is minor in comparison with Schuller's opera *The Visitation*. Yet such items can tell us something about the possible future of music, and it is unfortunate, though unsurprising, the jazz community being what it is, that *Improvisations* was scarcely heard of again (5).

Jazz Monthly, July 1959

The Brandeis Festival LP

When Brandeis University held its fourth Festival of the Creative Arts in 1957 at least one of the programmes represented a most unusual gesture. It consisted of six specially commissioned jazz pieces, and, for what little such distinctions are worth, three were from jazzmen, two from straight composers sympathetic to jazz, and one from a musician active in both spheres. Though universities are supposed to foster research and other original work, this for many years remained one of the few cases of such an institution doing anything practical to further jazz. To have promoted a concert at which a well known band marketed its familiar product would have been nothing, but here was created a situation in which something new might happen. And there was no aimless or self-indulgent experimenting, an encouragingly high standard being attained by all six composers. One of the pieces may be accounted a partial failure, yet these scores are a mine of ideas for further development.

It might be objected that such commissions, by removing normal commercial pressures, create an artificial situation, that music produced under such circumstances can offer no realistic insight on jazz potentialities, and that the point is proved by so few of the 'ideas for further development' having been widely followed up. But even now it is premature to say that, our perspective being too short. It must be remembered that at all periods of musical history the pieces which really made that history were in their own day the property of only a limited circle of initiates. True, such patronage will seldom be available for jazz until it is safely dead, but it is the worst sort of defeatism to discourage commissions because they are rare. And there is nothing artificial about the fine quality of the jazz which resulted on this occasion: the best of it affords us a glimpse of the sort of music we might be able to expect if jazz ever breaks away from the normally almost crippling limitations and sense of values of the entertainment business to which it has always been linked. Besides, a good piece of music is its own justification, and compared to its enduring value the conditions under which it was created are finally of little interest.

By the time these pieces were written, played and recorded (1) the expressive and technical resources of jazz were known to be very considerable, yet one of their fascinations is that they show us several composers employing the same basic procedures to quite different ends. This goes on at two levels, first being that of devices common to nearly all music. Examples include Jimmy Giuffre's and Charles Mingus's handling of ostinato basses, and Harold Shapero's and Gunther Schuller's use of the passacaglia idea. Second, it is equally instructive to hear the many ways techniques developed specifically by jazz musicians are here employed. Indeed, what these works are about is the creative use of procedures which in less propitious circumstances can readily become clichés. They prove, as good music often does, that, given imagination and fine craftsmanship, fresh results can be drawn from resources that might appear exhausted.

George Russell's *All about Rosie* is perhaps the most direct example here of musical thinking which, instead of being channelled by the common practice of jazz, employs it as a point of departure. It is based, he has said, "on a motive taken from an Alabama Negro childrens' song-game entitled *Rosie, little Rosie*". Among other things, Russell uses the superimposition of riffs approximately similar to that found, say, in Count Basie's *One o/clock jump* or in the Jimmy Lunceford *Yard dog mazurka*. But, in a manner perhaps learnt from Stravinsky, he selects phrases of varying lengths which, as the music proceeds, overlap in different ways both in relation to each other and to the beat. To put it another way, tension is induced by conflict between the basic pulse and the rhythmic units of the phrases. In the first movement, which shifts between 2/2 and 3/2, a most cogent musical argument is carried through via sequence and repetition which rises to an abrupt, logical, climactic end.

A similar process, in slow motion, can be heard during the following movement. This might be considered a study in how to retain the feeling of the blues without the form, and shifts meaningfully through several tonal areas. The control of material in both these movements almost deserves to be called masterly, the unobtrusive yet always telling changes in tone-colour being especially impressive. In fact this is that rarity, convincing written-out jazz polyphony, and should be heard in conjunction with Russell's scores of *You're my thrill* and *The end of a love affair*, recorded by Hal McKusick and discussed on a previous page. Russell is also able to provide a good basis for improvisation, and the very fast closing movement includes a superb piano solo from Bill Evans, followed with excellent ones by John LaPorta, Art Farmer, Teddy Charles and McKusick. Each of these pieces benefits from virtuoso performance, yet none more obviously than Russell's fleet but powerfully swinging finale. The movements are well differentiated yet the basic shape of the main *Rosie, little Rosie* phrase is detectable in all three, adding to the unity imparted by the composer's clearly defined style of writing.

Harold Shapero, too, based his contribution on borrowed material. This composer established his reputation with a group of three piano sonatas which are hard but grateful to play, are strongly influenced by Stravinskian neo-classicism, and, probably, by the anti-romanticism of some of Aaron Copland's earlier works. They are full of rhythmic and harmonic displacements which always suggested interesting possibilities if their composer ever applied himself to jazz. However, certain of Shapero's later pieces, such as the Symphony in Classical Style and the would-be-Beethovenian Piano Variations, show, both in content and technical method, too dependent an attachment to the past, and his turning to a long-dead composer for source material for a jazz score was not unexpected. The fact remains that Shapero brought it off, and *On green mountain* is one of the most successful, even the most exhilarating, of these six works.

As theme he uses Monteverdi's familiar *Zefiro torna e di soavi accenti*, but this is far from being a mere jazzing of the classics. A few pieces, like Duke Ellington's *Ebony rhapsody*, Art Tatum's *Elégie* and the Miles Davis/Gil Evans *Maids of Cadiz* succeed in doing just that because instead of merely applying jazz phrasing externally they rework the material in new terms. *On green mountain* takes the process much further and historically might be seen as a throwback to sixteenth-century parody and paraphrase techniques. Both Monteverdi's bass and melody are used, the former being a repeating, chaconne-type figure which Shapero harmonises in rich, quite modern chords for piano, vibraharp, bass and guitar. Over this he adds, without alteration, the first twelve bars of Monteverdi's tune. Preceded by an introduction and followed by a transitional section leading to the solos, the whole is a beautiful piece of orchestration, austere yet colourful.

For improvisational purposes Monteverdi is squared-up into a thirty-two-bar AABA chordal sequence taken at double tempo. To begin the solos Farmer was asked to stay close to the melody for eight measures, decorate it for eight, and then depart more and more into free improvisation. This he does well. Barry Galbraith, who plays outstandingly in the ensembles of each track, has one of his infrequent guitar solos, and after we have heard from LaPorta, a jubilant climax is reached with the re-entry of Farmer's trumpet.

Shapero finds an apt contrast and relaxation of tension after this by sounding the melody, in its revised form, on both muted trombone and french horn (very similar, yet different sounds, one hard, one soft) against bluesy counterpoint from McKusick. Jimmy Knepper has a good trombone solo, also, and Shapero most effectively lowers the tension again, preparatory to the return of the initial slow tempo, by means of interrupting the rhythmic flow with brief, irregular patches of silence. Most people able to respond to this piece will want, afterwards, to hear Monteverdi's version, and that is a compliment to both composers.

If Shapero's is the most optimistic work in this collection, Giuffre's *Suspensions* is the most hermetic, the most self-contained. And, like a natural, living organism, it grows from very small beginnings. It is in three-part, ABA, form, the opening section germinating from a little whole-tone and minor third accompanimental figure above which is added a blues-inflected melody. A feature of the related yet contrasting middle section is the opposition between its 5/4 ostinato bass and a swinging 4/4 line above.

It is an amusing comment on the unreality of musical dividing lines that Shapero, the straight composer, makes a sequence of improvisations the core of his piece while jazzman Giuffre writes out every note of *Suspensions*. All the same, he tried to write parts suited to the personalities of the musicians he knew would be performing, parts "with which they can express themselves as they would in a solo"—to quote from his notes for the original concert programme. Giuffre certainly overcame some of the notational problems in doing this, and *Suspensions* does sound like a group effort, but a head arrangement, not a collective improvisation.

'Hermetic' is one of the last words to describe Schuller's *Transformations*, for it tries to combine the jazz and straight music of the late 1950s. This being so, although Schuller's work in jazz is well known, a few comments on some of his straight compositions might be in order. The Symphony for Brass and Percussion (1950) would impress almost anyone at first, but especially those who have studied orchestration or even taken a particular interest in it. There is, indeed, something of showmanship in this work's relentless display of highly effective brass writing, and this is paralleled in some of Schuller's other early pieces. The Seven Studies after Paul Klee (1959) are visually-inspired, show a most sensitive ear, yet are little more than sequences of ingeniously mixed colours and textures. Here an accomplished manipulation of orchestral sound has overridden musical thought, and something similar happened with the rather weightier String Quartet dating from the same year as *Transformations*—1959. This includes the full panoply of the 1950s avant garde, including controlled (i.e. strictly limited) improvisation, etc., all made 'effective' and just a little glossy. What is wrong with these works is that, as with certain of André Hodeir's more overtly jazz-inclined pieces (2), command of a wide range of compositional techniques controls the invention, and hence what the music is saying, instead of it being the other way round. Such comments apply far less, if at all, however, to later pieces by Schuller, like his Symphony or opera *The Visitation* (both 1965).

Following on from his *Atonal jazz study* of 1948, *Transformations* begins as a straight piece into which fragments of jazz material are introduced. These grow and finally take over, making it into a jazz performance wherein Bill Evans again improvises very well. Then the work's two aspects, jazz and classical, are juxtaposed. The whole is carried through with a technical skill that makes some extended pure-jazz works sound unbearably jejeune, but its two entities remain separate, no fusion occurs, the avowed target is missed. Perhaps the two sides, classical and jazz, were differentiated with unnecessary sharpness in the first place. Schuller's next composition of this sort, *Conversation*, recorded by the Modern Jazz Quartet with the Beaux Arts String Quartet, marks a step forward. There still is no real integration, yet the two elements, by the very closeness of their contact, do enhance each others' essential qualities—something positive nearly happens.

It was with two later works, however, that Schuller achieved a breakthrough to the point where straight music techniques become vehicles of jazz feeling and (essential corollary) improvisational jazz devices respond to a straight composer's ways of musical thought. These are his *Variants on a theme of John Lewis* and *Variants on a theme of Thelonious Monk*, and the latter particularly benefits from two good improvisors, Eric Dolphy and Scott LaFaro, and one great one, Ornette Coleman, being close to top form. Yet music of this quality makes the categories that are supposed to undergo 'transformation' seem irrelevant, even meaningless. In both their composed and improvised parts the *Monk variants* are simply excellent music. However, to play the recordings of *Transformations*, *Conversation* and the *Lewis* and *Monk variants* in that order is to acknowledge that the first of these was a necessary beginning.

A different kind of transformation goes on in Mingus's *Revelations*, and a brief, purely external, description may give an idea of the variety he gets from his material, though none of its impact, nor of the piece's unity. A dark-toned statement from the lower instruments sets a brooding atmosphere, but unaccompanied solos by french horn, trumpet and trombone convey a feeling of freedom, of possibility. The opening returns, however, and its mood becomes ominous. Mingus gives a cry of "Oh yes my lord," which, especially with repeated hearings, sounds self-conscious, theatrical. A piano solo in 3/4 follows which, although clearly influenced by Negro church music, does not rely on that idiom's rather numerous clichés. This lessens the tension, and, for a while, the music takes on a quite romantic accent, related in feeling, though distinct from, the opening. In turn this toughens into something more energetic. We are back in 4/4 and over a tonic/dominant ostinato there is a churning collective improvisation in which everyone joins. This is the climax of *Revelations*, and, as we might expect, resolves back to the opening statement. But Mingus, good compositional tactician that he is, realises that it will not do, in this particular case, to end just as he began. So after the restatement follows another collective improvisation, as successful in its different way as the first. In it the music slowly disintegrates, evaporating into the far distance.

Although not so precisely demanding of his performers as, say, Milton Babbitt or Russell, Mingus takes greater risks than the other composers. The unity of his works depends not on their technical organisation, as with Babbitt's *All set*, nor on a highly personal musical language, as does *All about Rosie*, but is largely of an emotional order. One result of this, of course, is that when they are bad they are exceptionally bad, yet that does not concern us here for *Revelations* is among Mingus's best achievements of the period. It extends itself as a succession of moods, feelings, atmospheres, melting into and out of each other. This was something which had not then been widely attempted in jazz, although music, like poetry, is well equipped for it, good examples being *L'après midi d'un faune*—both the Debussy and Mallarmé versions.

Mingus's methods normally work very well for him, but, as is natural, they would not suit others. A problem for others is knowing how far to take the process of unification. If a composer works his material over too much there will be little new left for the soloists to discover. Indeed, that is sometimes the price of success—remember the absence of improvisation from *Suspensions*. Mingus is lucky in two ways. First as a virtuoso bassist he is always at the heart of the performance as few composers can now hope to be. Second, he usually knows—and one is sure this knowledge is instinctive—just how tight, or loose, a rein to keep. The collectively improvised climax and coda of *Revelations* are almost perfect instances of Mingus leading his players' expressive and instrumental resources into serving a higher and more complex form of organisation than that represented by their own individual efforts.

However, the greatest musician involved with this enterprise was Milton Babbitt, in whose *All set* extremely detailed calculation supplants the risks of empiricism. In the 1940s he began extending Schoenberg's method of twelve-tone composition into an actual system, serialising not only horizontal and vertical dimensions of pitch but also the parameters of duration, timbre, dynamics. The result was a highly complex network of inner relationships, and at first *All set* appears to be a welter of unrelated detail, with little evident short-term patterning. As Armin Klammer has suggested, the initial effect of music like this is "through purposeful determining, to make everything that is to come indeterminable by the listener" (3). Yet although so much is happening it is all significant, and, with repeated hearings, the correspondences which unify the whole gradually come into focus. The only one of these works that is in 4/4 throughout, *All set* in fact abstracts melodic, rhythmic, and at some points even harmonic, characteristics from the advanced jazz of the 1940s and makes interestingly different uses of Babbitt's procedures from those which obtain in other compositions of this period, such as his String Quartet No. 2 (1952) or Two Sonnets (1955) (4). Schuller, who conducted the Brandeis works, said *All set* was the most difficult to perform, but despite the incessant ferment of line and colour, reminiscent of a bank of many coloured lights of different wattage flashing on and off at different rates and in constantly changing orders, this music has a distilled clarity which the listener finally comes to recognise as the sign of a rare intellectual passion.

Jazz Monthly, June 1967

Around Paul Whiteman

Among the grosser simplifications of the supposed history of jazz is a notion that large bands, and the crafts of writing for and playing in them, were the virtually private creation of dedicated jazzmen following a straight and narrow path in company with such figures as Fletcher Henderson. This has confined our attention to conventionally accepted names, whereas the best hope of real comprehension lies, as ever, in the widest attainable listening experience. Once the mass of subsidiary recorded material from the 1920s has been taken into account the situation naturally looks more involved, yet specific musical events are often easier to understand through thus being set in a fuller perspective.

We have always been encouraged to think of popular music as a craven dilution of jazz, but this separation is false. Even publicity handouts from that time suggest the allegedly opposing forces often shared similar aims, even if these were not always ones of which we might now approve. Thus the American Negro press lauded Henderson's group as not "like the average Negro orchestra, but in a class with the good white orchestras, such as Paul Whiteman . . . not sloppy New Orleans hokum" (1). And before laughing at the slide-whistle solo on Whiteman's highly successful *Whispering* it is as well to remember a similar feature included three years later, perhaps in imitation, on King Oliver's *Sobbing blues*. There were unending cross-influences, for, so far as widening the music's expressive range and technical resources are concerned, the traffic was never in one direction only, there being precedents, often in nearly unmentionable places, for many of the supposed innovations of jazz, particularly in the orchestral field.

On early Whiteman tracks such as *Whispering* or *Japanese sandman* the rhythmic detail relates to ragtime and their overall sound to that period's instrumental jazz. *Sandman* has the more formal scoring, its introduction using quasi-oriental devices that later became very stale. Again, instead of feeling too supercilious, it is advisable for us to recall that these same tricks later appeared on respectable jazz records such as Duke Ellington's *Arabian lover* and Louis Armstrong's *Indian cradle song*. Similar comments apply to the self-consciously 'classical' piano introduction to Whiteman's *When day is done,* for, as comparison with the start of Armstrong's *You're next* shows, this was another practice which crossed the alleged barriers.

The use of quotations in jazz and popular music of the 1920s could be the subject of an amusing essay, ranging as it does from the snatch of *Bella figlia dell'amore* adroitly fitted into Armstrong's *Dinah* to Johnny Dodds's stilted use of *Vesti la giubba* in *Blue clarinet stomp*. The fragment of Chopin's Funeral March closing Ellington's *Black and tan fantasy* has long been recognised as emotionally most apposite, but Whiteman's quotations tend usually to humour, as in the glimpse of Rachmaninoff's Prelude in C sharp minor at the beginning of *Hot lips*, its solemn overtones sardonically at variance with the razz-a-ma-tazz of the following melody. The extract from *Tristan und Isolde* embedded in Whiteman's *The man I love* has wry aptness, and this sort of thing led to a kind of private wit not much associated with popular art. As with the lyrics of Alec Wilder's *Summer is a-coming in*, which are a trope on the medieval *Sumer is icumen in,* so the Whiteman arrangers who incorporated a few bars of Stravinsky's *Petroushka* into *Nobody's sweetheart* must have known that most of their listeners would never get the point, despite Petroushka indeed being nobody's sweetheart.

Garvin Bushell spoke informatively of the ragtime—as opposed to blues—orientation of early New York jazz (2), and his own recordings, besides others not necessarily cut in or near New York, support this. For instance, while a considerable advance in rhythmic control was achieved between Bushell's work on Edith Wilson's 1922 *What do you care?* and on Johnny Dunn's *Bugle call blues* of 1928, there is no corresponding increase of blues feeling. The ragtime affinities of Whiteman's early records, made chiefly at Camden, N.J., or New York, are, then, to be expected. And before complaining about a lack of blues inflections on his 1920 *Wang wang blues* we had best admit an equal deficiency in, say, Henderson's *Gulf coast* and *Potomac River blues* of three years later. The failure of Freddy Keppard's Creole Band twelve months before the Original Dixieland Jazz Band's 1917 success implies that from the start New York was not favourable to blues. And though we should need to know how the latter group was playing earlier in Chicago, it may be that their harsh, nervous brilliance owed more to New York than to their home town (New Orleans), and reflected, instead of creating, a trend.

Yet ragtime proved equally tenacious elsewhere, and, with the partial exception of Lamar Wright, there is little sign of blues feeling among the performers of Bennie Moten's *Crawdad blues* (1923). This is confirmed by such features as the banjo solo on *Moten stomp,* the interludes of *Dingdong blues* or the piano work of *12th Street rag* (all 1927). Among further recordings by Negro ensembles from that time showing a virtual incomprehension of the blues one may, almost at random, cite Mamie Smith's *Crazy blues,* the Kansas City Five's *Louisville blues* (with Bubber Miley), A. J. Piron's *West Indian blues,* the Stomping Six's *Jimtown blues,* Ellington's *Trombone blues* and the New Orleans Blue Five's *South Rampart Street blues.* There are plenty more, all suggesting that blues feeling cannot serve as a dividing line between 1920s jazz and popular music.

To hear *Bugle call rag* by Gus Cannon's Jug Stompers along with Ellington's version, also of 1928, or to set Keppard's *Salty dog* beside the recording by Lemuel Fowler's Washboard Wonders is to understand that jazz has long existed simultaneously on a number of different levels of sophistication. Within this context the persistence of ragtime, the almost actively resisted infiltration of blues into instrumental music, or the stylistically regressive qualities of, say, George Lee's 1928 *Meritt stomp* and *Down home syncopated blues* are unsurprising. Yet this conservatism must be related to players' attempts to extend their musical language, of which the pseudo-oriental colouring and incorporation of classical tags were minor instances. Tension between these forces partly accounts for the uncertainty of both style and method in so much jazz and popular music of this period.

A comic instance is the echo of tailgate trombone during the introduction to Whiteman's *Stairway to paradise*, but obviously more significant is the case of Oliver, who appeared so certain of his aims in the Creole Band titles of 1923 and so unsure afterwards. Thus his 1926 recording of Jelly Roll Morton's *Dead man blues* shows that he simply did not understand this composition's requirements and was unable, alternatively, to impose upon it anything of his own. It would be hard not to prefer the New Orleans Rhythm Kings' five-years-older version of *Farewell blues* to Oliver's, and comparison between the Creole Band's *Dippermouth blues* and the Dixie Syncopators' *Sugar foot strut* (the same piece retitled) teaches an obvious lesson, especially with the absurd passage following Oliver's solo on the latter. Diffuseness sometimes afflicts Oliver's bandsmen, too, and it is instructive to hear Omer Simeon on *Willie the weeper* in conjunction with Barney Bigard's more virtuosic yet more concise use of similar ideas on the Ellington *Jungle nights in Harlem*.

There are more than enough signs of confusion elsewhere, and the contrast between, say, George Temple's excellent trumpet and the appalling saxophone duet (following a curiously *sprechstimme* vocal!) on Fess Williams's *Make me know it* shows how uneven progress was. Similarly, as an orchestral treatment of such a melody, Henderson's 1925 *I'll see you in my dreams* is no advance on Whiteman's *Japanese sandman* of five years earlier: Whiteman's is better executed, yet both merely play the tune straight on one instrument or section while another fills in. Don Redman's arranging skill was based on a formal training then uncommon among Negro musicians, so comparison between his 1924-27 work for Henderson and the output of Whiteman's arrangers is apt. A disconcerting number of pre-Redman Henderson recordings, however, such as *When you walked out* and *My sweetie went away* (both 1923) are elaborations of Eastern dixieland, and Henderson did not appear to derive as much permanent benefit from Redman's stay as has been contended. Even in 1927 he was still having trouble with this sort of material, and, in its ensembles at least, his *Sorry* compares badly with Bix Beiderbecke's masterly version with Don Murray and Adrian Rollini. Five months later Henderson's *I'm feeling devilish* was replete with dixieland overtones although recorded immediately after a *Feeling good* heavily influenced by Beiderbecke's associate Frankie Trumbauer. Later still, his April 25th 1931 *Singing*

the blues closely follows the Beiderbecke/Trumbauer 1927 performance, while a further recording of April 29th is yet more faithful.

A few isolated tracks like Henderson's 1924 *Naughty man* show a
skilled use of the three-piece saxophone section which, if foreshadowed
by the reeds of Whiteman's 1922 *Stairway to paradise*, still anticipates
the beautifully integrated playing—and writing—so prominent on
Whiteman's *Song of India* (1926). Yet, generally speaking, the further
one penetrates into Henderson's recordings the less does he seem like
the leading innovator of orchestral jazz that we have always been
assured he is. Redman's story (2) of Henderson chasing all over New
York in search of a stock orchestration of *Milenburg joys* which they had
heard Sam Lanin play seems to underline this, and one suspects that,
especially after Redman's departure, he leant heavily on publishers'
stock orchestrations. This could account for the persistence of dixieland in that the appropriate recordings might have been based on
stocks taken off popular discs by the Original Memphis Five and
similar groups.

In fairness to Henderson, it should be noted that a far greater musician had a still more confused beginning. Ellington's 1926 band version of *Parlour social stomp*, for instance, is an extraordinary con-
glomeration of jazz, show music and several incompatible types of
rhythm; and the leader's own keyboard work on, say, *Oh how I love my
darling* is an unkempt mixture of genuine stride piano and Tin Pan
Alley ragtime dilutions. Later, during 1928 or '29, *Sweet mama* and
Jolly wog are still made up from bits and pieces, some good and some
bad, patched together without much sign of belonging, and this basic
compositional fault is apparent even in classics such as *Black and tan
fantasy*, with its two incompatible themes, or the latter part of *East St
Louis toodle-oo*. It lasted, indeed, until Ellington got his early style
completely together with the perfectly formed *Old man blues* of 1930.

Despite the muddle which many of these recordings portray, certain
general tendencies do emerge even from so random a selection of
Whiteman performances as has been reissued on LP. Although
widespread elsewhere, there is no sign on his records of the O.D.J.B's
influence, even on the 1920 tracks. Instead, and in sharpest contrast to
Henderson and others, a relatively independent path is sought nearly
from the beginning, though, as usual, parallels and precedents can be
found. *Hot lips* is as dull as can be, consisting basically of nothing more
than repetition of a single phrase, yet the idea of antiphonal response
between the sections has been grasped and is taken further at the close

of *Any time, any place,* where the brass riffs against the reeds' melody. Earlier in this 1920 performance there is a duet between that sour-toned trumpeter Henry Busse, who clings to the melody, and either Ross Gorman or Hal Byers on alto saxophone, who improvises round it. There is a similar equal-voiced duet in *My man* between Busse and Byers on soprano saxophone, and one can see how the idea of simultaneous extemporisation and melody-statement was beginning to come into use to add interest to a piece by systematically varying its texture. These duet passages substantially anticipate such things as Redman's and Coleman Hawkins's clarinet exchanges on Henderson's *Go 'long, mule.*

Real solos appear the following year—1922—with *Stairway to paradise,* which is more accomplished, too, in its diversification of textures and use of antiphony. Tommy Gott's trumpet solo, while not quite consistent in style, has more interesting ideas than, say, Elmer Chambers on Henderson's *Downhearted blues,* and he is one of a number of minor players of this period whose work deserves study. On *Stairway* it is worth noting the anticlimax as Busse follows Gott, stiff and corny as ever. Busse often appeared to disadvantage like this as Whiteman attracted better musicians, as in *Love nest,* where his muted solo is completely overshadowed by a brief later Beiderbecke contribution.

Altogether, it is more enjoyable to follow Whiteman's development than might be supposed. As noted, the overall sound of his earliest tracks, if sometimes inferior in detail, was close to that of jazz bands which recorded a few years later, particularly in the disposition of brass and reed parts. Here again, then, is something which never was peculiar to jazz, but in Whiteman's hands this sound gradually moved away from jazz orthodoxy. During the four years between *Stairway to paradise* and *Song of India,* for example, great advances were made in orchestral technique. The band's sound was now as personal, as instantly recognisable, as Ellington's later became, and had a far more consistent identity than Henderson ever attained on disc. It did not happen to be a jazz sound, yet that does not mean it was bad musically. Indeed, as Gunther Schuller has said (3), clean attacks, excellent intonation and well-nigh perfect internal balances do not necessarily equate with superficiality; and some of these Whiteman pieces are at least as instructive in their way as the numerous mediocre jazz recordings which chance to have a pedigree more in tune with received ideas. It is unfortunate the jazz audience never developed that proper respect for fine craftsmanship found among followers of the other arts, and it may be that this distrust for superlative performance is linked with a similar uneasiness about melodic beauty reflected in the suspicion with which such excellent musicians as Erroll Garner and Paul Desmond are regarded.

By the late 1920s almost every member of Whiteman's band was a superb instrumentalist, and Bill Challis, Lennie Hayton and Ferdé Grofé wrote very demanding scores that display constant ingenuity. During close listening to the band's records of this period one detects all kinds of differences in procedure, according, no doubt, to whether the score was by Grofé, Hayton, Challis or whoever. But without definite knowledge of who wrote what it is impossible to say anything about the work of these men or on the interactions between Whiteman's virtuoso ensemble and those who filled its library, and one regrets having nothing to contribute on this subject. Certainly they took the combination of delicacy, precision and versatility a long way, and one is struck by many passages showing real aural imagination. An attractive instance is the muted trumpet sounding across the violins and viola of *Love nest*; the effect is spoilt through Busse's sour tone, yet the string writing is superior to that heard on jazz recording sessions of decades later.

This increasingly skilled manipulation of the musical substance reminds us of the absurd notion, fashionable during the 1960s and beyond, that it was only "with bop [that] jazz moved into the world of *art*" (4). In reality, it was the great soloists and ensembles of the 1920s who affirmed the artistic status of jazz and with their recordings brought it to the attention of the international public it has retained ever since. But the high musical skill of bands such as Whiteman's led some part of the audience for American popular music to listen instead of to dance, and the best of his output, like that of certain European pioneers, helped create an atmosphere wherein jazz had some chance of recognition.

Whiteman's phenomenal success, right from 1920, when *Japanese sandman* and *Whispering* became one of the record industry's first million-sellers, proves that his music answered—and, despite, or perhaps because of, the evolution it underwent continued to answer—some need in America during the 1920s. Quite apart from his ambiguous effect on jazz, therefore, his career has a sociological aspect which gives him a place in the history of those times. However, he was almost as much misunderstood as the jazzmen themselves, though for nearly opposite reasons. A few lively minds such as Ravel, Ansermet and Milhaud grasped something of the value of jazz, but the minor academics who were the chroniclers of popular culture in America (5) were early put off by jazz musicians' relatively mild departures from European norms of pitch, etc. Whiteman's widespread success, however, attracted them. His indirect, though still largely uncredited, contributions to jazz, not only in terms of orchestral technique but in other respects mentioned below, were ignored. What they liked best was the unhappy tendency towards overelaboration which disfigured an increasing part of his output as the 1920s wore on, and it is this that was promoted, with a deal of naïve enthusiasm, as the great link between straight music and jazz. The sort of aggressive triviality these commentators liked best is typified by *Grand fantasia parts I and II*, described in the record company's files as "Wagneriana" and echoed decades later by Stan Kenton's perversions of that same composer. The ambivalence of Whiteman's role becomes most apparent, however, when we consider that the best aspects of his music were helping produce a climate sympathetic to jazz while the worst were partly responsible for the misrepresentation from which it has suffered ever since.

In a score like *When day is done* (1927) we can hear that differentiation of texture has gone too far, that the frequent tempo changes are out of scale with the performance's brevity. In the worst cases this sort of writing led to inflated brass parts which further unbalanced the textures, the strings neutralised the tone-colours, and the harmony's chromatic progressions cheapened the feeling to the point where we are uncomfortably reminded of Hollywood's synthetic products.

Yet there were precedents, prior gestures towards this kind of theatricality, such as the Pickett-Parham Apollo Syncopators' *Mojo blues* and *Alexander, where's that band?* of 1926. Noble Sissle's *Dear old southland,* featuring Sidney Bechet, is improbably stagey as well, but again outright condemnation is impossible for Bechet found it necessary to alter very little of his part when, years later, he made a small-group jazz recording of this piece. And Miley's solo apart, Ellington's 1926 *Animal crackers* sounds like the work of a pit band, the ensemble's rhythmic articulation having nothing to do with jazz.

Nor was the size of Whiteman's later orchestras new. James Reese Europe's band, playing a music derived from ragtime, had enormous groups of violins, banjos and mandolins, and in 1917 was billed as the Fifty Joy-Whooping Sultans of High-Speed Syncopation. Fred Bryant's rival group was the Fifty Merry Moguls of Melody, and another band was the Forty Black Devils Overseas. The twenty instrumentalists of, say, Whiteman's *Anything Goes* selection appear decently modest in comparison. So far as the violin family is concerned, according to Geechie Harper (6) their use by such leaders as LeRoy Smith was common as early as 1917, and even the Whiteman publicists' 'symphonic jazz' label was anticipated by groups like Dave Peyton's Symphonic Syncopators and titles such as Lloyd Scott's *Symphonic skronch*.

The actual light classics in Whiteman's later repertoire—e.g. Cui's *Orientale*—do appear to have been a gimmick, however. It is true the *Scherzo à la Russe* which Stravinsky wrote for him preceded the far more widely publicised *Ebony Concerto* for Woody Herman, yet there seems to have been no parallel to the genuine musical curiosity which led to Benny Goodman's adventures with Mozart and Bartók. The latter wrote *Contrasts* for Szigeti, BG and himself to play, and if their recording of this work is anything to go by (7), the composer must have been pleased with Goodman's spontaneous demonstration of the correspondences between jazz accentuation and the swing of Hungarian peasant rhythms which also had their origin in dance and song. (If this be doubted one may add that, at least as recorded by the composer (8), the syncopations of Bartók's Dance in Bulgar Rhythm No. 4, from *Mikrokosmos* Book VI, make it sound like a piece of superior Gershwin!)

Although it, too, must be related to general tendencies, we can be more positive about the beneficial side of Whiteman's influence on jazz, even if no particular detail can be ascribed to just one source. Pieces such as Challis's *Three blind mice* or Fud Livingston's *Humpty Dumpty*, both recorded by Beiderbecke during 1927, show us jazzmen intelligently expanding the resources of their music. The harmonic language, for instance, goes a long way beyond Ellington's, let alone Henderson's, and the impact of the better aspects of Whiteman's library is very apparent. Another sign of this affinity is Beiderbecke's *In a mist* and other piano solos, which, as Richard Hadlock has said (9), seem to be derived from the codas Challis wrote for his Whiteman and Jean Goldkette arrangements. The uncommon and fast-moving chord sequence of *Krazy kat* from the *Humpty Dumpty* session also deserves attention.

Yet this sort of exploration was in the air during the late 1920s to a greater extent than the jazzmen of that time, apart from a few master soloists, are now given credit for. Moten's *Dear heart* and *Slow motion* are crammed with contrasting musical incident, and several features of scores like Alphonso Trent's *Black and blue rhapsody* (1928), not least the unexpected key changes, underline Snub Mosely's statement (10) that this band played "symphony-type" arrangements. Comments by Harry Carney (11) and Armstrong (12) further emphasise jazzmen's admiration for aspects of the Whiteman output, while Zutty Singleton reminds us (13) of his influence on Fate Marable's riverboat orchestra, through which many fine musicians passed.

The inventive textural variety of, say, Gus Wilson's scoring of *Clementine* for Trent, or Taylor's Dixie Serenaders' *Wabash blues*, offer a different sort of confirmation, as, rather less happily, do the wa-wa trumpet section passages à la Busse on Henderson's *Go 'long, mule*.

Outside the fields of harmonic and melodic vocabulary, it was in the expressive use of tone-colour that Whiteman was likely to have most fruitful effect, but there was so much activity here that one can do no more than note a few random examples. These might include the clarinet solo with celeste backing on McKinney's Cottonpickers' *Laughing at life*, the guitar and baritone saxophone duet in Ross Gorman's *Sleepy time gal*, the three clarinets plus three muted brass behind Tommy Ladnier on Henderson's *Rocky mountain blues*. In this connection it is amusing to recall the pious horror expressed by some commentators during the mid-1950s over the 'non-jazz' instruments used by the West Coast school, for three-decades-old precedents could have been found for them all. Hear, for example, the oboe on Henderson's *Shanghai shuffle*, the bass clarinet in the Georgians' *Nothing but*, or the french horn on LeRoy Smith's *St Louis blues*.

The complications of the network of cross-influences through which jazz passed at that time becomes further apparent when we attempt to trace the effect which these players in turn had on their fellow musicians. If Hal Jordy's alto saxophone work on Norman Brownlee's 1925 *Peculiar* is set beside his more fluent contributions to Johnny Miller's *Dippermouth blues* and *Panama* of three years later it seems that he gained a sense of direction by using Trumbauer as a model. Yet Johnny O'Donnell's playing on, say, the Georgians' *Way down yonder in New Orleans* (1922) suggests this to be a vein of 'cool' expression that goes back further than Trumbauer, just as Frank Guarente's trumpeting on the same band's *Henpecked blues* or *Chicago* seems to anticipate Arthur Whetsol of the Ellington orchestra. Doc Cook's 1928 *Hum and strum*, with another Trumbauerish alto solo, does echo the white bands, and there is no denying the Beiderbeckian trumpeting on the Ross DeLuxe Syncopators' *Skad-o-lee*. We should also note Roy

Eldridge naming Red Nichols as one of his first influences (14), Carney mentioning Don Murray as one of his (11), Lester Young's statement that "I had a decision to make between Frankie Trumbauer and Jimmy Dorsey, you dig, and I wasn't sure which way I wanted to go" (15), and the fact that Speed Webb's band could play Nichols arrangements from memory (16).

Thinking about jazz was long conducted on such lines that influences of this sort were inadmissible, yet there is no getting round the recorded evidence and occasional off-guard remarks by the musicians themselves. There seems little point in denying, for example, that Henderson's *Copenhagen*, a rare musical success among his early recordings, is essentially a sophistication of an earlier version by Beiderbecke's Wolverines group. It is also salutary to hear Ellington's 1931 *Mystery song* in conjunction with Whiteman's *Sweet Sue* of 1928, and to recall that Billy Strayhorn's *Minuet in blues*, recorded by an Ellington small combo led by Barney Bigard, followed Whiteman's *Minuet in jazz*. It is interesting, also, to compare Ellington's use of low-register clarinets on *Crescendo and diminuendo in blue* and *The sergeant was shy* with the Casa Loma Band's earlier use of this same resource on *Study in brown*. The Casa Loma, though persistently misrepresented in the literature, had a considerable, even excessive, effect on other bands, as Henderson's *Blue rhythm*, Goodman's *Cokey* or Earl Hines's *Sensational mood* all show.

So one might go on. This has been an unavoidably discursive and deliberately inconclusive essay which has aimed at raising more questions than it answers, particularly as each question brings with it a ghostly army of secondary questions to which one hardly dare draw attention. This is because during the 1960s there was an explosive increase in the availability of subsidiary, or allegedly subsidiary, recorded material from the 1920s conscientious listening to which upsets, or should upset, most of our received ideas. Certainly it becomes obvious that there were very many threads in the fabric of that decade's musical activity, and orchestral jazz, even jazz itself, was only one among them. We may, as a matter of personal taste, regard jazz as the most valuable of these, yet it would have been poorer if isolated from the other musics to which it gave and from which it demonstrably learnt so much. Properly digesting this newly available material and adjusting our perspectives in accord with the more complex relationships and patterns of development it suggests will be the task of many years. Indeed, we may wonder if it is one that will ever be completed.

Jazz Monthly, July 1970

Notes

Charlie Parker

1 Tony Williams: 'Parker Discography', *Discographical Forum*, September 1968-September 1970.

2 Virgil Thomson: *American Music since 1910* (New York, 1970).

3 Henry Cowell: *Charles Ives and His Music* (New York, 1955).

4 For parallel comments on other Parker improvisations see Don Heckman: 'Bird in Flight', *Down Beat*, March 11th 1965.

5 Parker's complete Savoy recordings were issued on British Realm RM120-123 and 131 (four of the five original American Savoy LPs had the material chaotically out of sequence). The complete Dial sessions are on British Spotlite 101-106.

6 Quoted by David Sylvester in *The Listener*, March 12th 1970.

7 Charles Fox, *Jazz Monthly*, March 1959.

8 See Thomas Owens: 'Applying the Melograph to *Parker's mood*', *Selected Reports in Ethnomusicology*, Vol. 2, 1974.

9 Quoted in Robert Reisner: *Bird—the Legend of Charlie Parker* (New York, 1962).

10 Roy Carew: '1211 U Street', *Jazz Monthly*, March 1955.

11 For another viewpoint see Ronald Atkins's discussion of these Savoy recordings in *Modern Jazz: the Essential Records 1945-70* edited by Max Harrison (London, 1975).

12 Arnold Schoenberg: *Style and Idea* (New York, 1950; rev. ed. London, 1975).

13 Further reading: Lucien Malson: *Les Maîtres du Jazz* (Paris, 1952; rev. ed. 1972); André Hodeir: *Jazz—its Evolution and Essence* (London, 1956); Ross Russell: 'The Evolutionary Position of Bop' in *The Art of Jazz* edited by Martin Williams (New York, 1959); Max Harrison: 'Charlie Parker' in *Just Jazz 4* edited by Sinclair Traill (London, 1960); Michael James: *10 Modern Jazzmen* (London, 1960); Ross Russell: 'Charlie Parker and Dizzy Gillespie', *Jazz Review*, November 1960; Max Harrison: *Charlie Parker* (London, 1960); Nat Hentoff: *Charlie Parker—a List of Compositions Licenced by B.M.I.* (New York, 1961); André Hodeir: *Toward Jazz* (New York, 1962); Benny Green: *The Reluctant Art* (London, 1962); John Mehegan: *Jazz Improvisation* Vol. 2 (New York, 1962); Wilfrid Mellers: *Music in a New Found Land* (London, 1964); Ralph Ellison:

Shadow and Act (New York, 1964); Ira Gitler: *Jazz Masters of the 40s* (New York, 1966); William Lightfoot: 'Charlie Parker', *Keystone Folklore Quarterly*, Summer 1972; Ross Russell: *Bird Lives!* (New York, 1973); Lawrence Koch: 'Ornithology—a Study of Parker's Music', *Journal of Jazz Studies*, December 1974, June 1975; James Patrick: 'Charlie Parker and the Harmonic Sources of Bebop Composition', *Journal of Jazz Studies*, June 1975.

Fats Waller

1 *Sunday Times Colour Supplement*, June 10th 1962.
2 *Hear Me Talking to You* edited by Nat Shapiro and Nat Hentoff (New York, 1955).
3 Ed Kirkeby: *Ain't Misbehavin'* (New York, 1966).
4 *Jazz Review*, August 1960.
5 Further reading: Lucien Malson: *Les Maîtres du Jazz* (Paris, 1952; rev. ed. 1972); André Hodeir: *Jazz—its Evolution and Essence* (London, 1956); Charles Fox: *Fats Waller* (London, 1960); Willie 'the lion' Smith: *Music on My Mind* (New York, 1965); Richard Hadlock: *Jazz Masters of the 20s* (New York, 1965); Max Harrison: entry on Waller in *Jazz on Record* edited by Albert McCarthy (London, 1968); Gunther Schuller: *Early Jazz* (New York, 1968); Morroe Berger: 'The Outside Insider', *Journal of Jazz Studies*, October 1973.

Thelonious Monk

1 André Brassai: *Graffiti* (Stuttgart, 1960).
2 Stanley Dance: 'Towards Criteria' in *Jazzbook 1947* edited by Albert McCarthy (London, 1947).
3 Certain of these "specific ideas" are helpfully illuminated by some of André Hodeir's treatments of Monk themes, which are in effect musical instead of verbal commentaries. Instances are his variations on *Mysterioso* titled *Osymetrios I* and *II* (American Philips PHM200-073) and his atomisation of *Round about midnight* (American Epic LN3376).
4 Further reading: Lucien Malson: *Les Maîtres du Jazz* (Paris, 1952; rev. ed. 1972); Gunther Schuller: 'Thelonious Monk', *Jazz Review*, November 1958; Max Harrison: 'Thelonious Monk' in *Just Jazz 3* edited by Sinclair Traill (London, 1959); Grover Sales: 'Monk at the Black Hawk', *Jazz*, Winter 1960; Nat Hentoff: *Thelonious Monk—a List of Compositions Licenced by B.M.I.* (New York, 1961); Nat Hentoff: *The Jazz Life* (New York, 1961); André Hodeir:

Toward Jazz (New York, 1962); Wilfrid Mellers: *Music in a New Found Land* (London, 1964); Max Harrison: entry on Monk in *Jazz on Record* edited by Albert McCarthy (London, 1968); Jack Cooke: entry on Monk in *Modern Jazz: the Essential Records 1945-70* edited by Max Harrison (London, 1975).

Lionel Hampton

1 Reissued on French RCA 730.640, 730.641, 731.048, 731.053, 741.049 and 741.077.
2 Quoted in *Metronome Yearbook* (New York, 1956).
3 The American Contemporary C3502 issue of the 1953 *Walking at the Trocadero* session is to be preferred to the original French Vogue because on the former several incompetent clarinet solos by Mezz Mezzrow have been edited out.
4 For instance exaggerated condemnation of Berry can be found in Hugues Panassié's *The Real Jazz* (New York, 1942) and equally immoderate praise in the 1960 edition of the same book.

Teddy Charles

1 Teddy Charles and Ira Gitler: 'Dialogue on Modern Jazz', *Jazz*, Spring 1959.
2 George Russell: *The Lydian Concept of Tonal Organisation* (New York, 1959).

Bunk Johnson

1 American writers have persistently ignored this phase of jazz, and such works as Martin Williams's *Jazz Masters of New Orleans* (New York, 1967) and Gunther Schuller's *Early Jazz* (New York, 1968) are typical in making no attempt to discuss the musical value and historical meaning of the American Music and allied recordings.
2 Bruce King, *Jazz Monthly*, April 1967.
3 For a characteristic example see Hugues Panassié: *Dictionary of Jazz* (London, 1956).
4 *Jazz Monthly*, March and April 1959; see also July 1967.
5 Frank Driggs: 'Kansas City and the Southwest' in *Jazz* edited by Nat Hentoff and Albert McCarthy (New York, 1959); Ross Russell: *Jazz Style in Kansas City and the Southwest* (Berkeley, Calif., 1971; rev. ed. 1973).
6 Samuel Charters: *Jazz—New Orleans 1885-1957* (Belleville, N.J., 1958).
7 *Jazz Review*, August 1960.

8 *Record Changer*, November and December 1952.

9 Further reading: Virgil Thomson: *The Musical Scene* (New York, 1945); Morroe Berger: 'Jazz Prehistory and Bunk Johnson' in *Frontiers of Jazz* edited by Ralph deToledano (New York, 1947); Richard Hadlock: 'The State of Dixieland', *Jazz Review*, October 1959; Jerome Shipman: 'Bunk Johnson', *Jazz Review*, June 1960; Jerome Shipman: 'Two from Mainstream', *Sounds and Fury*, July/August 1965; Max Harrison: entry on Johnson in *Jazz on Record* edited by Albert McCarthy (London, 1968).

Hal McKusick

1 American RCA LPM1366.

2 American Decca DL9209.

3 George Russell: *The Lydian Concept of Tonal Organisation* (New York, 1959).

4 American RCA LPM2534.

5 *Jazz Review*, February 1960.

6 *Down Beat*, May 29th 1958.

7 Arnold Schoenberg: *Style and Idea* (New York, 1950; rev. ed. London, 1975).

8 George Russell: 'Where Do We Go From Here?' in *The Jazz Word* edited by Dom Cerulli (New York, 1960).

9 Further reading: Nat Hentoff: *George Russell—a List of Compositions Licenced by B.M.I.* (New York, 1961); Max Harrison: entry on Russell in *Jazz on Record* edited by Albert McCarthy (London, 1968); Olive Jones: 'Conversations with George Russell', *The Black Perspective in Music*, Spring 1974.

Jimmy Lunceford

1 See remarks by Jimmy Crawford, Lunceford's drummer, quoted in George Simon: *The Big Bands* (New York, 1967; rev. ed. 1974).

2 *Down Beat*, October 3rd 1968; see also comments by Willie Smith in the issue dated May 18th 1967.

3 *Sounds and Fury*, July/August 1965.

4 This is underlined by such unfortunate records as Oliver's *Sentimental Sy* (American Dot DLP3132).

5 In this case, however, the influence must have been through live performances as the recording of *Shake your head* did not appear in America until the days of LP reissues.

6 Martin Williams, *Saturday Review*, March 15th 1969.

7 Billy May: *Jimmy Lunceford in Hi-Fi* (American Capitol TA0924).

8 Ralph Gleason: *Celebrating the Duke* (Boston, Mass., 1975).
9 *Jazz Review*, March/April 1960.
10 Quoted in Leonard Feather: *Encyclopaedia of Jazz* (New York, 1960).
11 Quoted in Simon—see Note 1.
12 *Jazz Review*, January 1959.
13 Simon (see Note 1) quotes Lunceford as saying in 1942, "We do a couple of hundred one-nighters a year, fifteen to twenty weeks of theatres, maybe one four-week location, and two weeks of vacation. We cover about 40,000 miles a year".

Music for Brass

1 American Columbia CL941 (the second side of this LP is occupied with Gunther Schuller's Symphony for Brass and Percussion, conducted by Dimitri Mitropoulos).
2 Quoted in Leonard Feather: *Encyclopaedia Yearbook of Jazz in the 60s* (New York, 1966).

Continental Jazz

1 A few books such as Horst Lange's *Deutsche 78er Discographie der Jazz und Hot Dance Musik 1903-58* (Berlin, 1966) and Robert Pernet's *Jazz in Little Belgium* (Brussels, 1967) represent attempts to close this gap, at least on the discographical and historical levels.
2 French Pathé C054-10656.
3 *Aux Frontières du Jazz* (Paris, 1932) and *Jazz from Congo to Metropolitan* (New York, 1944).
4 *Etudes* (Paris, 1927).
5 Examples: Armstrong's *Oriental strut* (1926), Ellington's *Japanese dream* (1929), Bechet's *Egyptian fantasy* (1941).
6 *Le Coq et l'Harlequin* (Paris, 1921).
7 Albert Bettonville and André Gillet: *European Recordings of Louis Mitchell* (Brussels, 1957); B. A. L. Rust: *Jazz Records 1897-1931* (Hatch End, 1962).
8 Reproduced in *Melody Maker*, July 14th 1956.
9 Czechoslovakian Supraphon DV10177/78.
10 Examples: Bohumil Čipera's *Logarithm 6*, Luděk Hulan's *Outcry*, Milan Řežábek's *Picnic* (all on Czechoslovakian Supraphon SUA15599) and the compositions of Pavel Blatný (Supraphon 0 15 0528).

James P. Johnson

1 *Jazz Review*, August 1960.
2 Quoted in Richard Hadlock: *Jazz Masters of the 20s* (New York, 1965).
3 Tom Davin: 'Conversations with James P. Johnson', *Jazz Review*, June, July, August, September 1959, March/April 1960.
4 *Jazz Review*, December 1958.
5 See Gunther Schuller: *Early Jazz* (New York, 1968) for diagrammatic representations of the cross-rhythms of *Keep off the grass*, *Scouting around*, etc.
6 Winthrop Sargeant: *Jazz Hot and Hybrid* (New York, 1938).
7 *Jazzmen* edited by Frederic Ramsey and Charles Smith (New York, 1939).
8 For example in Hugues Panassié: *Discographie Critique des Meilleurs* [sic] *Disques de Jazz* (Paris, 1958).
9 See Eric Thacker: 'Gottschalk and a Prelude to Jazz', *Jazz Monthly*, March 1973. This composer's dates are 1829-69.
10 Further reading: Ross Russell: 'Grandfather of Hot Piano' in *Frontiers of Jazz* edited by Ralph deToledano (New York, 1947); Rudi Blesh and Harriet Janis: *They All Played Ragtime* (New York, 1950; rev. ed. 1971); Willie 'the lion' Smith: *Music on My Mind* (New York, 1965); William Schafer and Johannes Riedel: *The Art of Ragtime* (Baton Rouge, La., 1973).

Dizzy Gillespie

1 Further reading: Richard Boyer: 'Profile of Dizzy' in *Treasury of Jazz* edited by Eddie Condon (New York, 1956); Michael James: *Dizzy Gillespie* (London, 1959); Ross Russell: 'Brass' in *The Art of Jazz* edited by Martin Williams (New York, 1959); Michael James: *10 Modern Jazzmen* (London, 1960); Max Harrison: entry on Gillespie in *Jazz Era—the 40s* edited by Stanley Dance (London, 1961); André Hodeir: *Toward Jazz* (New York, 1962); Henry Woodfin: 'Dizzy Gillespie 1946-50', *Jazz Monthly*, October 1964; Ira Gitler: *Jazz Masters of the 40s* (New York, 1966).

David Mack

1 British Columbia 33SX1670.
2 The best introduction to the subject is Schoenberg's own 1941 essay 'Composition with Twelve Tones' in his book *Style and Idea* (New York, 1950; rev. ed. London, 1975). This should be followed with Josef Rufer's *Die Komposition mit Zwölf Tönen* (Berlin, 1952) and

George Perle's *Serial Composition and Atonality* (London, 1962; rev. ed. 1972).

3 Paul Hindemith: *A Composer's World* (New York, 1952).

4 Quoted in Rudolph Reti: *Tonality, Atonality, Pantonality* (London, 1958).

5 George Russell: 'Ornette Coleman and Tonality', *Jazz Review*, June 1960.

6 André Hodeir: *Toward Jazz* (New York, 1962).

7 Sidney Finkelstein: *Jazz—a People's Music* (New York, 1948).

Ornette Coleman

1 André Brassai: *Graffiti* (Stuttgart, 1960).

2 Charles Ives: *Essays Before a Sonata* (New York, 1920).

3 Quoted in the sleeve note of Ornette Coleman: *Change of the Century* (American Atlantic 1327).

4 Quoted in Peter Dickinson: 'Edgard Varèse 1885-1965', *Ricordiana*, April 1966.

5 Igor Stravinsky: *Poétique Musicale sous Forme de Six Leçons* (Cambridge, Mass., 1942).

6 This concert, organised by Victor Schonfield, took place at the Fairfield Hall, Croydon, London, on August 29th 1965. It was the equivalent of Charlie Parker visiting Britain in the late 1940s, or Louis Armstrong in the late '20s—neither of which events, needless to say, ever occurred. Coleman's part of the Croydon programme was recorded on Freedom FLP40102/3.

7 *Jazz and Pop*, January 1965.

8 *The Village Voice*, January 6th 1966.

9 Quoted in Calvin Tomkins: *The Bride and the Bachelors* (New York, 1962).

10 Quoted in A. B. Spellman: *Four Lives in the Bebop Business* (New York, 1966).

11 H. R. Hitchcock: *Rococo Architecture in Southern Germany* (London, 1968).

12 Quoted in the sleeve note of Ornette Coleman: *Music of Ornette Coleman* (American RCA LSC2982).

13 From the Croydon concert programme notes.

14 Further reading: George Russell: 'Ornette Coleman and Tonality', *Jazz Review*, June 1960; Wilfrid Mellers: *Music in a New Found Land* (London, 1964); Terry Martin: 'The Plastic Muse', *Jazz Monthly*, May, June, August.1964, May 1965; Don Heckman: 'Inside Ornette Coleman', *Down Beat*, September 9th 1965; Jack Cooke: 'Coleman Revisited', *Jazz Monthly*, July 1966; Wilfrid

Mellers: *Caliban Reborn* (London, 1967); Jack Cooke: 'Ornette and Son', *Jazz Monthly*, July 1967; Max Harrison: entry on Coleman in *Jazz on Record* edited by Albert McCarthy (London, 1968); Ekkehard Jost: 'Zur Musik Ornette Colemans' in *Jazzforschung II* edited by Friedrich Körner and Dieter Glawischnig (Graz, 1970).

Tadd Dameron

1 Malcolm Lowry: *Dark as the Grave* (London, 1969).
2 American Prestige D7842.
3 Quoted in Ira Gitler: *Jazz Masters of the 40s* (New York, 1966).
4 American Riverside RLP419.
5 Further reading: Jack Cooke: 'Tadd Dameron', *Jazz Monthly*, March 1960; Bill Coss: 'Tadd Dameron', *Down Beat*, February 15th 1962; Max Harrison: entry on Dameron in *Jazz on Record* edited by Albert McCarthy (London, 1968); Henry Woodfin: 'Tadd Dameron', *Jazz Monthly*, April 1973.

Duke Ellington

1 *Hear Me Talking to You* edited by Nat Shapiro and Nat Hentoff (New York, 1955).
2 Constant Lambert: *Music Ho!* (London, 1934).
3 A. J. Bishop: '*Creole rhapsody*—an Analysis', *Jazz Monthly*, November 1963.
4 A. J. Bishop: '*Reminiscing in tempo*—an Analysis', *Jazz Journal*, February 1964.
5 Robert Crowley: '*Black, brown and beige* after 16 Years', *Jazz*, Spring 1959; see also Alexandre Rado: 'Un Oeuvre Maudit: *Black, brown and beige*', *Jazz Hot*, February 1969 and Brian Priestley: '*Black, brown and beige*—an Analysis', *Composer*, Spring, Summer, Winter 1974.
6 For brief comments on these experiments by a member of the band see Freddie Jenkins: 'Reminiscing in Tempo', *Storyville*, April/May 1973.
7 Albert McCarthy, *Jazz Monthly*, June 1957.
8 For details of Powell's post-jazz output see Leslie Thimmig: 'Music of Mel Powell', *Musical Quarterly*, January 1969.
9 Further reading: Roger Pryor Dodge: 'Harpsichords and Jazz Trumpets' in *Frontiers of Jazz* edited by Ralph de Toledano (New York, 1947); Lucien Malson: *Les Maîtres du Jazz* (Paris, 1952; rev. ed. 1972); Vic Bellerby: 'Duke Ellington', *Jazz Monthly*, November, December 1955, February, April 1956; André Hodeir: *Jazz—its Evolution and Essence* (London, 1956); Burnett James:

Essays on Jazz (London, 1961); Demètre Ioakimidis: 'Un Pianiste Nommé Ellington', *Jazz Hot*, March, April, May, June 1961; André Hodeir: *Toward Jazz* (New York, 1962); Wilfrid Mellers: *Music in a New Found Land* (London, 1964); Luigi Sanfilippo: *General Catalogue of Ellington's Recorded Music* (Palermo, 1964); Gunther Schuller: *Early Jazz* (New York, 1968); Brian Priestley: 'The Far-Eastern suite', *Jazz Monthly*, March 1969; Demètre Ioakimidis: 'Ellington—a Time of Transition', *Jazz Monthly*, February 1973; Antonio Berini and Giovanni Volonté: 'Cinque Suites', *Musica Jazz*, July 1974.

Jelly Roll Morton

1 Reissued on American Riverside RLP9001-12.
2 Richard Hadlock, *Jazz*, Spring 1959; for a different view see Larry Gushee, *Jazz Review*, November 1958.
3 An analysis of *State Street special* is included in Max Harrison: 'Reconsiderations—Jimmy Yancey', *Jazz Review*, March/April 1960.
4 For a general discussion of this question see Frank Tirro: 'Constructive Elements in Jazz Improvisation', *Journal of the American Musicological Society*, Summer 1974.
5 Further reading: Alan Lomax: *Mister Jelly Roll* (New York, 1950); Guy Waterman: 'Jelly Roll Morton', *Jazz Review*, December 1958; William Russell: 'Morton and *Frog-i-more rag*' in *The Art of Jazz* edited by Martin Williams (New York, 1959); Kenneth Hulsizer: 'Morton in Washington' in *This is Jazz* edited by Kenneth Williamson (London, 1960); Max Harrison: 'Notes on Jazz Composition', *Jazz Monthly*, April 1963; Wilfrid Mellers: *Music in a New Found Land* (London, 1964); Max Harrison: entry on Morton in *Jazz on Record* edited by Albert McCarthy (London, 1968); Gunther Schuller: *Early Jazz* (New York, 1968); William Schafer and Johannes Riedel: *The Art of Ragtime* (Baton Rouge, La., 1973).

Gil Evans

1 Quoted in Nat Hentoff: 'Birth of the Cool', *Down Beat*, May 2nd and 16th 1957.
2 This is incorrectly titled *The troubador* on all issues.
3 *Jazz Review*, September 1959.
4 André Hodeir: *Toward Jazz* (New York, 1962).
5 Sleeve note of George Russell: *Jazz Workshop* (American RCA LPM2534).
6 George Russell: 'Where Do We Go From Here?' in *The Jazz Word*

edited by Dom Cerulli (New York, 1960).

7 This little-known detail is given in Leonard Feather: *Jazz—an Exciting Story of Jazz Today* (Los Angeles, 1959).

8 Miles Davis: *Pre-Birth of the Cool* (Italian Cicala BLJ8003); the relevant scores are, of course, by Gil Evans, not Bill Evans, as given on the sleeve.

9 Quoted in the sleeve note of Gil Evans: *Great Jazz Standards* (American Pacific Jazz 28).

10 *Jazz Monthly*, March 1966.

11 For example André Hodeir (see Note 4); Charles Fox: 'Experiment with Texture' in *Jazzmen of Our Time* edited by Raymond Horricks (London, 1959); Max Harrison: 'Miles Davis—a Reappraisal' in *This is Jazz* edited by Kenneth Williamson (London, 1960).

12 Whitney Balliett: *The Sound of Surprise* (New York, 1959).

13 American Mercury MG20442.

14 All on American Creative World ST1049.

15 American Verve MGV8612.

16 Several Evans LPs have been given misleading new titles on reissue. For instance *Gil Evans plus 10* reappeared as *Big Stuff*, *New Bottle Old Wine* as *Roots*.

17 For example Budd Johnson: *Blues à la Mode* (American Felstead FAJ7007).

18 For instance on *Monk at Town Hall* (American Riverside RLP12-300).

19 Claude Lévi-Strauss: *Le Cru et le Cuit* (Paris, 1974).

20 Further reading: Don Heckman: 'Gil Evans on His Own', *Jazz Review*, March/April 1960; Nat Hentoff: *Gil Evans—a list of Compositions Licenced by B.M.I.* (New York, 1961); Wilfrid Mellers: *Music in a New Found Land* (London, 1964); George Endrey: 'Gil Evans', *Sounds and Fury*, July/August 1965; Gian Mario Maletto: 'Le Storiche Incisioni di Miles Davis per la Capitol', *Musica Jazz*, March 1967; Don DeMichael: 'Miles Davis', *Rolling Stone*, December 3rd 1969; Michael James: entry on Evans in *Modern Jazz: the Essential Records 1945-70* edited by Max Harrison (London, 1975).

Jazz: a People's Music

1 Sidney Finkelstein: *Jazz: a People's Music* (New York, 1948).

2 Rudi Blesh: *Shining Trumpets* (New York, 1946).

3 These were mainly scattered essays such as Roger Pryor Dodge's 'Harpsichords and Jazz Trumpets', reprinted in *Frontiers of Jazz* edited by Ralph deToledano (New York, 1947), and William

Russell's pieces on boogie pianists, reprinted in *The Art of Jazz* edited by Martin Williams (New York, 1959).

Martial Solal

1 Edmund Wilson: *The American Earthquake* (Garden City, 1958).
2 American Epic LN3376.
3 French Vogue LDM30065.
4 After a careful restudy of the performances I retain this comment from my original text despite its being half denied by Solal during an interview he gave Martin Williams in the latter's *Jazz Masters in Transition* (New York, 1970). In this same conversation Solal admits that he never heard the recordings with Bechet again after they were completed.
5 French Columbia CTY40181.
6 French Columbia CTX41228.
7 French Columbia CTX40306.
8 Stockhausen's *Mikrophonie II* is for twelve singers and an electric organ; it combines electronic music with live performance. The sounds are picked up with directional microphones and modified by ring modulators whose outputs emerge from four loudspeakers. Thus the original music of the organ and voices is heard along with a transformation of itself.
9 American Verve 68526.

Miff Mole

1 Gunther Schuller: *Early Jazz* (New York, 1968).
2 *Hear Me Talking to You* edited by Nat Shapiro and Nat Hentoff (New York, 1955).
3 Reissued on British Parlophone PMC7120 and 7126.
4 Burnett James: *Essays on Jazz* (London, 1961).

Serge Chaloff

1 *Metronome Yearbook* (New York, 1956).
2 *Jazz Review*, December 1958.
3 Louis Armstrong: *Satchmo—a Musical Autobiography* (American Decca DXM-155).
4 Anna Kavan: *Ice* (London, 1967).
5 Further reading: Alun Morgan: 'Serge Chaloff', *Jazz Monthly*, October 1957; Ira Gitler: *Jazz Masters of the 40s* (New York, 1966); Michael James: entry on Chaloff in *Modern Jazz: the Essential Records 1945-70* edited by Max Harrison (London, 1975).

The 'Spirituals to Swing' Concerts

1 American Vanguard VRS8523-4. Though it in no way affects the quality of the music considered here, the suggestion has been made, by Brian Priestley in *Jazz Monthly*, July 1969, that several of these performances—*Blues with Helen, Mortgage stomp, Don't be that way, I ain't got nobody* and perhaps *Mule walk* and *Carolina shout*—were not recorded at the concerts but are later 'recreations' done in a studio.

2 See also John Hammond: 'An Experience in Jazz History' in *Black Music in Our Culture* edited by Dominique-René de Lerma (Kent, Ohio, 1970), and James Dugan and John Hammond: 'An Early Black Music Concert from Spirituals to Swing', *The Black Perspective in Music*, Autumn 1974.

Lennie Niehaus

1 Lennie Niehaus: *Vol. I The Quintet* (American Contemporary C3518).

2 *Vol. II The Octet No. 1* (C3540).

3 *Vol. III The Octet No. 2* (C3503).

4 *Vol. V The Sextet* (C3524).

5 *I Swing for You* (American Mercury MG36118).

Mátyás Seiber and John Dankworth

1 Igor Stravinsky and Robert Craft: *Conversations with Stravinsky* (London, 1959).

2 American Columbia CL842 (recorded 1955).

3 American Candid 8004 (recorded 1960).

4 American Atlantic 1365 (recorded 1960).

5 In fact, a recording of *Improvisations* appeared in 1962 on British Saga XIP7006; it was soon deleted, however, and has not been reissued. Seiber died in 1960.

The Brandeis Festival LP

1 First issued as *Adventures in Sound* (American Columbia WL127) and reissued as part of a two-LP set, *Outstanding Jazz Compositions of the 20th-Century* (American Columbia C28-831). Later, independent recordings were made of Russell's *All about Rosie* by Gerry Mulligan's Concert Band (American Verve MGVS8415) and of Babbitt's *All set* by the Contemporary Chamber Ensemble (American Nonesuch H71303).

2 *American Jazzmen Play André Hodeir* (American Savoy MG12104); *The Paris Scene* (MG12113); *Kenny Clarke Plays Hodeir* (American

Epic LN3376).

3 *Der Reihe* Vol 2 (Bryn Mawr, Penn., 1958).
4 'The Brandeis Festival Album' by Louis Gottlieb in *Jazz*, Spring 1959, gives some indications of the serial organisation of *All set*. For respectively elementary and advanced comments on his methods see Babbitt's 'Some Aspects of Twelve-Tone Composition' in *The Score*, June 1955, and Twelve-Tone Invariants as Compositional Determinants' in *Problems of Modern Music* edited by Paul Lang (New York, 1962). For his reply to aesthetic and other objections to this music see Babbitt's 'Who Cares if You Listen?' in *The American Composer Speaks* edited by Gilbert Chase (Baton Rouge, La., 1966).

Paul Whiteman

1 *Chicago Defender*, February 20th 1926, quoted without identification in the anonymous sleeve note to *The Birth of Big Band Jazz* (British London AL3547).
2 Garvin Bushell: 'New York Jazz in the 1920s', *Jazz Review*, January, February, April 1959.
3 Gunther Schuller: *Early Jazz* (New York, 1968).
4 A. B. Spellman: *Four Lives in the Bebop Business* (New York, 1966).
5 Examples: Gilbert Chase: *Seven Lively Arts* (New York, 1924); Henry Osgood: *So This is Jazz!* (Boston, Mass., 1926).
6 *Jazz Monthly*, April 1969.
7 American Columbia 70362-3.
8 American Columbia ML4419.
9 Richard Hadlock: *Jazz Masters of the 20s* (New York, 1965).
10 *Jazz Monthly*, March 1960.
11 *Jazz Journal*, June 1961
12 *Hear Me Talking to You* edited by Nat Shapiro and Nat Hentoff (New York, 1955).
13 Martin Williams: *Jazz Masters of New Orleans* (New York, 1967).
14 *Down Beat*, September 19th 1956.
15 *Jazz Review*, September 1959.
16 *Jazz Monthly*, November 1968.

Index

155, 167, 191, 199, 205
Beck, Joe, 144
Beethoven, Ludwig van, 67, 84, 126, 179
Behind the eight bar, 65
Behounek, Kamil, 78
Beiderbecke, Bix, 30, 88, 132, 136, 143, 149-50, 159, 160, 187-8, 189, 192, 193, 194
Belgium stomp, 63
Bella figlia dell'amore, (Verdi), 185
Belle of the ball, 170
Bellerby, Vic, 202
Bellonzi, Charles, 156
Bells and chimes, 112, 114
Bemsha swing, 155
Bennet, Tony, 68
Berg, Alban, 115, 168
Berger, Morroe, 196, 198
Berini, Antonio, 203
Berman, Sonny, 163
Berry, Chew, 37-8, 39, 197
Best things in life are free, 65
Bettonville, Albert, 199
Bigard, Barney, 129, 187, 194
Big Chief Battle-axe, 52
Big foot, 65
Big stuff LP, 204
Bilbao song, 145
Billie's bounce, 18, 19
Bird feathers, 142
Bird gets the worm, 20
Bird in Igor's yard, 58
Bird of paradise, 62
Bird's nest, 105
Birk's works, 94
Birth of Big Band Jazz LP, 207
Bishop, A. J., 122, 202
Black and blue rhapsody, 193
Black and tan fantasy, 185, 188
Black, brown and beige, 122, 202
Black Diamonds Band, 76
Black mysticism, 112
Black saint and sinner lady, 127
Blake, Eubie, 84
Blakey, Art, 44, 147
Blatný, Pavel, 199
Bleeding-hearted blues, 25
Blesh, Rudi, 148, 200, 204
Bley, Paul, 112
Blue because of you, 38
Bluebells goodbye, 52
Blueberry rhyme, 83
Bluebird, 20
Blue clarinet stomp, 185
Blue hound bus grays, 65
Blue moods, 87
Blue 'n' boogie, 89

Blue Rhythm, 62, 194
Blue Rhythm Band, 62
Blues à la Mode LP, 204
Blue Serge (Burns), 162
Blue Serge LP (Chaloff), 15
Blue serge (Ellington), 140
Blues for Fats, 86
Blues for Pablo, 138, 139, 140
Blues with Helen, 167, 206
Blues with Lips, 166
Body and soul, 163
Bolden, Buddy, 49
Boo woo, 166
Boplicity, 136-7, 139
Bopscotch, 162
Boswell, James, 62, 63
Boulez, Pierre, 93, 105
Boyer, Richard, 200
Brassai, André, 30, 32, 107, 114, 196, 200
Breakfast ball, 62
Broad way blues, 112
Brom, Gustav, 79
Brooks, John Benson, 58
Broonzy, Big Bill, 166
Brown, Lawrence, 33
Brownlee, Norman, 193
Broz, Lumir, 79
Brubeck, Dave, 139, 166
Bruce, Ralph, 102
Bryant, Fred, 84, 191
Buckner, Ted, 64, 66
Budo, 135
Bugle call blues, 186
Bugle call rag, 186
Bunko, 170
Burian, E. F., 77
Burns, Ralph, 124, 162
Burrell, Kenny, 140
Burroughs, Alvin, 37
Bushell, Garvin, 185-6, 207
Busse, Henry, 189, 190, 193
Buzzing around with the bee, 33
Buzzy, 19, 21
Byers, Hal, 189
By the river of St Marie, 66, 67

Cage, John, 110, 112, 113
Call, The, 112
Callender, Red, 54
Calloway, Cab, 36
Call the police, 68
Cameo, 102
Cannon, Gus, 186
Cannonball blues, 31
Caprice rag, 86
Caprice Viennois (Kreisler), 134
Caravan, 79

214

215

217

220